CLASSICS IN EDUCATION
Lawrence A. Cremin, General Editor

☆   ☆   ☆

THE REPUBLIC AND THE SCHOOL
Horace Mann on the Education of Free Men
Edited by Lawrence A. Cremin

AMERICAN IDEAS ABOUT ADULT EDUCATION
1710–1951
Edited by C. Hartley Grattan

DEWEY ON EDUCATION
Introduction and Notes by Martin S. Dworkin

THE SUPREME COURT AND EDUCATION
Edited by David Fellman

INTERNATIONAL EDUCATION
A Documentary History
Edited by David G. Scanlon

CRUSADE AGAINST IGNORANCE
Thomas Jefferson on Education
Edited by Gordon C. Lee

CHINESE EDUCATION UNDER COMMUNISM
Edited by Chang-Tu Hu

CHARLES W. ELIOT AND POPULAR EDUCATION
Edited by Edward A. Krug

WILLIAM T. HARRIS ON EDUCATION
(in preparation)
Edited by Martin S. Dworkin

THE *EMILE* OF JEAN JACQUES ROUSSEAU
Selections
Translated and Edited by William Boyd

THE MINOR EDUCATIONAL WRITINGS OF
JEAN JACQUES ROUSSEAU
Selected and Translated by William Boyd

PSYCHOLOGY AND THE SCIENCE OF EDUCATION
Selected Writings of Edward L. Thorndike
Edited by Geraldine M. Joncich

THE NEW-ENGLAND PRIMER
Introduction by Paul Leicester Ford

BENJAMIN FRANKLIN ON EDUCATION
Edited by John Hardin Best

THE COLLEGES AND THE PUBLIC
1787–1862
Edited by Theodore Rawson Crane

TRADITIONS OF AFRICAN EDUCATION
Edited by David G. Scanlon

NOAH WEBSTER'S AMERICAN SPELLING BOOK
Introductory Essay by Henry Steele Commager

VITTORINO DA FELTRE
AND OTHER HUMANIST EDUCATORS
By William Harrison Woodward
Foreword by Eugene F. Rice, Jr.

DESIDERIUS ERASMUS CONCERNING
THE AIM AND METHOD OF EDUCATION
By William Harrison Woodward
Foreword by Craig R. Thompson

Desiderius Erasmus

concerning

the Aim and Method

of Education

By WILLIAM HARRISON WOODWARD

With a Foreword by
CRAIG R. THOMPSON

CLASSICS IN

No. 19

EDUCATION

BUREAU OF PUBLICATIONS
TEACHERS COLLEGE, COLUMBIA UNIVERSITY
NEW YORK

Foreword ©1964 by Teachers College
Columbia University

Library of Congress Catalog Card
Number 64–18613

First published 1904
Reprinted by permission
of the Cambridge University Press

Manufactured in the United States of America
By Edwards Brothers, Inc.
Ann Arbor, Michigan

Contents

Foreword

By CRAIG R. THOMPSON

"Better unborn than untaught," says the adage. In one of Erasmus' colloquies, *Puerpera* (1526), a friend who speaks with unmistakably Erasmian voice gives a young mother advice about her baby. Nursing the child properly is her first responsibility, he tells her, but after that must come nurture of the mind by good education. She asks him in turn to explain the best methods of sound mental and moral training, and he promises to do so.

To keep such a promise was no difficulty, for by 1526 Erasmus had already written an impressive number of books or tractates on principles and methods of education, and he was to produce still more.[1] They were written not for the benefit of a family or friend but for teachers and

---

[1] These may be grouped as follows, with dates of first publication. (Some of the dates given by Woodward must be corrected.)

Curriculum and method: *De ratione studii* (1511), *De pueris instituendis* (1529).

Grammar, syntax, composition, and style: *De duplici copia verborum ac rerum* (1512), *De constructione* (revision of a Latin syntax by William

pupils in many lands. He preferred to instruct by his pen, not in person or before a class; but the number of his works on curriculum, pedagogy, and related topics, their lucidity and persuasiveness, and his fame as a scholar and man of letters gave him an extraordinary international standing as an educator. Certain of his books were used in European schools for many generations.

For these reasons, and because of the inherent interest the writings of Erasmus have for students of intellectual and social history, a judicious account of Erasmian doctrine belongs in this series of *Classics in Education*. The most convenient summary is still William Harrison Woodward's *Desiderius Erasmus concerning the Aim and Method of Education*, a volume which includes selections from several of Erasmus' essays. Woodward (1855–1941), a graduate of Christ Church, Oxford, was Lecturer and later Professor of Education at the University of Liverpool from 1892 to 1907. While there he wrote a trilogy on Renaissance education: *Vittorino da Feltre and Other Humanist Educators* (1897), the book on Erasmus (1904), and *Studies in Education during the Age of the Renaissance, 1400–1600* (1906). These surveys, well organized and clearly written, deserved the approval and widespread use they received.[2]

Lily) (1515), translation of Theodore Gaza's Greek grammar (1516, 1518), *Antibarbari* (1520), *Ciceronianus* (1528), *De recta Latini Graecique sermonis pronuntiatione* (1528), epitome of Valla's *Elegantiae* (1531).

Material for writers: *Adagia* (ancient aphorisms and proverbs, with commentary) (1500), *Parabolae sive similia* (1514), *De conscribendis epistolis* (1521), *Apophthegmata* (1531).

Dialogues: *Colloquia familiaria* (1518).

Handbook on manners: *De civilitate* (1530).

Editions, translations, or commentaries on works by Cicero, "Cato," Terence, Euripides, Curtius, Isocrates, Libanius, Lucian, Livy, Ovid, Seneca, Plutarch, Suetonius, Demosthenes, Aristotle, Galen, Xenophon.

[2]One caveat, however: the versions of *De ratione studii* and *De pueris*

Here we are concerned with Erasmus as an educator, not
as a literary artist, textual scholar, divine, or moralist. Yet
these are not altogether practicable distinctions, for in the
Erasmian conception of education, grammatical, literary,
and moral instruction were inseparable components. Most
educators since Plato have postulated as self-evident an
authentic connection between letters and ethical training;
and from the time of the Christian schools of the Roman
Empire until the twentieth century, most Western educators took for granted that a moral education meant one
conducted under Christian auspices. Erasmus shared the
conviction of Christian scholars that the character of education is ultimately religious and, indeed, Christian. His
friend Dean Colet, when refounding St. Paul's School in
London (1509–1512), wrote under the heading "What
Shall be Taught":

> As touching in this school what shall be taught of the masters
> and learned of the scholars, it passeth my wit to devise and deter-
> mine in particular, but in general to speak and somewhat to say
> my mind: I would they were taught always in good literature
> both Latin and Greek, and good authors such as have the very
> Roman eloquence joined with wisdom, specially Christian au-
> thors that wrote their wisdom with clean and chaste Latin either
> in verse or in prose, for my intent is by this school specially to
> increase knowledge and worshiping of God and Our Lord Christ
> Jesu and good Christian life and manners in the children.

Undoubtedly Erasmus had reservations about the Latinity
of some of the Christian authors Colet esteemed, but he
endorsed Colet's moral and religious purposes.

Medieval opinion took for granted that education was
a function of the Church—as in fact it had to be then—
and that consequently schools and masters should be an-

---

instituendis appended to Woodward's book are paraphrases as much as
translations, are incomplete, and contain at least a few interpolations.

swerable to ecclesiastical authority. By the sixteenth century, however, lay schools and a degree of lay influence or
management were noticeable. Colet, an ecclesiastic, vested
control of his school in a body of laymen and appointed a
layman as high master. Yet the increasingly evident disposition of citizens and the State to do some things formerly
left to the Church did not imply hostility to religion,
though here and there it may have had undercurrents of
anticlericalism. No conflict between the schools and religion as such existed in sixteenth-century society. When
reading about Erasmus' ideas on education we should keep
in mind that he wrote to and for a society that was in
theory, and by law, Christian. This point may seem obvious enough, but readers whose presuppositions are those
of a democratic, pluralist, and largely secular society do
not always make sufficient allowance for it.

Important as this consideration is, it is not the leading
fact about his work as an educator; if it were, there would
be little excuse for reprinting a book about him. The main
reason for his place in the history of education is his superiority and influence as an expositor of what is commonly
called "humanistic," "classical," or "liberal" training. Each
of these words has its own complex history and would require rather elaborate semantic and historical treatment
if its meanings were to be defined or investigated fully.
Academic people are forever talking about "liberal education" and "the humanities," but in a vaguely descriptive
and imprecise manner, which takes little account of the
ancestry of such ideas. In education, as in philosophy or
literature, the history of an idea may be part of its meaning. At any rate, when dealing with terms like the ones
quoted, we should be aware of their history and know
something of the kind of world in which they were current.
Woodward's book is helpful toward these ends, but sixty

years ago he could assume of his readers certain kinds of information and scholastic experience no longer general.

The forces or phenomena most influential on conceptions and methods of education during Erasmus' lifetime are usually summed up as the Renaissance and humanism. Though these terms scarcely seemed to need definition in Woodward's time and seldom received it, they have been subjected to repeated analyses since his day and are now words to conjure with in historiography. And because specialists in the history of art, literature, economics, philosophy and religion, and government use different approaches to the epoch, their jargon as well as their judgments about it differ markedly.

The Renaissance, as a period in European history, extended from the fourteenth century (in Italy) to the seventeenth. For education, its most relevant phenomena were the cult of antiquity, humanism, and printing. The first two are complementary; the third is no less important for our own schools than for those of the Renaissance, but its European development coincided roughly with that era. Without printing, the educational effects of the Renaissance could not have occurred.

What Erasmus and other educators of his time meant by the Renaissance was a literary and scholarly movement originating in Italy.[3] It signified, first of all, what seemed to them nothing less than the "rebirth" or "recovery" of letters, that is, of ancient texts unknown or undervalued

---

[3]This statement must not, of course, be taken to slight the extremely important and pervasive changes in painting, sculpture, and architecture that are also identified with the Renaissance. What we are concerned with here is the Renaissance as it appeared to educators.

Moreover, the geographical and chronological boundaries of the Renaissance warn us against oversimplifying it. Erasmus, after all, was a native of Holland, not of Italy, and belonged not to the first but to the second generation of humanists north of the Alps.

in previous centuries, of more accurate and more elegant Latinity, of the study of Greek. "Latin speech, that was almost lost, is now after long absence recovered and come again," says an early sixteenth-century schoolbook.[4] Such an opinion as this may seem uncritical today to the partisan of medieval studies, but no matter; it was typical of its time. Closer study and wider dissemination of classical texts, enthusiasm for the cultural achievements of antiquity, and a more sophisticated attitude toward many of its aesthetic, ethical, and civic ideals characterized the Renaissance in the judgment of Erasmus. Old wine was poured into new bottles. The spell of antiquity and the reinterpretation of it in literature, criticism, philosophy, and art led to new and fruitful methods of scholarship, new modes of thought, new perspectives, new refinements in taste. That these were not always so novel or profound as their champions believed does not seriously diminish the character of the Renaissance as a conscious reaction against older standards and practices (i.e., those that we call "medieval") or its magnitude as a major era in intellectual history.

When used with reference to educational ideals and intellectual cultivation, the term *humanitas* represents a legacy from Cicero. It designated a literary education and thus, by implication, emphasized the centrality of human experience as the theme of such training. When we use *humanitas* or "humanism" to describe Renaissance curricula and pedagogy, these terms are virtually synonymous with "classical education," provided we refer to the content and value of the classics as well as to their form. Essentially, humanism was the study of the humanities; the humanities were Latin and Greek, the "classical" lan-

[4]Horman's *Vulgaria,* edited by M. R. James (Oxford, 1926). p. 122.

guages.[5] *Studia humanitatis* included Latin and Greek literature, rhetoric, history, and moral philosophy, studies distinct from the professional subjects of the universities —law, medicine, theology—though of course not unrelated to them.

These are general statements, subject to addition or modification as we move about from one city or region to another in the fifteenth and sixteenth centuries, for as a cultural phenomenon and an educational program humanism did not exhibit exactly the same characteristics always, everywhere, and for everyone. Some historians argue strongly, for example, that in certain centers—Florence, above all—humanistic studies, by providing new insights into history, affected political thought and policy, and therefore civic life, in very significant ways. However that may be, the impressive fact about humanism for the history of education is its reliance on Latin and Greek[6] as the chief instruments of pedagogy, with all that this reliance assumes about the nature of the classical world and

[5]Erasmus is often described as a "Christian humanist," a term formerly acceptable because passably clear, but now unfortunately ambiguous. If by "Christian humanism" we mean the interaction between classical culture and Christianity in the thought and work of Erasmus and like-minded men, the phrase makes sense. The trouble is that nowadays "humanism" is used by writers on ethics and religion as a counter to "supernaturalism" or "theism." Thus, an Anglican bishop could say in a recent popular book: "Not infrequently, as I watch or listen to a broadcast discussion between a Christian and a humanist, I catch myself realizing that most of my sympathies are on the humanist's side" (John A. T. Robinson, *Honest to God*, Philadelphia, 1963, p. 8). If "Christian" and "humanist" are antithetical terms, then to call Erasmus or anybody else a Christian humanist is nonsense, and chaos is come again. But if "humanist" is used in its older and stricter sense, meaning a person of literary and specifically classical cultivation, Erasmus was certainly the humanist par excellence in his day.

[6]Renaissance educators paid lip service to the third learned tongue, Hebrew, which was taught in a few secondary schools; but ordinarily it was a subject of the university rather than the school.

the uses of education. Renaissance educators believed, with an assurance amounting to certitude, that antiquity furnished the most illuminating and artistic examples of human experience. In Greek and Latin literatures they found, or believed they found, the finest models of expression and human wisdom. Ancient classics are "humane" and "humanistic" because they deepen our understanding of human history and values. Therefore they are supremely civilizing forces. They furnish standards of taste; the achievements of classical antiquity in art, architecture, law, literature, and philosophy are accepted as permanent models of excellence. Intelligent study of these models was considered the best training for young minds, intelligent application to modern life of lessons learned from antiquity, the promised end. The purpose of Erasmian education was to produce, by such training, civilized men who could perform private and public duties.

When described so summarily, Renaissance humanism may appear to beg many questions, but the fact remains that it was enormously influential for centuries. It provided the operative principle of "liberal" education, and in some parts of the world it still does. This is why a recent book on the classical tradition can even assert with some justice that Erasmus "is the greatest man we come across in the history of education."[7] We have enlarged the scope of liberal education, but in doing so, we retain the humanities—language, literature, philosophy, history—as central. The basis of liberal training in the Renaissance was letters, *bonae litterae:* Erasmus' favorite expression for the kind of education he prized and indeed the only kind about which he cared. Latin and Greek were "good letters" because, as he wrote in 1511, virtually everything worth

[7] R. R. Bolgar, *The Classical Heritage and Its Beneficiaries* (Cambridge, England, 1954), p. 336. An excellent book.

knowing had been set forth in those two tongues. When Erasmus wrote this statement, it was scarcely an exaggeration.

How effective classical study was in most schools, how much the authentic principles of humanistic education were honored in teaching and learning the Latin language —think of Holofernes in *Love's Labour's Lost*—are legitimate questions, which are not easy to answer. But similar questions can be asked as readily about any scheme of secondary education. Learning Latin may have been something of a tribal "puberty rite"[8] and all that, but it met the supposed requirements of the tribe; and though narrow in our eyes, it utilized the only body of knowledge available for educating. Letters commanded a respect and enthusiasm comparable to that enjoyed today by scientific studies. The early generations of humanists thought of themselves, quite rightly, as the party of progress. They felt the fervor of discovery, of communion with greatness, the satisfaction of serving a good cause.

That studies of all kinds owe a debt to the invention of printing is a truism, but it cannot be overemphasized. Thanks to printing, books became much more plentiful and much cheaper. Printing and philology together made possible better texts and uniform readings, and facilitated reference to them. Thus, printing gradually changed schoolbooks, the quality of schoolwork, and the practices of teachers and pupils. Imagine the difference between merely hearing a teacher expound a text or taking down laboriously everything he dictates and having a text of your own, besides (in the more fortunate schools) printed dictionaries for ready reference. Until the time of Erasmus, this was not possible. Or consider the business of taking

[8]Walter J. Ong, "Latin Language Study as a Renaissance Puberty Rite," *Studies in Philology*, LVI (1959), 103–124.

notes from your own reading. With skill in taking notes,
able students could grasp and retain more material than
a reader could have hoped to cover before printing made
texts cheap and plentiful. To us, note-taking is an obvious
tactic; actually it was an important innovation. Erasmus
gives careful directions about it in *De copia,* and some of
his own works of most value to students—the *Adagia,* for
instance—were products of it.

In both theory and practice, Erasmian education was
predominantly grammatical and rhetorical. Sixteenth-
century attitudes toward Latinity had nuances lost on us,
assumptions surprising and doubtless distasteful to our
age. The terms "grammar" and "rhetoric" were as inclu-
sive as our phrase "language and literature," or more so.
A grammarian had as wide a range of activity as a teacher
of English today; a competent grammarian, Horman tells
us, must be "well broken in all faculties of learning."[9] And
what could be more important to master than rhetoric,
which conferred understanding and control of the numerous schemes (figures of arrangement) and tropes (figures
of thought, images) essential for every speaker and writer?
"Language most shows a man: speak that I may see thee,"
says Jonson, echoing a Socratic dictum. Language differ-
entiates the well-bred from the ill-bred person, the learned
from the ignorant. Anyone foolish enough to be careless
of words deserves the ridicule he incurs. God is not offended by a solecism, remarks Erasmus, but neither is He
pleased by it.

Grammar and rhetoric were not supreme ends in themselves, but means. The goal of rhetorical training was eloquence. In Erasmian humanism, "eloquence" implied that
critical intelligence and breadth of mind which, when
conjoined with moral virtue, denote the educated man.

[9]*Vulgaria,* edited by M. R. James (Oxford, 1926), p. 145.

Clearly eloquence demanded, in addition to knowledge of rhetoric, long practice in composition and declamation. That is why Erasmus has so much to say on methods of composition, and why sixteenth-century educators—Roger Ascham, author of *The Schoolmaster,* is a familiar example— argued so vigorously over methods of teaching it. There was general agreement that after gaining proficiency in grammar and learning to vary and amplify words and phrases, the next major step should be imitation of good models. "Imitation" is a concept that is now even less in favor than "rhetoric," but when we meet it in sixteenth-century writings we must try to recognize it as a fundamental principle of humanism. Imitation demanded close study of approved models, with deliberate efforts to apply the lessons of this study to one's own writing—not so very different, after all, from what is attempted or what used to be attempted in "freshman composition" courses. No suggestion of anything slavish or injurious to "originality" attached to imitation; rather the contrary. The sixteenth century did not worry excessively about originality in composition but set its sights on the achievement of form. Form means order; disorderly writing is the bad fruit of disorderly thought, whether in the sixteenth or any other century. A tough-minded modern writer, George Orwell, was convinced that the political troubles of his own time were "connected with the decay of language."

Erasmus' *De copia* (1512), an authoritative manual on composition prepared at Colet's request for St. Paul's School, brings us somewhat closer to matter as well as form. In it, he discusses the mutual relations between ideas, or subject matter, and language, teaching the proper use of schemes, tropes, and synonyms. A writer's or speaker's task is always twofold: he must possess knowledge—and all knowledge is relevant to rhetoric—and express it appropriately. Effective expression requires *copia* and *amplifica-tio,* so that a thought may be varied or elaborated in many different ways. In *De copia,* Erasmus illustrates by giving no fewer than 150 variations of the sentence, "Your letter pleased me very much." Copiousness calls for imagination, in addition to an ample vocabulary and a thorough knowl-edge of proverbs, quotations, similes, and fables. Here, too, Erasmus was helpful, for he edited the century's most popular collection of proverbs and quotations, the *Adagia,* and compiled other collections of aphorisms *(Apophtheg-mata)* and similes *(Parabolae sive similia).* Another famous work of his, the *Colloquia,* began as exercises in idiom de-signed for teaching Latin but turned into a book of dia-logues on a fascinating variety of subjects. The *Colloquia,* read both by boys in school and by adults out of school, was one of the enduring works of Renaissance literature and remains an unsurpassed introduction, for the modern reader, to the daily life of the early sixteenth century.

Like many other men, Erasmus wrote only in Latin. To infer from this circumstance that scholars despised and totally neglected vernacular languages would be an exag-geration. They used Latin for the sensible purpose of reaching particular classes of readers. All formal educa-tion was based on Latin. In England, for example, it was the only language used in grammar schools until Eliza-bethan times; and boys were punished for speaking their own tongue, as willful boys had an annoying habit of doing. (Even Erasmus permits the vernacular to make a brief entrance at one stage of composition, however: the master may propound in his own language a topic for pupils to treat in Latin or Greek.) English at home, yes; but everybody agreed that the function of grammar schools was the teaching of Latin: study of grammar[10] and rheto-

[10]Erasmus had no patience with attempts to teach too much gram-

ric, analysis of texts, training in prosody, regular practice in writing and speaking Latin. Tradition authorized this course, reason recommended it, and no parent-teacher association existed to interfere with it. One's native language would look after itself; the main business of formal schooling, until the child was fourteen, was to teach Latin. Everybody knows Montaigne's account of how, from infancy, he learned only Latin and was not allowed to hear a single word of French, a language of which he knew nothing before he was six years old. In his day there was no doubt that Latin was the language most necessary to learn. It was a living language, the medium of international communication, as of traditional and of most contemporary scholarship. It was a practical subject: the only avenue to the law, medicine, and the Church. And if, incidentally, one went abroad to study, one did not have to learn a foreign tongue first; the language used in every university, as in every church, was the same—Latin.

By giving us a standard of comparison and compelling us to translate constantly, command of a foreign language sharpens our sense of our own tongue. Renaissance educators were fond of citing the example of Cicero's acknowledgment of his debt to the study of Greek. A system which produced Shakespeare, Marlowe, Jonson, Spenser, and Milton, however much may be said against it, cannot be said to have completely spoiled one's chances of artistic expression in English. None of the great English writers, until one or two generations ago, studied English literature in the university. Montaigne, it is true, forgot his Latin, or so he says; and we cannot regret that he wrote

---

mar at first. The pupil, who already knows some Latin words and phrases learned in his earliest school days, should begin to learn fundamentals of grammar as he begins to read and continue to learn grammar as he progresses in reading.

his *Essays* in French. But he did so because they were tentative, informal pieces, not addressed solely to learned readers. On the other hand, Erasmus wrote everything, even personal letters, in Latin, except for a very few in Greek.

Greek was a language much admired, but though cultivated conscientiously by the humanists, it never threatened the primacy of Latin. For all its importance to the theologian and man of letters, it was a dead language, whereas for the professional world Latin was still useful as a spoken tongue. Sir Thomas Elyot, in *The Governor* (1531), urged that Greek and Latin be taken up at the same time, when a boy is seven; but ordinarily the grammar schools postponed Greek for several years, until the pupil was well along in Latin. No one was more emphatic on the urgency of Greek to the world of scholarship than Erasmus, one of whose claims to eminence was his edition of the Greek New Testament, the first to be published (1516). He edited and translated Greek texts, translated a Greek grammar for students, and outlined a program for the teaching of Greek in the schools. Ordinarily Greek was little used as a spoken language in schools, but written Greek was taught in the same manner as Latin: drill in grammar, memorizing, reading of simple texts as soon as possible, then composition.

As Woodward's chapters show, Erasmus has much to say on elementary as well as secondary training: on teachers, texts, discipline, education for girls—which he strongly supports—and other topics of concern to an educator whose doctrine is both humanistic and humane. In some of his sympathies and ideas he was ahead of his time, in others not. He did not invent humanistic education, nor was he by any means its only distinguished advocate; but he was perhaps its most accomplished one.

From the standpoint of most members of our own society, a program of schooling based on the close study of Greek and Latin authors seems a luxury for the very few, an irrelevance for the rest. Classical education of the kind prevalent from the sixteenth through the nineteenth century is gone, at least from this country; and it will not experience a renaissance. Fortunately, however, some of its values are still widely respected and sought after. It may or may not be true that mental discipline and an understanding of man's history and of his persistent traits can be gained as well from other types of education as from the classical curriculum. But if, in our efforts to impart such discipline and understanding, we believe that the humanities or liberal arts have a major role, then we pay classical education the compliment of imitating it. Our schools try to preserve its values by teaching a variety of humanities, including modern languages, instead of concentrating on Greek and Latin. How well this scheme works is a matter of opinion, but it is one to which we seem committed.

BIBLIOGRAPHICAL NOTE

This list gives titles, with dates of recent editions, of selected works available in English.

Most of the writings of Erasmus cannot be found in English. Some of his religious works were translated in the sixteenth century, but only one or two of these versions have been reprinted. His letters to 1517 were translated by F. M. Nichols (London, 1901–1917). Other important works in English are *Enchiridion,* translated by Ford Lewis Battles, in *Advocates of Reform,* edited by Matthew Spinka, Library of Christian Classics (Philadelphia, 1953), and by

Raymond Himelick (Bloomington, Ind., 1963); *The Praise of Folly,* translated by Hoyt H. Hudson (Princeton, N.J., 1947); *The Education of a Christian Prince,* translated by Lester K. Born (New York, 1936). A new translation of the complete *Colloquies,* by Craig R. Thompson, will be published shortly. The essential parts of *De copia* are in *On Copia of Words and Ideas,* a translation by D. B. King and H. D. Rix (Milwaukee, Wis., 1963).

On sixteenth-century translations of Erasmus, consult, in addition to Woodward's list, the entries under "Erasmus" in the *British Museum Catalogue of Printed Books* and the *Short-Title Catalogue of Books Printed in England . . . 1475–1640.*

The best introductions to the life and times of Erasmus are P. S. Allen, *The Age of Erasmus* (Oxford, 1914) and *Erasmus: Lectures and Wayfaring Sketches* (Oxford, 1934); R. W. Chambers, *Thomas More* (London, 1948); Johan Huizinga, *Erasmus of Rotterdam,* translated by F. Hopman (London, 1952); Margaret Mann Phillips, *Erasmus and the Northern Renaissance* (London, 1949); Preserved Smith, *Erasmus* (New York, 1923).

For interpretations of the Renaissance, see Hans Baron, *The Crisis of the Early Italian Renaissance* (Princeton, N.J., 1955); Jacob Burckhardt, *The Civilization of the Renaissance in Italy,* translated by S. G. C. Middlemore (New York, 1930); Douglas Bush, *The Renaissance and English Humanism* (Toronto, 1939); Wallace K. Ferguson, *The Renaissance in Historical Thought* (Boston, 1948); Denys Hay, *The Italian Renaissance in Its Historical Background* (Cambridge, England, 1961); Paul Oskar Kristeller, *Studies in Renaissance Thought and Letters* (Rome, 1956); *New Cambridge Modern History* (Cambridge, England, 1957), Vol. I; Erwin Panofsky, *Renaissance and Renascences in Western Art* (Stockholm, 1960); Preserved Smith, *The Age of the Reformation*

(New York, 1948); Roberto Weiss, *Humanism in England during the Fifteenth Century* (Oxford, 1957).

Valuable analyses of the classical tradition in the West can be found in R. R. Bolgar, *The Classical Heritage and Its Beneficiaries* (Cambridge, England, 1954); Gilbert Highet, *The Classical Tradition* (Oxford, 1949); Paul Oskar Kristeller, *The Classics and Renaissance Thought* (Cambridge, Mass., 1955); J. E. Sandys, *A History of Classical Scholarship* (Cambridge, England, 1906–1908).

Some Tudor vulgaria, English sentences with Latin translation, have been reprinted and often make delightful reading. The best are Horman's, edited by M. R. James (Oxford, 1926); Stanbridge's and Whittinton's, edited by Beatrice White, Early English Text Society (London, 1932); and an anonymous one by a Magdalen School master, *A Fifteenth Century School Book,* edited by William Nelson (Oxford, 1956). Among specialized studies may be mentioned T. W. Baldwin, *William Shakspere's Small Latine and Lesse Greeke* (Urbana, Ill., 1944); Hanna H. Gray, "Renaissance Humanism: The Pursuit of Eloquence," *Journal of the History of Ideas,* XXIV (1963), 497–514; E. H. Harbison, *The Christian Scholar in the Age of the Reformation* (New York, 1956); Pearl Hogrefe, *The Sir Thomas More Circle* (Urbana, Ill., 1959), Chapter 5; J. H. Lupton, *A Life of John Colet* (London, 1909); Walter J. Ong, "Latin Language Study as a Renaissance Puberty Rite," *Studies in Philology,* LVI (1959), 103–124; J. K. Sowards, "Erasmus and the Apologetic Textbook: A Study of the *De duplici copia verborum ac rerum,*" *Studies in Philology,* LV (1958), 122–135; Craig R. Thompson, *Schools in Tudor England,* Folger Booklets on Tudor and Stuart Civilization (Washington, D.C., 1958); Foster Watson, *Vives on Education: A Translation of the De tradendis disciplinis* (Cambridge, England, 1913).

Desiderius Erasmus

concerning

the Aim and Method of Education

by

WILLIAM HARRISON WOODWARD
Professor of Education in the University of Liverpool
Author of *Vittorino da Feltre*

CAMBRIDGE :
at the University Press
1904

PREFACE.

THE scope of the present study of Erasmus is defined by its title. I have directed attention to one aspect only of his work and personality. That aspect of Erasmus is of profound importance. Indeed it may be reasonably maintained that of all his activities none was more congenial to him, none more characteristic, none of more influence in his own age and subsequently than that which was concerned with Education.

Yet although the limitations of the subject have not been lost sight of, it has been, from the nature of it, necessary to take a wider view of the attitude of Erasmus to the problems of his time than a hasty reading of the title of this book might suggest. For it is obviously impossible to understand and to present aright the Erasmian ideal of the fit training of the young unless the presuppositions upon which it rests are duly examined. Thus a brief historical review of the literary life of Erasmus was called for, though it seemed well to make clear the limits of the purpose for which it was compiled. Much that fills so large

a space in the approved biographies of Erasmus has
been in effect ignored, as but remotely affecting the
subject of this enquiry. On the other hand I have
endeavoured to realise with precision the appeal which
Antiquity made to Erasmus and the message which he
believed it to convey to the modern world. Compared
with this his share in the Lutheran conflict seems to
me to be, in a serious appraisement of Erasmus, as
unimportant as it was to himself distasteful.

The deepening interest in educational enquiry which
marks the present time will, we may confidently hope,
extend to the study of the aims and achievements of
the educators of the past. Next to the great Italian
Masters of the Quattrocento Erasmus makes claim for
serious recognition. The actual degree of his influence
in Germany and England it is difficult to assess, and
writers have differed in their judgments. But if it
should be provable that Erasmus left less direct impress
upon school organisation or methods than certain of
his contemporaries, the reason will be found in the fact
that he was on crucial points so far in advance of public
opinion, that he took so wide, so truly humanist, a view
of the scope of education that in the troubled times of
sectarian partisanship his day was not yet. In certain
regards we must feel as we study such a work as the
De Pueris statim ac liberaliter instituendis, contained in
English dress in the present volume, that he speaks
with a note unexpectedly "modern." As we realise
therefrom the depth of Erasmus' conviction of the
respect due to the rights of the child we understand, what
we may have already suspected, how far a prevalent

type of criticism of Humanist methods has been based
upon ignorance of the facts.

It is indeed of the first importance that the student
of the history of educational thought should be led to
acquaintance at first hand with the men whose doctrines
are under discussion. Only upon this condition can the
study of the subject be regarded as worthy of serious
recognition as an aspect of literary and historical
enquiry.

In the study of Erasmus the text is the first, the
second and the third authority: and I have built up
my exposition upon repeated readings of the treatises,
prefaces, and letters pertinent to the subject. The
range of Erasmian literature is notoriously immense.
To distinguish the works which have proved specially
prolific of suggestion is scarcely possible. But two
may be here singled out as of first rate importance to
students of Erasmus. The *Letters of Erasmus* by
Mr F. M. Nicholls carries down the correspondence to
1509: a second volume which is, I am glad to know,
to appear very shortly, will include the year 1517. The
correspondence of Erasmus so far as it is of biographical interest—in a very wide sense—is presented
in an English version, with most careful apparatus of
preface and note. Without necessarily accepting every
disputed attribution or date, I can affirm that no more
valuable aid to the understanding of Erasmus down to
the Cambridge period has yet seen the light, whether
in this country or in Germany. The second work to
which allusion is made is the analysis of the psychological presuppositions of Erasmus' educational doctrine

of Dr Hermann Tögel, *Die pädagogischen Anschauungen des Erasmus in ihrer psychologischen Begründung*. The author, however, is prone to see everything in terms of Herbartianism, to the detriment of his historical perception.

I desire to express my obligations to Miss May Allen, Mr John Sampson, University Librarian, and Mr E. Gordon Duff, for kind assistance at different stages of my work. Miss Allen has been particularly helpful in the bibliographical section.

THE UNIVERSITY, LIVERPOOL,
    February 1, 1904.

PART I.

CHAPTER I.

AN OUTLINE OF THE LIFE OF ERASMUS, MAINLY
IN REGARD TO HIS CAREER AS A SCHOLAR.

ERASMUS was born at Rotterdam on October 27th, 1466[1].
He and his brother Peter, some three years his senior, were the
offspring of a union unsanctified by the Church. His parents
were Gerard of Gouda and Margaret, the daughter of a physician
of Zevenberge. Their marriage had been obstructed by the
family of Gerard, but at the time of the birth of Erasmus there
would seem to have been a legal bar to the union, in the fact
that the father was in priest's orders[2]. The connection of
Erasmus with Rotterdam rests probably on the circumstance
of his mother's residence in that city when he was born.

There is no ground for doubt that the name *Erasmus* was
given him at baptism after a Saint and Martyr held in reverence
in the Low Countries and in England[3]. The common prae-
nomen *Desiderius* was added as a Latin equivalent by Erasmus
himself; *Roterodamus* completed the triple designation with
which Roman usage made him familiar. The first edition of

---

[1] The evidence for 1466 is set out by Richter, *Erasmus-Studien*, p. v;
Nicholls, *The Epistles of Erasmus*, p. 474, has arrived at the same conclusion. The date usually given is 1467.

[2] See Nicholls, *Epistles*, p. 14.

[3] Erasmus was a martyred Bishop of Campania, who suffered under
Diocletian.

the *Adagia* (1500) bears the full title: *Desyderius Erasmus Roterodamus.*

The common assumption that Erasmus was a name fancifully devised by its bearer to express in Greek form the meaning 'beloved' contained in the Flemish Gerrit or Gerard is unnecessary.

The circumstances of their birth inevitably clouded the home-life of the two boys, and we know that throughout his career Erasmus felt the slur which was cast upon his mother's name and his own. As late as 1516 he sought for formal relief from the disability attaching to his origin by papal dispensation. Moreover, it is not unlikely that this same "invidious bar" may have materially influenced his guardians in the action which they took in respect of his future career at the time of his parents' death. And when towards the close of his life Erasmus became involved in bitter controversies, religious and literary, he found opponents not unwilling to envenom their warfare by a taunt so ready to their hands.

At four years of age Erasmus was living with his mother at Gouda where he attended a school kept by Peter Winckel, afterwards his guardian. Later we find him entered as a pupil in the Cathedral Choir School at Utrecht. When nine years old he was taken by Margaret to Deventer where he attended the famous school attached to the Church of St Lebuin, of which Alexander Hegius[1] was the head-master, and Sintheim, a scholar of distinction, an assistant. The Deventer school was not one of the schools of the Brethren of the Common Life; nor was Hegius a member of the Order, though certain of his assistants probably were. The school had great repute in the Low Countries and in the Rhine-land, and at this period contained possibly six hundred pupils. We cannot trace any definitely humanist note in the instruction of the junior classes. Erasmus in later years complained bitterly both of the teaching and

[1] Hegius went to Deventer school in 1465 and died, still head-master, in 1498. Nicholls, p. 17.

of the books employed, as well as of the brutality of the discipline[1]. It is difficult not to feel that, like Locke at Westminster, Erasmus derived from Deventer life-long impressions of profitless and unhappy experiences of his school days. Hegius, probably, had but little share in his education, for Erasmus left the school in 1480, before he had reached the higher classes. But he tells us that he there saw that much greater scholar Rudolphus Agricola, who on his return from Italy in that year was staying at Deventer, where he visited the school and perhaps took an occasional part in the teaching. We may safely infer that the man from whom Erasmus learnt most was Sintheim, whose repute for learning and for skill in teaching survived in North Germany for half a century. We are told that Hegius and Sintheim were men of true humanist instincts and represented the wider educational aims and more intelligent methods which the Italian masters had set forth in the famous schools of Mantua and Ferrara. But we gather from Erasmus' recollections that Deventer exemplifies once more the gulf which in the actual working of a school separates ideals from practice. The "love for sound learning" has not always proved to be readily translateable into terms of class-work, instruction and exercises. Hegius and Sintheim were men of scholarship; but their assistants, the text-books, the range of possible subjects, the available methods of instruction, were inevitably those of the time. So we find Erasmus as he looks back upon his school days writing: "Deventer was a school still in the age of barbarism. We had the *Pater meus* (joint declension of noun and adjective) and the tenses dictated to us for learning by heart; the accidence of Ebrardus Graecista and the ridiculous verses of John Garland were read aloud. From Hegius and Sintheim the school drew some savour of true Letters: and so by contact with boys in Sintheim's class I got glimpses of higher things. Hegius himself gave on rare occasions lessons to classes grouped together."

[1] *Op.* i. 514 F.   Infra, p. 205 seqq.

In the tract *De Pueris* we find allusions of the same kind, which relate, we cannot doubt, to his own school experiences. Erasmus admits that at Deventer he imbibed a strong taste for learning, though with the qualification that he could only indulge it by stealth, and in spite of, rather than by the aid of, his masters. It is perhaps wise not to take this reservation very literally.

In the autumn of 1480 Erasmus had reached the third class, "Tertia" (the eighth, Octava, being the lowest), when he lost both father and mother within a few months of each other. He was thereupon taken from Deventer to be entered at the school of the Collationary Brothers at Bois-le-Duc. He left Deventer a boy of fourteen, a studious youth, probably of poor physique, and shrinking from too intimate converse with other boys, with whom he had little in common and in whose hands the knowledge of the shadow resting on his home-life was an inevitable instrument of torture. Yet the change to Bois-le-Duc was by no means for the better if we are to accept the criticism which Erasmus at a later period recorded upon the school of the Brethren. We must, however, remember that Erasmus cannot be treated as a judicial witness in respect of the period which followed the death of his mother in 1480. It has generally been assumed[1] that his entry upon the monastic life and his subsequent ordination were steps forced upon him by the self-seeking action of his guardian ; that a chain of circumstances was deliberately forged to fetter him ; that he was cajoled into accepting a decision from which there was no escape. It is enough to say here that a candid examination of all the evidence we can collect from Erasmus' own writings which date from that period leads his biographers to a different conclusion. His reminiscences, recorded at a much later period, upon which the version usually current is based, are

[1] This not unnatural interpretation of the references made by Erasmus to his early life is found in every biography except in those of Emerton and Nicholls. But the facts seem to be as they are stated above.

so evidently coloured by subsequent experiences and reflections that we cannot accept them as a sincere account of the actual facts. The boarding school of the Brethren of the Common Life at Bois-le-Duc was, he asserts, "a very seed-bed of monkery," and as a place of education worthless. It is, of course, possible that this and other Houses of the Brethren had declined from the high standard of religious life and of intellectual interests which marked them at Deventer, Liège and elsewhere. We have no contemporary evidence of any kind to guide us to a judgment of the level of studies or of spiritual fervour of this particular monastery. Erasmus undoubtedly inveighed all his life long against monastic schools for boys; his famous dictum[1]—"schola sit publica aut nulla" —is certainly aimed at the schools kept by the monastic orders. It is probable, also, that the monastic career was presented by his schoolmasters to the shrinking, studious boy, of no fortune, no prospects, of weakly constitution, and of discredited origin, in its best light. To the friends of the young Erasmus it might well seem without insincerity a suitable calling. And there is reasonable ground for believing that to Erasmus himself his choice proved for some years at least sufficiently congenial.

He remained in the school until the close of 1482 or a little later. His guardians, he tells us in 1515, vied with the Brethren in bringing moral pressure to bear upon their charge. He was then between 16 and 17 years of age, and allured by the promise of unrestricted opportunities of study he yielded, and in 1483 entered as a novice the Augustinian monastery of Emmaus at Stein near Gouda. This was his home for the next ten years; here in due course he made full profession, and took the vows; here finally in 1492 he was ordained priest. Erasmus' career was thus finally determined.

The period of his residence at Stein is of no little significance as a stage in the development of Erasmus as a man of Letters. It is clear that he found there some attractive

[1] *De Pueris*, etc., i. 504 C. Infra, p. 204.

companionship and much tranquil leisure for scholarly reading. He wrote, we may suppose for his own amusement, certain Latin poems that have been preserved. There are amongst them a few religious poems, in sapphics ; satires in the Horatian manner ; elegiacs after Tibullus. But three prose works are of more importance in revealing the trend of his interests. The first, written when he was 18, is an Epitome of the *Elegantiae Linguae Latinae* of Laurentius Valla[1], the great Italian scholar, the contemporary of Vittorino and Poggio, to whom later humanists looked up with justice as the chief restorer of Latinity. This compendium was circulated in MS. and found its way into the hands of students in distant centres of learning. Erasmus is unwearied at this time in urging upon his correspondents the solid worth of Valla's work, in spite of the known antipathy of churchmen to his memory. We have in the second place two slighter compositions, rhetorical in treatment yet none the less expressing genuine conviction on the part of the writer, a piece in denunciation of war, always a favourite theme of Erasmus, and an oration in grateful memory of a lady who had befriended his orphanhood. Thirdly, he has left a formal epistle *De Contemptu Mundi* (1486) in which with evident sincerity he sets forth the attractions of the monastic life, in a fashion which confirms that general spirit of content with his quietist career which breathes through all the letters of this period which have survived.

It is not an easy problem to appraise at their true value the complaints which Erasmus, at a much later date, levelled against destiny in making him a monk. Two things seem clear : the first is that he has left no contemporary record of his discontent ; the second, that his bent to literature and scholarship was fostered by the leisure of the ten years spent at Stein, as it could hardly have been by any other mode of life. In 1493 Erasmus had gained repute enough to have become known to

---

[1] On Valla's contribution to scholarship see p. 104 : and on Erasmus' early respect for his achievements, *Op.* iii. 1 c (Nicholls, p. 72).

the Bishop of Cambrai, whose service he now entered. This appointment enabled him to gain dispensation from residence in the monastery, whereupon the Bishop sent him to the University of Paris, where he resided at the Collège de Montaigu as a student in Theology. The absorbing interests of the University were scholastic Divinity and Logic. Grammar was treated mainly as a branch of Dialectic. The New Learning was but feebly represented. Robert Gaguin was perhaps the best scholar teaching regularly in the University. His chief performance is a Latin history of France, a poor humanist history of the imitative sort, on the model of the histories— themselves lifeless copies of Livy—of Bruni and Poggio. Erasmus wrote a laudatory letter to the writer on seeing the work in manuscript. It was thought good enough to print as a prefatory epistle (Sept. 1495) to the work. This letter attracted the notice of certain readers, amongst whom was Colet, who reminded Erasmus of this occasion of his first acquaintance with his name.

Erasmus, although in the faculty of Theology, devoted himself chiefly to the classics, and made a beginning with Greek. In this he was almost wholly self-taught, for Greek literature had attracted as yet very few students outside Italy. He seems to have preached at the Augustinian Abbey Church of Ste-Geneviève. He was already acquiring that distaste for scholastic learning, particularly as represented in Scotus, and in the mediaeval grammarians, which he so loudly expressed as his own classical feeling became more defined. But it is probable that leave of absence from the monastery was at first conditional upon the devotion of a fixed proportion of time to the study of Theology. This will explain why Erasmus, becoming resentful of restraint upon his freedom, writes with an accent of self-pity of this enforced occupation with the mediaevalists. He was groping his way to the standpoint of historical divinity and of plain literary method in exegesis, which was characteristic of his maturity. Meantime he earned

his living as a teacher of Latin, and became recognised as one
of the ablest scholars in residence. About 1495 he came into
contact with English students, and transferred his quarters to
the boarding-house in which certain young Englishmen of
position lived for purposes of study. Amongst them was
Lord Mountjoy, a young man of eighteen, who proved one
of Erasmus' most forbearing patrons. Erasmus was fortunate
in his English pupils, to whom he was indebted for much consideration at the time, and for valuable interest in subsequent
years. Apart from teaching, Erasmus was a most industrious
student, and in spite of a severe illness contracted through the
unhealthiness of his surroundings—Paris was noted for its ague
and fever—he was absorbed in Latin scholarship. He wrote a
little handbook on epistolary composition, but we have no other
published work from his pen at this period.

Erasmus was a poor man, with no resources beyond his
earnings as a teacher. He had the tastes and the necessities
of a scholar, conscious of considerable powers but at the same
time of a bodily condition which rendered him dependent on
a certain standard of comfort. He began to cast about for the
means of support sanctioned by the custom of the age among
men of learning. He wanted a patron, liberal, but not exacting. To the scholar of the Renaissance generosity lost all
its grace if accompanied by expectation of definite work in
return. The patron should be content with the consciousness
that it had been permitted him to come to the aid of genius.
There is indeed nothing peculiar to Erasmus or to his age in
this attitude. A certain Lady of Veer was approached through
a friend in the interests of Erasmus. Here was a poor scholar
of great promise anxious to establish his position by acquiring
the degree of Doctor; desirous also of enlarging his attainments by a sojourn in Italy; a man of such ability might be
counted on to reflect renown upon an enlightened patroness.
As all his biographers have admitted, the correspondence of
Erasmus with his ally who had the ear of the lady—who

yielded not very adequately to persuasion—leaves an unpleasant savour. Irritable self-conceit, shameless importunity, perfect indifference to the person importuned, are all in evidence ; it is hard to banish a sense of contempt for a scholar who could play so sordid a part.

Yet we must remember that Erasmus was by profession a scholar, at a time when scholars had yet, in Western Europe at least, to establish their claim to professional status and respect. His was a career in which no external standards of capacity were so far understood or accorded recognition. The only measure of desert was the scholar's own claim : he was above criticism, for no one but another scholar could test his excellence. Hence the man of Letters in the earlier days of the New Learning was apt to be abnormally sensitive, resenting a judgment upon himself which was less flattering than his own, ever suspicious of lack of appreciation, and filled with a sense of his own serious importance. It was an inevitable stage in the evolution of the scholar's position in the new society. The pedant or the charlatan became in time distinguishable by consent from the man of real power, as standards of merit which were readily understood were slowly formulated with the increasing security of learning. This irritable self-consciousness may be compared with that of the modern actor, or, less aptly, with that of the prophet of a new school in art or music, where, for lack of accepted canons of excellence, criticism is perforce individual and provisional. We understand the sensitiveness of the artist and forgive him if he likes his own criticism best. As regards importunity, Erasmus was conscientiously assured that he had it in his power to add something to the learning of his age. He knew, too, as we also know, that in his begging neither avarice nor ambition of place had part or lot. We can sum up the matter by saying that if Erasmus did not rise above the fashion of his day and the precedents of his class, in the larger view his motives were not wholly unworthy. It proved of no slight import to the world that Erasmus should, with whatever importunities, gain what he needed to go on with his studies.

In the middle of 1499 Erasmus left Paris to accompany Lord Mountjoy to England. This was the first of several visits to this country and left behind it on the mind of the traveller a most grateful impression. He was welcomed as one of themselves by the group of scholars, with Colet at their head, which centred at Oxford; and in London he was at home with More and Warham. It was, during this winter of 1499, that Erasmus laid the foundation of that affectionate intimacy which united him to More and Colet until their deaths. Undoubtedly his intercourse with these two kindred minds strengthened in Erasmus the determination to devote himself to classical study. Colet urged him further to utilise his attainments in the service of historical theology: and from this time we find frequent reference to such a purpose in the correspondence of Erasmus. Colet, indeed, attracted all that was best in him; and the peculiar intellectual habit of the Oxford scholar—his historical and objective view of knowledge —made warm appeal to Erasmus' own literary and scholarly instinct. He was thus able to appreciate to the full the method upon which Colet treated the Pauline Epistles, the subject upon which he was at that period specially engaged. It is not surprising that he tried to secure Erasmus for Oxford, as a co-worker in the cause which he had so closely at heart. But Erasmus became at once suspicious of an attempt to fetter his liberty. Indefatigable now and always as a student he would only work in absolute freedom. His aims must be of his own choice; he would pursue them where and how his own waywardness should determine. To overlook this charac-teristic is to misunderstand the man: with him this passion for independence was thoroughly genuine and had in it nothing of mere self-conceit. It is evident from the letters which he ad-dressed to Colet before leaving England that he was still uncertain whither his intellectual tastes would lead him. He did not wish the question to be pre-judged by any one else, not even by Colet. That there existed an intimate relation between sound (*i.e.* classical) literature and sound (*i.e.* pre-scholastic) divinity he was already assured. But it was still possible that his dominant interest might lie in the ancient literatures. And in any case it was clear to him that his equipment in learning was wholly inadequate to the task of attacking historical divinity as a scholar should. He had already resolved that "a little more knowledge and a little more power of expressing it" were the pre-requisites of any service which he could render to the world. Whether while at Oxford he spent any time upon Greek we do not know, nor whether he saw Grocyn and Linacre, the pioneers there of the New Learning. But before the end of 1499 he had determined to return to Paris.

In February of the following year he was at work there, absorbed in the classics but especially in Greek. "My Greek studies are almost too much for my courage, while I have not the means of purchasing books nor the help of a master." Throughout the spring he was engaged upon the first collection of the *Adagia*, a compilation of proverbs, maxims and witty utterances drawn from classical authors. It appeared in June 1500 with a dedication to Lord Mountjoy, to whom Erasmus was doubtless indebted for timely help at the period. The book gave evidence of a wide range of reading. His knowledge of Greek was in spite of difficulties rapidly increasing. About this date he begins to quote it in his letters. He records that he is at work upon Homer "refreshed and fed by the very sight of his words even when I cannot always understand him." Driven from Paris by the plague he carried off his books to Orleans, or St Omer, but longed to find himself again at the University where alone books and a teacher were to be had. When he had attained to some moderate competency in Greek, "without which the amplest erudition in Latin is imperfect[1]," he will devote himself entirely to sacred

---

[1] iii. 968 D. Infra, p. 135.

literature.   To earn money he edited the *De Officiis* of Cicero.
By this date (1501) Erasmus had acquired a notable power of
expression in Latin; both in speech and in writing : and by his
industry and his acute observation he had accumulated a store
of knowledge upon the material of the language, which was
surpassed perhaps by his great predecessor, Valla, alone.   He
was laying the foundation for his book *De Copia Verborum et
Rerum*, the *Similia* and an enlarged *Adagia*.   For all that
he insists that "he has almost deserted the Latin Muse for the
Greek," and that he "would pawn his coat for a codex of an
author whom he had not yet read."   He began to work at
Euripides and Isocrates in July 1501, and is revelling in his hardly
won powers of construing.   He tried to compile a commentary
on the *Epistle to the Romans*, but gave up the task for lack of
sufficient knowledge of the original.   At this time, too, we
meet with a half-formed project of an edition of the Letters of
St Jerome.   But in such a task "how large a space must be
filled by comment upon the literature, the antiquities and the
history of the Greeks[1]."

In 1502 Erasmus removed to Louvain.   His travels during
the years 1499–1505 throw an interesting light upon one or
two aspects of the life of the time.   We perceive for instance
the real meaning of the constant visitations of the plague,
which year after year broke up Universities even in so important a city as Paris, bringing in its train risks and losses of
most serious import.   Next, the habit of travel in spite of the
time and expense involved.   Erasmus is constantly on the
move.   Crossing the Alps is no doubt a grave and costly
venture, but a scholar regarded a visit to England, Germany,
Switzerland more lightly than he did a century ago.

At Louvain, Erasmus was at once pressed to accept the
chair of Rhetoric in the University, an offer which with equal
promptitude he declined.   He had no intention of staying
long at Louvain.   So far as the scarcity of texts would permit
he was absorbed in Greek.   He began to prepare versions from

[1] iii. 67 D (Nicholls, p. 289).

Lucian and from Euripides, partly by way of earning money from patrons, partly to supply a need of students. We must remember the extreme scarcity of Greek MSS. and of printed editions during the period preceding the activity of the Aldine Press and the rival houses, of the Giunta, Gryphius and Plantin. There was as yet no printer of Greek texts out of Italy: and Greek copyists were rare. Aldus published the *Dialogues* of Lucian in 1504: Erasmus spent much of his time translating from this text. It is not difficult to imagine that Lucian's thrusts at the philosophers of his day appealed peculiarly to Erasmus, who had begun to expend his sarcasms upon the schoolmen. There was, too, much in common between Lucian and his translator in the humour of their outlook upon life and the overflowing wit with which they told what they saw. These months devoted to the *Dialogues* bore other fruit than the volume of translations of 1506: they rendered possible the *Praise of Folly* five or six years later.

Once more in Paris in 1505, Erasmus resumes communications with his English friends, especially with Colet, now Dean of St Paul's. He sent him one or two of his books in MS., amongst which was the *Enchiridion*, a simply written manual of Christian conduct, but not the Lucian. The work upon which he was particularly engaged was a new find of which he was very proud, a volume of *Annotations on the New Testament* by Valla, the first attempt to apply the method of linguistic criticism to Scripture[1]. To Erasmus such a line of enquiry was thoroughly congenial, falling in, as it did, with his conviction of the essential importance of the literary point of view in the study of all ancient documents. As soon as this book was issued from the press (April 1505) Erasmus left

[1] The aim of Valla's *Notes* was to correct errors in the Vulgate by reference to the original Greek. In these *Notes* we may see the first suggestion of the edition of the Greek Testament with its version and notes which Erasmus published in 1516.

Paris for another visit to London, on the invitation of Lord Mountjoy.

No city in Europe, except Rome, possessed such attraction for Erasmus as London then held out, in the presence there of the well-known group of English scholars, with Colet at their head. Linacre, Grocyn, More and Warham were either in the capital or close at hand. Erasmus it seems looked to receive a sinecure benefice at the hand of the Archbishop. It is significant that the method of approach to this desirable end was the presentation of a version from Lucian to Bishop Fox and a translation of the *Hecuba* to Warham. During this English visit the University of Cambridge passed a Grace enabling Erasmus to take the degree of Doctor of Divinity, but it is certain that he did not avail himself of it. It is probable that he did not journey either to Oxford or Cambridge during the year that he remained in this country. The time seems to have been spent in or near London, much of it in company with More, who joined his guest in translating Lucian. More's first published work is contained in the volume of the *Dialogues* in Latin dress published at Paris by Badius in 1506. Erasmus left England in May of that year to fulfil a project conceived more than ten years before.

The position of Erasmus in the world of Letters was already assured. In Louvain, Paris or London, wherever indeed the new light had won its way, his repute was above question. He had undoubtedly command of the best Latin style of his time out of Italy. He was widely read in Roman literature, classical and patristic. Men of position in affairs, in scholarship and in the Church came to him as a friend and adviser. It rested with himself alone to gain fame as a great Teacher in any seat of learning in Europe. But Erasmus knew how much more he had yet to know before he could put forward any such claim. It was borne in upon him with increasing force that he must first make himself known to the

Italian scholars and sit at the feet of the Greek teachers who even yet had not crossed the Alps.

He took with him two pupils and their English tutor, and in July 1506 was well on his way by Paris, Lyons and Savoy. It is characteristic of Erasmus that finding himself for the first time amidst the most striking scenery in Europe he left no word which conveys the impressions which it made upon him. Instead we have a classical lucubration on Old Age, composed, we are told, to while away the tedium of the August days in the High Alps. Only once, in the very last years of his life, did Erasmus record the sensations evoked by great scenery, when the view from the Lake of Constance struck his fancy.

At Turin[1] he received the degree of Doctor of Theology, and pressed on, early in September, to Bologna. Thence in November he crossed the Apennines to Florence. We turn hopefully to his correspondence. But what do we find? Not a word which reveals that he was under the spell of the beauty of the city, that he recognises the dignity of its civic life, the distinction of its architecture and art. He gives us no clue, moreover, to any perception of the living significance of Florence in the history of learning. We may perhaps understand that Erasmus might have little feeling for the *Heiterkeit* of the Italian spirit, and less for the art which expressed it. But as a humanist he knew himself to be on classic ground, where Chrysoloras had taught Greek first in Western Europe, where the great manuscript treasures had been collected, the city of Poggio, of Ficino, of Poliziano. Erasmus made no acquaintances; he translated more Lucian, and grumbled at his lot. It was a principle with him to refuse to learn or even to recognise vernacular languages. Thus he found himself cut off from intercourse in a society proud of its Tuscan speech. "You speak to a deaf man," he said to Ruccellai, who pressed

[1] Upon the Italian journey the indispensable authority is P. Nolhac, *Érasme en Italie*.

his Italian upon him: and in Italian as in English he remained
dumb to the end.

In December Erasmus was again in Bologna, where he was
an amazed spectator of the entry of Julius II, a victorious
general taking possession of a vanquished city.   He now gave
up the use of the monastic dress, thus decisively refusing to
be longer identified with the obscurantists of the Church.
Bologna was favourably circumstanced for Greek studies, and
in its University Erasmus made the first of those friendships
which were the charm of his Italian sojourn.   The year (1507)
which he thus spent was of high importance in his intellectual
development.   He had come to Italy, in his own words, chiefly
for the sake of Greek, and found himself amid a circle of
noteworthy scholars, with leisure and passable health.

Towards the end of 1507 he was in correspondence with
Aldus Manutius, the great printer, respecting a new and
corrected edition of his versions from Euripides, when he was
met by an offer that he should transfer himself to Venice and
there prepare for publication a new and larger collection of
Adages.   At the close of the year Erasmus was installed as a
member of the Aldine household, his pupils got rid of and he
himself enjoying what could be had nowhere else in Europe,
the society of a community of scholars and craftsmen using
Greek as their living language.   His position in the circle is
not very clear.   He acted in some capacity as adviser and as
assistant to Aldus ; but his time must have been chiefly
absorbed by the compilation of the *Adagia*, which by aid of
friends and of books became a wholly new work.   Amongst
the scholars whom from time to time he may have seen almost
daily were John Lascaris, Marcus Musurus and Urban of
Botzen, all Greek scholars of the first rank, and engaged in
editorial work for Aldus.   It is indeed difficult to overstate the
debt due from Erasmus to Aldus at this critical stage of his
career.   Thanks to his friendship Erasmus had gained ex-
ceptional facility in Greek, and had definitely entered the

inner circle of Greek scholars. He had formed profitable relations with the greatest publisher of his age, the man who in a true sense rendered Greek learning possible to Western communities. In his preface to the *Adagia* and in the actual text of the work Erasmus records his immense obligation to Aldus and to his colleagues in searching for MSS. for purposes of the work and in diligent help in interpretation. But it irked Erasmus to feel such obligations; some years later he wrote a spiteful dialogue (the Colloquy upon *Sordid Wealth*) in abuse of Asulanus, the father-in-law of Aldus and manager of his household. The abuse is vented upon the parsimony of the Aldine table; but the Italian standard of living was probably as beneficial to Erasmus as it was novel and unpleasant. And in any case we may be certain that he lived there only because he chose to do so. One hopes that there may be some key to the puzzle which has escaped record. Towards the end of the year 1508 as the great Aldine *Rhetores Graeci* was in process of publication—to have a share, however slight, in preparing such a work was no slight privilege to Erasmus—he left Venice for Padua, where he attended the lectures of Musurus and mingled in the learned society of the famous University—"locupletissimum optimarum disciplinarum emporium," he calls it. He formed a good opinion of the integrity and seriousness of the Paduan humanists.

Erasmus had again taken charge of a pupil, a son of James IV of Scotland, the youthful Archbishop of St Andrews. Going by Ferrara and Siena he reached Rome on March 1, 1509. Once more, it would be interesting to find in his letters or writings—then or subsequently—traces of some deep impression made upon him by the ruins of Rome. But there is, in effect, nothing. On the other hand, the dignity of the scholarly society in which he at once took his place, was wholly to his liking. He did not fail to remark, however, the divorce between learned Churchmen and the Christian spirit, which was nowhere more noticeable than in the Rome of Julius II. "Rome," he says,

" is nothing but a site strewn with ruins and remains—monuments of disaster and decay......take away the papal See and the papal Court—would Rome to-day be more than a name ? " To Erasmus, full of conviction that the genius of Ancient Rome was still the unique force of civilisation, there was no attraction in the picturesqueness of its fallen greatness. The libraries of Rome were open to him, and Cardinals and Secretaries vied with one another in shewing him kindness : though he is, perhaps, a little too anxious to impress his northern friends with the fact. Raphael was at work in the Vatican, Michelangelo in the Sistine Chapel, and Erasmus may well have seen both of them there. But in the presence of the glowing noon-day of Italian art he remains untouched. Nor do the scenery, the light, the colour, the vegetation of the southern land affect him. He moves through all these things as a student, an observer of human life, seeing much that, apparently, he does not notice, yet, perhaps, also acquiring much that he does not overtly record.

But when Erasmus hastened north again in the spring of 1509 to greet the new King Henry of England we know that he went out of Italy a different man. He had come into direct relations with the princes of the Church, and had watched the working of the great ecclesiastical machine, with no enthusiasm but without serious moral repulsion. He had established his own status by acquiring an Italian degree. He had entered into intimate relations with scholars, editors, and publishers, and had been admitted by them to a place in the inner circle of European scholarship. He had gained, what he specially came to gain, a sound working knowledge of Greek. His new edition of the *Adagia* proved him to be a learned man and a versatile student of ancient literature; but Erasmus was now more than that. He was almost alone in the gift of bringing all he learnt to bear upon his view of human life. When he reached England in July, 1509, he brought with him not a little of the practicality of a keen-sighted and accomplished man of the world. This too in the main he owed to Italy.

The accession of Henry VIII was regarded, not in England only, as an event of the highest importance to humanity. " What may we not expect from a prince of so extraordinary— almost divine—a character? How like a hero he appears to us, with what prudence he bears himself, what love he shows for truth and justice, what favour to men of letters....... If you could but see how wild with joy everyone here is...the very earth dances, the earth flows with milk and honey....... Our King is ambitious, although not for gold, but for excellence, for fame, for immortality!" It is not easy for us to realise with what sanguine hopes men regarded the advent of the new reign. The culture of Italy, the wealth of Spain, the peaceful arts of trade and exploration—were all bound up in the accession of the young king. Erasmus was summoned from Rome to be the representative of the new learning. It was in the same year that Colet worked out his scheme for a great school of St Paul's. In this year also the conflict, significant of a far fiercer struggle, which raged around the person of Reuchlin, was stirred up in Germany.

Erasmus found a home at Cambridge, where in 1510 he was made Lady Margaret Professor of Divinity, and took up his residence at Queens' College. He seems also to have done a little teaching, public and private, in Greek ; though his success in enlisting interest in the subject was disappointingly small. Apart from this far from exacting occupation Erasmus worked hard during the five years he spent in England. First of all, soon after his arrival he prepared and sent to the Press from More's house in London, the *Moriae Encomium* or *Praise of Folly* (1509), that extraordinary satire upon the life of his day which he had conceived and partly worked out during his recent journeys across Europe. The monk, the scholastic theologian, the courtier, the dominant types of mankind in Erasmus' immediate world, are, especially, depicted with keen insight and biting sarcasm. Like almost everything that Erasmus wrote, it was a sermon for the times, and a potent solvent of accepted stupidity and pretence. No book of Erasmus had so instant recognition, such striking effect on opinion. Here was a man who not only knew his books, but knew his world not less.

Apart from the *Praise of Folly*, the literary activity of Erasmus lay mainly in two different directions. In the first place he was stimulated by Colet's interest in his new school to a definite concern in education. For four years he was in constant communication with the Dean, guiding him in choice of books and men. Certain important contributions to the work of teaching were made by Erasmus immediately for Colet's behoof. We need only mention here the tract *De Ratione Studii* (of which a version is given in the present volume), which he sent to Colet in 1511. It is based perhaps upon the recollection of his own experience of teaching in Paris and Italy. The work on Latin composition, which he called after a phrase of Quintilian *De Copia Rerum et Verborum*, was issued in the same year. This is a very remarkable storehouse of material for rhetorical uses, the product of five-and-twenty years of observation of the style, usages, figures, and sentence-forms of the classical authors. The work deserves much more careful attention than has been devoted to it during the past two hundred years, but the great Latinists of the 16th and 17th centuries owed to it the same debt that Erasmus, Melanchthon, and Budaeus admitted as due from themselves to Valla. Erasmus issued also a small metrical compendium of rules of conduct known by the name of the *Cato pro Pueris* or *Disticha Catonis*, printed by Wynkyn de Worde in 1513. The *Concio de Puero Jesu*, an *Oration in honour of the Child Jesus*, was composed for recitation by the scholars of St Paul's. Erasmus was, like Colet, already deeply considering the right methods of training little children and the provision of sound aids to teaching rudiments. Thus in

1513 at the request of William Lily, the High Master of the
school, he revised the little text-book of elementary Latin
syntax, intended to supplement the Accidence which had appeared a year or two before under Lily's own name. This went
through a large number of editions in Erasmus' lifetime; the
Giunta and Aldine Presses, printers at Cracow, at Deventer,
Vienna, Paris, poured editions on to the market. It survives
in a greatly altered form in the Eton Latin Grammar of our
own day. The usual title of the book in the 16th century
was *De Constructione octo Partium Orationis Libellus.* The
Institutum Hominis Christiani, or the *Elements of Christian
Training*, is a Latin metrical version of the greater part of
Colet's *Cathecyzon*, or rudiments of religion, a little manual
of faith and conduct, written in simple direct language, which
he set forth for use in his school of St Paul's. We may
mention two other products of the Cambridge period : the
Latin version of Theodore Gaza's Greek Grammar, which
we know that Erasmus used at Cambridge, and which was
published in Basel (1516) a few months after he left England.
To Henry VIII he dedicated (1512) a translation of a treatise
of Plutarch (from the *Moralia*) upon the *Distinction between
a Flatterer and a Friend*; and he completed another from the
same source : *On the Art of keeping oneself in Health.* Both
had a certain educational reference. Erasmus, it is evident,
revealed at this time a special interest in schools and instruction. His residence at Cambridge, therefore, with its
opportunities for intercourse with Colet, is particularly important from the point of view of the present study of Erasmus
in relation to the progress of educational thought and practice.

Cambridge, moreover, enabled Erasmus to bring towards
completion two great enterprises in the field which he hence-
forward claimed to be peculiarly his own, that of the application
of scholarship to historical Christianity. I refer to the edition
of the *Letters of Jerome*, and the text of the Greek Testament.
The former had been for twenty years the subject to which

Erasmus had always turned with keen interest. Jerome represented for Erasmus all that was most learned, sober, eloquent
in Christian theology. To produce an edition worthy of the
great Latin Father was an ever-present ambition. Thus on
hearing that the printing-house of Froben, at Basel, successor
to the great Amerbach, was ready to undertake at their own
cost the issue of this favourite child of his scholarship, Erasmus
left England (1514) and made his way thither.

Between 1514 and 1517 Erasmus can scarcely be said to
have had a settled home. The true centre of his interests lay
in Basel, where from 1515 onwards Froben and his partners
were engaged not only upon the two great works just mentioned,
but upon several others from Erasmus' pen. In 1515 the
Epistolae Obscurorum Virorum appeared in Germany. They
were, naturally enough, ascribed to the author of the *Moriae
Encomium*, and the whilom translator of Lucian : though
Erasmus was anxious to disown any share in this famous *jeu
d'esprit*, he admits that he never laughed at anything so help-
lessly in his life. But he was just now writing the dedication
of his two great works to Leo X and Warham, and outwardly
was in a serious mood. The Greek Testament, with all its
importance as the *Editio Princeps* of the original text, is still
far from being a scholarly recension. Textual criticism of
Greek authors was still in an embryo stage. Manuscript
sources were very imperfectly known, and the particular codices
used by Erasmus were not of importance as authorities. The
importance of the edition lies in the motive and method which
it reveals. To go back to the origins,—that was invariably
Erasmus' principle : to get behind the gloss of the grammarian
to the plain text of the author, behind the gloss of the dialectic
theologian to the actual teaching of the apostolic age. To be
afraid of facts was superstition and the denial of the prerogative
of human reason. In relation to this general principle we are
concerned indirectly, at least, with the attitude of Erasmus to
the monuments of historical divinity.

Part of the period to which reference has just been made (1515–1519) was spent at Louvain with visits to London and Brussels. Francis I had in 1515 ascended the French throne, amid such hopes as had been stirred in England a few years ago. The great Budaeus wrote from Paris to Erasmus offering him, apparently on the new king's behalf, a position of distinction and a rich benefice. This offer came to nothing; but Erasmus accepted (1516) a sinecure post as Counsellor to Charles I of Spain, who became later the Emperor Charles V. Whereupon Erasmus indited for his behoof the *Institutio Principis Christiani*, a tract treating of *The Duties of Kingship*. The work has no very great interest in relation to education in general, but in spite of its inevitably, but reasonably, laudatory tone, it expresses clearly the views which Erasmus and More had in common on government, peace, and the functions of a true king. It was held in high esteem by a man of so practical temper as Sir Thomas Elyot, who urges that it should be " as familiar alway with gentlemen at all times and in every age as was Homer with the great King Alexander or Xenophon with Scipio....There never was book written in Latin that, in so little a portion, contained of sentence, eloquence, and virtuous exhortation a more compendious abundance." In the same year, 1516, Froben published the famous collection of dialogues on incidents of daily life and intercourse known as the *Colloquies* under the title of *Colloquiorum Formulae*. They had been written by Erasmus from time to time as exercises in the teaching of conversational Latin. Some of them date back to the days of his tutoring work in Paris twenty years previously. In their definitive form in the Basel edition of 1523 they contain Erasmus' riper views on a wide range of topics; and not a few are directly concerned with his ideas on training and instruction. The whole volume, however, is evidence of Erasmus' method of uniting scholarship with didactic purpose : what was begun as an aid to composition, has developed into a manual of comment on life and conduct.

It was full of satire on obscurantism in the fields of religion and knowledge, and in the changed atmosphere induced by the Lutheran conflict it roused the suspicion of the authorities. The condemation of the *Colloquia* by the University of Paris, as undermining to the Faith, led to its almost universal adoption as a school book in schools influenced by the Reform. The result was that no book of Erasmus, not even the *Moria*, had so wide a vogue. It was pirated in every country in Europe.

In 1517 Erasmus was busily engaged in advising upon the organisation of the new Collegium Trilingue at Louvain, a school or college intended to establish liberal learning upon an assured footing. Hebrew, Greek and Latin formed the curriculum, and scholars of the highest repute were sought for it. It is interesting to note the collocation of the three languages. This had as a fact little or no theological significance. It was due much more to the conception of the philological importance of Hebrew as the primitive language, and of the light which the study of it might throw upon the classical tongues. Erasmus clearly found much to attract him in Louvain at this time. But he met the offer of a chair in the new Collegium with a prompt refusal; no doubt it was hardly expected that he would accept even a titular responsibility, much as he enjoyed giving advice on the election of the professors and framing the schemes of study. In 1519 he determined to settle in Louvain amongst friends so congenial to his pursuits. For the University city was a centre of keen intellectual life, well placed for meeting scholars, and not less so for visits to France, England or the Rhinelands. Moreover it contained several printers of repute, so that about this time we find Erasmus issuing many editions of his smaller works from Louvain. And in spite of piracies his income from publishers must have been considerable.

The stirrings of the German revolt from Rome opened a new chapter in the career of Erasmus. His attitude to the

earlier controversies of the Reformation has been frequently
and elaborately argued, and only indirectly concerns us here.
This at least must be said. The Lutheran conflict brought
Erasmus much anxiety and no little misfortune during his life.
But it is still more certain that it did equal injury to his fame
after death, in that it has thrown his master-aims and activity
into wrong perspective in the eyes of his critics and biographers. Erasmus was not a Dogmatist, still less an ecclesiastic or politician, least of all a fighting partisan. He was a
scholar, a teacher preparing well-sifted authorities for others to
make such use of as the changing needs of the times might
demand. Unfortunately for himself he had a keen scent for
self-deception in loudly vocal people, and a pretty trick of style
in exposing it. But it is true to say that the only region in
which he had any thought-out system to offer for guidance of
a practical world was the region of Latin scholarship and
of education. And Erasmus knew it. His shrinking from
partisan declarations was but the recognition of the fact that
both in theological dialectic and in ecclesiastico-political fighting, the two dominant sides of the Lutheran struggle, he was
no expert, and had neither the gifts nor inclinations to become
one. So far as ideals went, Lutheran separatism was utterly
distasteful to him. He was for his years an old man, of uncertain health ; but Erasmus can only be called a coward by
those to whom partisanship is the one note of courage.

Louvain did not escape the clouds and thunder of the
"great Day of the Lord." Always prone to a restless desire
for change, Erasmus persuaded himself that he must go in
search of a quieter atmosphere, where pronouncements on the
controversy would not be expected of him. This haven of
peace he decided that he would best find at Basel under the
shelter of the Frobenhaus. There in the spring of 1522 he
was welcomed by his old friends, and there he installed himself
in the home where he spent the happiest period of his later
life. He had now entered upon the last stage of his vigorous

and productive career. The Lutheran trouble, indeed, pursued him in spite of his flight from it. He had hoped great things from the election of Adrian VI (1522) as successor to Leo X. For the Archbishop of Utrecht, though as a Pope he was a failure, was a man of very different type to the Borgia, the Rovere, and the Medici. Erasmus had known him well and respected him for his sincere life and his solid intellectual gifts. Through Adrian he was led to take an overt part in the pamphlet warfare now raging. His tract on *Free Will* set out with excellent temper his view of human nature in relation to the Divine Will. As we should expect, he is not very forcible in taking up a controversial position; he sees, here as elsewhere, both sides of the question. But he believed, and had always believed, that the human spirit is by creation not merely capable of, but prone to, a rational and wholesome activity. His spiritual analysis was never deep: Plutarchian, perhaps, in its plain common-sense method. Thus Erasmus was an easy victim to Luther's dialectic: as Luther said of the controversy, "it was as easy as it was disagreeable to confute so superficial a treatise from so profound a scholar." But the duel waxed hotter. Erasmus quickly became "that poisonous serpent Erasmus of Rotterdam." Melanchthon was invoked from Basel to mitigate the harshness of the conflict. But the young man of 24, a scholar no less than his correspondent, saw, what Erasmus was never to see, that the problem of the new age was not to be solved by scholarship alone. The result of it all was that Erasmus drew insensibly nearer to the Roman side. He was ageing rapidly, and was unable to face the illimitable possibilities involved in the collapse of that ancient ecclesiastical order which meant to him, as we shall see, so much besides itself. His real abiding interests remained steadily to the fore; he resolutely put aside the controversy, which in its methods absolutely, and in large measure in its aims, was repellent to him.

The Basel period (1522–1529) was, therefore, mainly given

to literary activity. Of interest in the field of pure scholarship we have the *Ciceronianus* (1528), a dialogue on Latinity
in which Erasmus appeals for a living Roman speech fit to
be the vehicle of expression for modern needs and practical
life. He had begun to interest himself in the discussion as
to the limits of Imitation in style in 1526, and had no doubt
watched with amusement the controversy on the subject which
had arisen in Italy so far back as the day of Poliziano and
Cortesius. He ridiculed, with his own peculiar sting, the
mere Ciceronian who had reduced Latin to a purely imitative
language, relying on the accident of Cicero's vocabulary or
usage of inflectional forms. Erasmus' instinct was perfectly
right in perceiving that such a canon implied the death of
Latin as an instrument for modern life. But though he could
appeal to such scholars as Poliziano and Pico, he roused
against himself fierce controversialists of the younger type,
like Julius Caesar Scaliger and Étienne Dolet, with the whole
school of Padua. The unfortunate champion of common-sense
was battered by a vituperation which had a truly theologic
wealth of epithet and innuendo[1]. The treatise *De Recta
Latini Graecique Sermonis Pronunciatione,* which was regarded
as the last word upon the subject of Greek pronunciation, for
northern peoples at least, appeared in the same year. His
work on *Christian Matrimony, Institutio Christiani Matrimonii,* had, like the *De Re Uxoria* of Francesco Barbaro
written just a century before, a section—perhaps in each case
the most interesting part of the work—on the bringing up of
children. This dialogue is our best source for insight into
Erasmus' thoughts on girls' education. In 1529 he printed
also the *De Pueris statim ac liberaliter instituendis,* the
ripest of his educational tracts, which is contained, in an
English dress, in the present volume. Meantime he was
applying himself still with marvellous energy, under stress of
grievous bodily pain, to the origins of Christianity. The

---

[1] Upon the import of Ciceronianism see infra, p. 51.

Paraphrases, or free Latin versions of the Gospels, had been begun at Louvain or Cambridge, and were all published by 1524. They met with signal condemnation at the hands of controversialists of both camps. The works of St Ambrose were printed in the year of Froben's death (1527); the entire works of St Augustine in 1528–9 in ten folio volumes; St Chrysostom in five volumes in 1530. These dates will serve to indicate the untiring industry with which Erasmus kept his printers employed, although Erasmus' actual editing in some cases was but slight. The year of 1532 saw the publication of the great edition of the Comedies of Terence, always Erasmus' favourite classic: this is, perhaps, the most valuable, in a critical sense, of his classical recensions.

Froben died in 1527: his death was a great personal loss to Erasmus, although the work of the printing-house did not slacken. This event, coupled with the spread to Basel and the upper Rhine of the Reformation controversy, provoked once more the wandering spirit in Erasmus. It is not otherwise easy to explain his removal to Freiburg in 1529. For he had been probably happier at Basel than he had been anywhere else since he left England in 1514. He had friends, repute, congenial work, and adequate means, in spite of his confessed bad management in affairs. The atmosphere of the city was tolerant yet keen. But he fled to the strongly Catholic Imperial city which stands on the edge of the Black Forest, where the hills sink to the broad plain of the Rhine. There he hoped, he tells us, to find a more peaceful home, where no one would pester him to interest himself in the conflicts of the day. But the Diet of Augsburg sat in the following year (1530), and Erasmus began to moot the project of going still further away from such centres of disturbance, to Italy perhaps, or at least to Burgundy. The old restlessness was not to be laid, and it was steadily aggravated by the nature of his illness. It was no special mark of discontent or irritability, as some biographers represent it, but the revolt of a temper passionately devoted to study against all that seemed to hinder him from the highest level of productive energy. In 1536 he declares Basel to be after all a better residence than Freiburg, and is once more welcomed by the Froben circle, the best friends left to him, for Colet and More, the gracious figures of his brighter time, were already dead. In the very last year of his life he sent to the press the *Ecclesiastes,* a significant work, so reasonable, and, in the best sense, Evangelical in tone, on the *Office of the Christian Preacher,* followed by his edition of Origen. Working "till death itself wrested the pen from his hand," he ended his strenuous life on July 12, 1536.

CHAPTER II.

CHARACTERISTICS.

§ 1.   ERASMUS AND ANTIQUITY.

IT is a proof of the intimate relation which subsisted between the Revival of Learning and the social *milieu* which rendered it possible, that a hundred years intervened between the residence of Chrysoloras at Florence and the beginnings of Greek studies in Paris or Oxford.   The formative epoch of the Renaissance, the Quattrocento, was over before the northern peoples were fit to receive it, or were able to assimilate it, and reproduce it in the special shape which the history and genius of each nationality determined.

Of the various factors, differing in origin and character, which constitute the movement to which we give the title of Renaissance, the impulse to revive the form and the spirit of the antique world was but one.   In Italy by virtue of causes readily intelligible this factor of the Renaissance filled a larger space and had subtler effects than in northern countries.   One reason for this difference is, no doubt, that the undue self-consciousness, with the consequent artificiality and affectation, which mark the Italian Revival, had, so to say, worn through to the surface before the translation of the new ideal of culture beyond the Alps.   For in Italy itself, by the time that the fifteenth century had reached its close, the more vigorous minds had already shed, or were shedding, the encumbrance of mere imitativeness.   In language, in art, in building, in literary form and in political thought, a truly new world had begun to arise. Amid the vast material which the past century had heaped together with such industry and enthusiasm the genius of Da Vinci, of Machiavelli and Michelangelo was busy sorting and re-ordering; not now with the purpose of re-erecting in patient obedience the monuments of antiquity, but to create a dwelling for the modern spirit. Now it was the fact that Germany and Western Europe were socially and politically a hundred years behind Venice or Florence, that enabled them to receive the impulse of the Renaissance at the stage when its true vitalising force began to stand out from the immaturities of its early development.

The career of Erasmus covers exactly this period of transition. His powerful intellect, of a markedly objective and receptive type, was well-fitted to be the instrument of conveying and interpreting a many-sided movement of the human spirit. Like the Revival itself, he too passed through—as an ardent student, perhaps, must always pass—his period of idolatry, of imitation, of conscious affectations. The years of his youth and early manhood partly coincided with the reign of scholarship of that type. But with him also this was but a stage in development. Gradually the New Learning became to him an instrument of life, actual and modern; a thing of use, to be adapted to intelligible needs, a source of illumination amid the hard experiences of ordinary men. In his maturity Erasmus showed himself a man of practical aims, with whom wisdom and scholarship were means to social well-being.

It is the problem of Erasmus' personality to determine the relative place occupied in it, first by religion and next by humanist impulse, and to understand the nature of the reconciliation at which he arrived. Neither of these two currents of interest was at any time in his life operative to the exclusion of the other. But it is true to say that up to the time of quitting Stein in 1493, at the age of 26 or 27, his pre-occupations had been in the main with religion; and that for the

next twenty years, a stage in his development even more
critical, he was absorbed in the study of the ancient literatures.
It would be impossible to account for the unexpected evidences
of mediaeval sentiment and ways of thought even in the
maturity of his powers, when the monastic concept of life had
become wholly abhorrent, had we not before us the fact of the
contented life which for ten years he led as an Augustinian
monk.   In the same way the intensity of his first humanist
enthusiasm may explain certain odd inconsistencies in his view
of the place to be filled by the antique in the modern world.
That it is impossible to "classify" Erasmus was reluctantly
admitted by his friends and by his enemies long before he
died ; it has remained impossible ever since.   His personality
indeed is more complex than his contemporaries knew.   But
the Age itself was a strange conflict of Old and New, of unreconciled forces, of methods and of aims alike uncertain.
And the receptivity of Erasmus' nature made it inevitable that
he should reflect the contradictions which indeed his training
and environment worked into the fibre of his spiritual self.

The presumptions involved in the Christian ideals of
Erasmus will be touched upon later.   We must here estimate
the significance to him of the concept of antiquity which he
found current amongst humanists when (about 1493) he sur-
rendered himself first to their influence.   From the writings of
Italian scholars he found that the ancient civilisation was
treated as the living heritage of their nation.   It was in no
sense regarded by them as an extinct order.   On the contrary,
it was a Golden Age, an ideal yet real past, worthy to evoke
both patriotic pride and eager imitation.   In this ancient
culture the share of Rome was to the humanist by far the
more important.   The function of the scholar was to bring
home to the citizen of Florence and Milan that Cicero, Vergil
and Augustus belonged to him : that in that notable epoch
were conceived and in large part realised the highest ideals of
culture, of social order, of justice, of peace, and, not least, of

human personality. To some scholars, indeed, like Vittorino, the absence of Christian faith was an indelible blur upon the picture; to Beccadelli, to Valla, or to the Roman Accademia, there was no blur. The language of Rome was the perfection of all speech; the various literary forms elaborated in the Augustan age were the ideals of all composition; in sculpture, architecture, military art, in agriculture and all technical crafts the Roman practice, if we could completely understand it, would prove the absolute standard for all time. There was no doubt in the mind of the Humanist that in the literature of Greece and Rome was contained all knowledge useful to man in each department of his life. To reproduce the antique order seemed the inevitable corollary from such an argument; but, as Italian Popes and Princes failed to respond to the ideal sufficiently to induce political self-effacement, the dreams of scholars were restricted to restoring the realm of ancient know-ledge, literature and art. How did this strike Erasmus?

Let us remember carefully the social environment in which Erasmus lived. The constant factors of his experience were unceasing wars, plague, famine, gross vice, coarseness, cruelty, political tyranny, indifference to spiritual and intellectual light. In the stir and movement of the sense of nationality he per-ceived an inevitable hindrance to order and peace: local character, ambition, languages, were so many barriers to unity of culture, to progress through intercourse, to amelioration of common life. The Church instead of commanding respect as the symbol of a world-order, was debased, ignorant, and a source of danger. The New Learning, then, opens to him a window from which he looks out upon another world. Like the Italians he recognises in it a Golden Age of humanity. Its notes of distinction were, first, its universality: government and order were then secured to mankind: there was one law and uniform justice: war was impossible. Again, language was one, with free intercourse thereby opened between all peoples; whilst Learning laboured under no obstacles of race and speech.   It was co-extensive with civilisation, the true Humanitas.   Next, the material conditions of life were favourable even to the poorest.   The dignity of the City, the prosperity of the country, were such as no one might realise in the France or Germany of his day.   Lastly, the level of attainments, scientific, artistic, or political, was infinitely in advance of anything that had been reached in subsequent ages. In literature the supreme heights had been gained in the oratory, poetry, and philosophy of Greece and Rome.   It was possible to hope for a gradual recovery in favoured lands of the wisdom and content which the ancient world enjoyed from the Indus to the Atlantic.   Whether the modern world could attain to the standard of culture reached by the ancients was doubtful.   That it should surpass it was hardly conceivable, though Erasmus had his sanguine moments.   In any case the way to progress lay through the study of the great past.

No doubt the remoteness in time of the Roman empire, and, still more, the lack of critical knowledge of its history and inner life conduced to easy idealisation.   Still we must recognise—it is worth repeating—whence came the impulse to such belief: from a desire, never dormant, for a time when men's lives might be passed in peace and order, and human well-being rest on the sure basis of enlightenment.

It is, however, a misreading of the man to ascribe to him the dream of a mere reproduction of the Roman world either as a political or as a social system.   Of the two factors which render such an ideal to us unthinkable, Christianity and the spirit of nationality, Erasmus gave its due weight to the first alone.   But that factor he realised to the full.   His own keen sense of reality saved him from the affectation of neo-paganism in any of its forms.   In such revivals he saw only a futile attempt to resuscitate a dead body; whereas his aim was to unite and reconcile the ancient spirit with the new.

Now the relative place to be given to each of these two elements varies partly with the stage of his development, partly with his mood, or the precise object with which he writes. We cannot formulate a consistent doctrine from his writings or his practice. But the uniform belief of his working life may be thus expressed. A thorough study of ancient literature could, as nothing else, enlarge knowledge and elevate human motives. Acquaintance with the history and political writings of Greece and Rome would tend to raise the standard of government and to stimulate patriotic duty. By widening men's interests, by the application of arts long since lost, by abolishing war, by encouraging reason and illumination, society would be lifted on to a new plane—and this could only be effected by harking back to the wisdom stored in the historic past. He believed, also, that Christian doctrine could not be rightly understood without a rich acquaintance with the thought amid which it first grew up. Finally, as the ancient world held the key to the amelioration of the present, no education of the young was possible which was not built upon Greek and Roman models and administered through classical literature as its chief instrument. But we must not forget that the classical civilisation was not, to Erasmus, merely a *past*. He was unable to view it as a purely historical phenomenon. It was an ideal to be defended or to be criticised: and modern progress signified approximation to that ideal, or at least to such aspects of it as were reconcileable with the Christian spirit. Here comes in the limitation of his outlook to which allusion has been made above; his blindness to the true mark of modern history, the function of nationality. In his passionate desire for the fruits of peace he sees only in national aspirations so many forces making for war and exclusion. When he concerns himself with current politics it is mostly with unwillingness and fitfully: he longs in his heart for a republic of enlightenment which knowing no country shall be coterminous with humanity.

There is no question that in this ideal of a universal order we have also one principal clue to the dread with which he regarded the Lutheran revolt. If to the barriers of political system and of vernacular languages were added an aggressive spiked fence of national churches and theologies, what hope was left for the peaceful advance of mankind? The centrifugal force of the Reformation dismayed Erasmus: for it boded a rude awakening from his dream of the priceless gift which the spirit of the ancient world was offering to the new. And this was a humanity bound together, in one faith and one culture, by the bond of universal peace.

The appeal which Antiquity made to Erasmus thus rested, in large part, upon its aspect as a social ideal. But its attraction can only be fully accounted for by a relation still more intimate: the special sympathy which he felt for the intellectual and moral temper of the old civilisation. In other words Erasmus found in Antiquity not only a social ideal, but the very pattern of his own personal attitude to thought and action. The spirit of Erasmus was, as has been said, of the type which moves freely only amidst ideas capable of easy verification and clear statement; mostly of a concrete order, of direct human interest, of definite applicability to life and action. It is probable that Erasmus had little poetical feeling —his criticism of the Choruses of the Greek drama alone implies as much[1]—nor do we find in him serious evidence of historical imagination. But we mus describe him as conspicuously deficient in all that concerns philosophical speculation, and mental analysis that passes below the surface of thought or morals. Thus he is never really at home with Plato; the earlier philosophers have no attraction for him.

---

[1] Erasmus is speaking of his versions of the two plays of Euripides (1506): 'in no other instance does antiquity appear to me to have played the fool so much as in this sort of choruses, in which eloquence was debased by an excessive affectation of novelty, and in aiming at verbal miracles all grasp of reality was lost.' The whole passage should be read: Nicholls, *Epistles*, pp. 431—2. In 1507 Erasmus' knowledge of Greek was still slight, and the chorus of a Greek play was beyond him.

The great mediaevalists, with their gropings after a profound unifying concept in knowledge, were not properly appraised by him, or by any humanist. The dogmatic aspects of theology, particularly as they became drawn into the whirlpool of the Lutheran controversy, were repellent to him. Yet he often speaks—as do all humanists—of *philosophia* and *sapientia*. But in these words he is in effect referring to Cicero, Seneca, or Plutarch. "Philosophy" meant primarily to Erasmus and the Italians (Ficino, Pico and Sadoleto are notable exceptions) the clear self-evident working morality current in the best minds of the period between Caesar and the Antonines. In the same way, "doctrine" was the historic faith set out in the Gospels, and the social conduct based upon it. There is no trace of mysticism in his attitude towards religion : the quality is wholly alien from his temperament. Hence it was not difficult for him to reconcile the best moral teaching of the old world with Christianity, and to regard literature as, in skilful hands, a practical guide to action. In this he took up the ordinary humanist position. The tolerance towards others, the calm and reasonable judgment of ourselves, the hopeful estimate of humanity, which he found in Plutarch, were peculiarly characteristic of his objective way of regarding human nature. Then it is noticeable that of the Greek poetic or speculative spirit, in its deeper sense, Erasmus has little or nothing. Lucian and Plutarch he knows well. The world of Pythagoras, Aeschylus or Plato is all but closed to him. The practical wisdom of the Roman statesman-moralist is that which is most congenial to his temperament, and coincides most nearly with his outlook upon life.

Reading Antiquity with these limitations the entire culture of the ancients struck him as marked by the same intelligibility, the same restraint. In politics as in literature there was a corresponding concreteness and absence of elusive generals. As contrasted with mediaeval conceptions in which abstractions played so large—and to Erasmus so irritating—a part, he found

the antique world singularly actual, definite and realisable.
There is no doubt that his instinct was sound so far as it concerned Roman thought. It would even be true to say that
such Aristotelian phrases as that of men φύσει δοῦλοι, or of
αὐτονομία, were less doctrines based on *à priori* speculation
than convenient expressions of political experience. In any
case the "theory" of the Roman Empire set out through the
Aeneid is merely a statement of the actual situation under
Augustus. How wide a gulf separates such generalising from
the theory of the Secular and the Religious Power of the
12th and 13th centuries, of the Functions of Government
of the 17th, or of the Rights of Man of the 18th! Similar
characteristics exist outside the region of politics, in the
literature, the art, the building, in the entire moral and intellectual interpretation of the World as presented by his
favourite Roman authors : all was objective, descriptive ; there
was nothing to call either for the mystic or the analytic spirit
in their understanding.

Antiquity, then, as Erasmus read it, made this two-fold
appeal to him : the first, that of a social-cultural ideal, capable
of being harmonised with the Christian ideal, and so fit for the
modern age ; the second, that of an intellectual type deeply
congruous with his own. It is in the operation of this double
attraction that we find the explanation of his zeal for the study
of the ancient world, and, it may be added, the key to certain
limitations and inconsistencies which we shall note in his
interpretation of it.

Antiquity thus understood was in truth the "New World"
to the humanist ; the "Old World" was that of expiring
Scholasticism, effete, puerile, in its second childhood. Scholasticism had recognised only one aspect of human nature—
thought ; and the forms of thought had been so reduced to
rule, summary and dogmatic exposition as to lose all interest
for intelligent men. The other sides of human life, literature,
art and passion, had been either ignored or repressed. They

had remained, perforce, unreconciled with the dominant culture, and stood without as lawless aliens. Now in the New Age these were to claim their rightful place by support of the great precedents of the world of Greece and Rome. But Erasmus, with German and English humanists behind him, was disposed to make conditions.

§ 2. THE RECONCILIATION OF THE ANTIQUE WITH THE CHRISTIAN SPIRIT.

The humanists of the Quattrocento, in their task of basing upon the ancient literatures the edifice of a new education, were by no means uniformly concerned about the relation of their ideal of knowledge to religion. On the one hand Vergerio, Vittorino and Ficino—to take one type—were always conscious of a problem to be faced and a reconciliation to be effected[1]; whilst Filelfo, Valla and Beccadelli appeared frankly indifferent to any such issues. Over against both stood the obscurantists, who decried all pagan culture as the enemy of Christianity and a direct danger to morality. To this class belonged Giovanni Dominici, the Friar of Santa Maria Novella; not a few of the preaching Friars were conspicuously of the same opinion; and with them must be reckoned as at least in partial sympathy Savonarola[2]. These no doubt

[1] "Nel Vergerio l' umanista ed il credente mai si contradicono, ma vivono quasi a dire l' uno per l' altro," *Epist. Verg.* p. xix.

On Vittorino, see Woodward, *Vittorino*, pp. 27, 241. L. Bruni rests his defence of ancient learning upon the predominance of noble types of character in the classical masterpieces: he also urges that unedifying "fictions are not to be taken literally." *Op. cit.*, p. 131.

Ficino and the Platonic Academy professed as their central aim the philosophical reconciliation of Christianity and antiquity.

[2] On Dominici, who was very bitter, see Rösler, *Kard. J. Dominicis Erziehungslehre*, esp. pp. 28—9: and Dominici, *Regola del Governo*, p. 134. G. da Prato declaimed at Ferrara (1450) against Terence and other poets, denouncing all who copied, translated or taught them. On the other hand

represented a large number of earnest-minded Italians of the fifteenth century, to whom the revival of antiquity was a movement to be cautiously watched if not wholly deplored.

It was inevitable that the champions of the New Learning in northern countries should find themselves confronted by similar scruples more widely held. In explanation it may be urged that in Italy patriotic enthusiasm claimed an unqualified allegiance to the revival of the ancient culture. Or it may be argued that, historically, the Teutonic spirit has shown itself more sensitive than the Italian to the supremacy of the moral sanction and has been, therefore, more readily affected by a discord between creed and practice. This divergence of attitude may plausibly be connected with distinction of national type. For we feel that much that is characteristic of a citizen of Florence or Venice of that age is hardly conceivable in respect of the burgher-life of a northern community, even of Augsburg, Nuremberg or Bruges, which in wealth or artistic interests most resembled an Italian city. The "complete man" of the Renaissance, whether a man of action or an artist, pursuing his ends in serene detachment from the moral factor, with the single aim of *virtù*, personal distinction,—such a type of individuality was only developed in its fulness south of the Alps. When he appears in the north, as in Thomas Cromwell, for example, he seems incongruous, almost monstrous. At the same time we must allow for the effects produced by the intrusion of the Reform at a period so early in the development of the northern Revival of Letters; for whether for Catholic or for Protestant the new interest in religion brought conduct still more definitely into consciousness. Calvin and the Council of Trent had at least this in common that both expressed reaction against a non-moral view of life. Erasmus, therefore, as a chief agent in the

Alberto da Sarteano, a popular preaching Friar, in the same city, affirmed that the study of the classics in right hands redounded to true religion. Sabbadini, *Vita di Guarino*, pp. 146—7.

transfer of the Renaissance to the German and English peoples was confronted with this problem. The inevitable conflict of ideals and their reconciliation as the Teutonic peoples reached it may be regarded indeed as typified in him. An enquiry into his attitude towards this issue is amongst the most instructive of those which concern Erasmus.

It is obvious that the present-day historian of the Renaissance approaches the question from a very different point of view from that of a scholar of the time, and that as a consequence the stress of the argument on either side will be found to have varied. For to us the ancient world is primarily a historical phenomenon, to be weighed and criticised with the detachment which suits a historical enquiry. Four centuries ago, however, the Roman culture was a practicable ideal of life, and as such was advocated or opposed with the zeal of partisanship. A purely objective view of antiquity was in those days of enthusiasm an impossibility, and a rational judgment of its phenomena unattainable.

In endeavouring then to disentangle and to interpret the attacks upon profane learning with which the scholars of the Revival were familiar we may classify them under three groups. The first includes the arguments drawn from the antagonism between the spirit of the antique and of the Christian world in respect of the ideal of human perfection. Such arguments, now disconnected from the comparison of the old culture with the new, have lost none of their force and touch the entire question of the relation of morals to the art of living. Another group of objections rested upon the evil example set by scholars, artists or rulers who had yielded themselves to the full impulse of the New Learning[1]. There are, thirdly, arguments of the more usual type, which were suggested by mere superstition and ignorance. We discern in the writings of Erasmus his attitude to criticisms determined in these three directions, which may be considered in order.

[1] On this see Burckhardt, *Civilisation of the Ren.*, p. 273.

The contrast between ideal excellence accepted in Italy at the Renaissance—viz. *virtù*, or distinction expressed in individuality, personal force and self-assertion—and the corresponding Christian virtue of humility, self-repression, and surrender to external Will, is the most striking of all the oppositions involved. It might be worth enquiring how far the Italian concept of *virtù* was in fact a product of interest in, and absorption of, the antique spirit; at any rate it was identified with it by those who combated the Revival. This passionate sense of Personality was beyond doubt a characteristic note of the new Italy and expressed itself in various ways. The craving for Fame, during life or after death, and the interpretation of immortality in the Horatian sense ("non omnis moriar"), was one of the commonest and most significant of these manifestations. Closely akin were a desire to provoke envy, and the hatred of a mere conventional status, much more of any conditions likely to imply contempt. Parents have no right to allow their son to be born in a city of mean repute or to give him a name of which he might feel ashamed[1]. The pursuit of thoroughness in political aims (as with Machiavelli or Cesare Borgia) or in technical skill (as in Cellini), unhampered by moral law, was perhaps the aspect of *virtù* which most disturbed northern observers. Hardly less typical of the same quality were the egoism of the humanist orator, always forcing his personality to the foreground[2], and the overweening sense of importance of the scholar, even the smartness of the *bravo*. It is not that self-consciousness was peculiar to this particular age, but that it was accepted as natural, as praiseworthy, as a notable element in distinction. Nearly allied to this was the concept of the present as the sole object of concern to men of intelligence. This was in large

[1] Cp. Vergerius, *De Ingen. Moribus*, in Woodward, *op. cit.* p. 96.

[2] The art of delivery was scarcely second to that of composition, so that the scholar was actor as well, whereby we can understand that the floodgates of egoism were thrown wide.

measure a direct consequence of the passion for the antique world.   By not a few enthusiasts the doctrine of a future life was vaguely held or wholly ignored[1].   The Papacy, which set the temper of the current religion, was from time to time frankly secular in motive and demoralising in effect.   The cult of grace of form in art and Letters, in personality, in society, was accompanied by the abeyance of idealism in thought and belief.   It was easy to show that absorption in pagan culture did as a fact induce a habit of viewing and appraising thought and action in all departments as things separable from spiritual truths.   This secularisation of knowledge, motives and life was most noticeable in the ecclesiastical sphere, in the latter half of the fifteenth century, and that was due, it was alleged, to the influence of humanism.

As regards the argument from example, the poems of Beccadelli, the epigrams of Janus Pannonius[2], the moral obliquity of Filelfo or Valla pointed to a danger lest a new sanction to immorality might be pleaded from the authority of ancient practice.   The devout Churchman was aroused by the difference of standard as to personal purity, by the nature of many classical myths, by the very grace of the language in which these were clothed by the poets.   Even the affectation of paganism, such as the use of classical forms to describe the institutions and the mysteries of the Church, appeared to serious people as a grave risk.   The crimes and the unscrupulous policy of rulers and statesmen, avowedly disciples of classical learning, were taken as evidence of its perilous influence upon character.

The objections of the remaining group are less worthy of

[1] Erasmus records that he discussed the subject of immortality with a scholar in Rome who rested his denial of a future life on the authority of the elder Pliny: Nolhac, *Érasme en Italie*, p. 77.   Cp. also Eras. *Op.* iii. 189 A.

[2] He was a pupil of Guarino, and became a Hungarian Bishop.   But his poetry was in the vein of Martial.

respect. The new light had a disturbing effect upon certain accepted opinions in the ecclesiastical world. Valla had exercised his scholarship in demolishing the evidence for the famous Donation of Constantine: he had shown how to apply critical methods formed from classical reading to the study of the New Testament. It was reasonably feared that many sacred Arks would be touched if principles of enquiry drawn from secular learning were to be accepted. The *Praise of Folly*, the *Colloquies*, and the *Epistolae Obscurorum Virorum* reveal the presence of other perils. A knowledge of Greek invariably turns a man into a heretic [1]. To understand Hebrew means that you are becoming a Jew. Every statue of Venus or Apollo is the abode of a demon. Monks recalled the story that when Boniface consecrated the Pantheon of Agrippa the devils had been seen escaping through the opening in the dome [2]. To teach Christian youth the old mythology was to invite Satan to re-occupy his ancient seat.

How then did Erasmus regard the conflict? His standpoint was inevitably determined, as has been said already, by the complex conditions—of mind and temperament, of training and experience—which moulded his spirit. To take the outward or historical determinations first, we know that the young Erasmus was brought up under the influence of the deep affection of his mother and that down to his twenty-sixth year his surroundings were those of a sheltered, studious and not too robust existence. All was conducive to the outlook upon life of a serious though enquiring Churchman. The following period of about twenty years (1492–1510) was for him a time of wavering aims, of which a breaking loose from mediaevalism in an intellectual sense and a rapidly growing interest in Antiquity were the characteristic marks. When the full

---

[1] One of Guarino's stories was of a Friar who derived "Ethnici" (i.e. the heathen) from Aetna, a mouth of Hell, from which they sprang.

[2] See the story in Gregorovius, *History of the city of Rome*, ii. p. 110 (Eng. transl.). The date, A.D. 604.

impulse to Greek studies was upon him there is no doubt that he passed through a stage in which the inducement to yield himself wholly to classical enthusiasm was keenly felt. From 1499 to 1506 he was much absorbed in Greek; but at this time the influence of Colet and More proved of singular moment in determining his bent. We know from his correspondence how deeply he appreciated the sobriety of the English type of scholarship, and that association of learning with Christian life and with public duty which his friends so conspicuously exhibited. The reconciliation, therefore, of the old and the new was accomplished before his eyes, in that practical fashion which harmonised with his own temper. The visit to Italy which followed (1506) took place when he was just forty years of age. His tastes and habits, and his intellectual attitude were well nigh fixed. The specific object of his journey had been settled long before. It was as a student of Greek that he set out; and as a most industrious student he lived at Bologna, Venice and Padua. Thus he saw in Italy just what he had prepared himself to see, and it has been shown above that the limitations of his interests were very definite. Politics scarcely affected him, art not at all. He had no taste for any form of sumptuous self-indulgence; the grosser side of paganism had no attraction for him. The scholars into whose society he was chiefly thrown, Bombasius, Aldus, Musurus, were all men of fine character and strong mental balance. In Rome, indeed, he was in contact with another type of society. But Erasmus quickly detected the unreality and affectations which characterised its humanism. His solid sense was amused rather than disturbed by the playing at paganism and the condescensions to Christianity of eminent scholars. It may be affirmed that his experience of Rome showed him that the dream of a reproduction of the ancient world was of the nature of a make-believe, which could work nothing for good, and perhaps very little for evil. Erasmus, however, was not blind to the importance of the fact that the sanction of the religious capital of the world should at this period be so freely accorded to ancient Letters.

Erasmus returned in 1509 to the wholesome atmosphere of his English friendships. He has now reached, once for all, the conviction that the line of progress lay in the direction of the incorporation of antique wisdom into the frame-work of a purified Christian thought and society. The culture of Greece and Rome could play a part for modern men only by adaptation to the actual world. Moreover, he saw his own share in the work marked out for him. It was, in part, to aid education in its task of fitting man to absorb the noble gift of the ancient civilisation : in part, to apply the method of scholarship to the historical origins of Christianity.

The Reformation scarcely affected the mental attitude of Erasmus, unless perhaps to strengthen his consciousness of this particular duty of enlightenment by education and learning which he had taken upon himself. Nothing that he wrote during the later period of his career marks any serious modification of the point of view which he had attained before the Lutheran revolt.

So much for the outward determinations. Passing next to consider the religious temper of Erasmus, we are aware that he was constantly accused by his enemies of a lack of one of the deeper instincts of the Christian consciousness, the sense of the depravity of human nature. It has been already admitted that his spiritual analysis was never very profound. He held a view of humanity which was certainly optimistic in respect of the individual and of the race. The working of the *Logos* "outside the Covenant" was with him a matter of sincere conviction. He found evidence of it in the lofty thought and moral ideals of Socrates, Cicero and Vergil. Defective training, evil circumstances, made men bad : by nature they were created for good. Such a view of the human spirit led easily to an attitude towards the great past which was in itself a reconciliation. It was natural to seek a parallel between

Christian aspiration and conduct and those of the nobler figures of paganism. The parallel, indeed, became an identity. As to the corruptions of antiquity they were, like the evils of the Christian world, but deflections. Each must be judged by its best examplars and its highest moments.

Given this point of view it is easy to see that the conflict between ancient and modern ideals did not exist for Erasmus in an acute form. He had little fear of pagan license, less of pagan superstition, for his own reasonableness made such dangers inconceivable.

However, Erasmus was always ready to weigh the doubts of people of whose intelligence and earnestness he was assured. His method of meeting them in the present case was characteristic. It is, he holds, partly a question of degree, partly of ends. There may be too much weight attached to speculation, or to rhetoric, too much interest in mythology, or too much craving for reputation for learning[1]. Character and usefulness in life are primary ends: scholarship is but a means, a precious means indeed, to such ends. A sense of the right application of knowledge to life is a crucial test of a true teacher. Hence selection of authors is a special function of every master. For example, only the most serious obligation will justify anyone in treating Martial. Such admissions Erasmus makes readily enough. But in truth he feels that the problem must be settled by the broad aims with which the ancient learning is advocated. Allow that its main tendency is for good—for religion, for wisdom, for efficiency in life—the question of details will solve itself[2].

Hence we do not find one uniform line of defence in

---

[1] Eras. *Op*. iii. 923 D and 688 F.

[2] For example, in spite of the undeniable importance of the religious end in education, he will not yield so far as to substitute Christian late Latin poets for Vergil or Lucan. *Op*. ix. 93 E. The Psalms are holier than the *Odes* of Horace, but if your object is to learn good Latin you must choose Horace. *Op*. i. 922 B.

Erasmus' writings. In the *De Ratione* (1511) he is hardly
conscious that a difficulty exists. The *Ciceronianus* (1528) is,
on the other hand, a warning against the pagan temper. But
there was no yielding of his position, even when Melanchthon
and most humanist Reformers seemed to abate their ideal of
scholarly education under stress of religion. The *De Pueris*
(1529) and the preface to the *Tusculans* (1532) are pitched in
the key of earnest conviction that the light of which the times
stand in so sore need is to be found not in Scripture alone but
in the organised experience and wisdom of antiquity.

It may with some fairness be alleged of Erasmus that he is
too anxious to disown as his aim the true self-abandonment of
the scholar in his subject. It was the corollary of his "practical"
temper ; his want of sympathy with speculative thought[1]—
ancient and mediaeval alike—is only an illustration of it. Yet
we may say that his actual practice was better than his
principle.   In the region of language and in the editing of
texts he provided material, genuine products of research, for
others to use.

Erasmus, however, was not content with resisting attacks
upon Antiquity in the supposed interests of religion. He has
several positive arguments to bring forward from the history of
Christianity. The first is that the universal Graeco-Roman
culture rendered possible the spread of Christianity. The
next, that its foundations lie in the ancient society and cannot
be considered apart from it. The use of classical learning for
the explanation of the truths of religion is manifold and indispensable. Hence a real knowledge of divinity is impossible
without Greek : the New Testament is perverted in the hands
of one ignorant of the liberal disciplines. In the third place,
Erasmus, like all humanists, dwells upon the approbation of

---

[1] " I am not unjust to philosophy, but she is only an adjunct to
knowledge." *Op*. ix. 103 D. Detailed study of philosophy leads to arro-
gance, and is bad for healthy common sense. He had never forgotten the
scholastic theology of his Paris days.

ancient literature recorded by Basil, Jerome and Augustine[1]. This proves that no inconsistency exists between the two great fields of knowledge. How much did not Basil or Chrysostom owe to Plutarch[2]? Finally, the study of grammar, logic, of the orators, poets, and moralists was, as a mere fact of history, of first-rate importance to the early ages of the Church: and the Church had not refused to use them—so far as it could understand them—ever since.

One further argument he derives from the study of historical Christianity: that pagan stories may be utilised for religious and moral edification by the method of Allegory. This reliance upon an arbitrary and uncritical treatment of literature strikes us as inconsistent with Erasmus' main canon of interpretation. But he has drawn it from the Greek Fathers, notably Origen; and we have here another instance of the want of precision in Erasmus' logical thinking. For purpose of edification he surrenders, unconsciously perhaps, one of his most characteristic principles of criticism. He affirms that all phenomena in Nature may be regarded as reflections of moral states. Hence the place of allegory in exposition. Scripture does not satisfy us if we limit ourselves to literal interpretation: for example, the stories of Esau and his birthright, of Goliath, of Samson. Much of the Old Testament, indeed, may be perilous to morals, if taken literally. He then proceeds to affirm that poetry, especially Homer and Vergil, and the entire Platonic philosophy, are "allegorical," and offensive myths may in this way be rendered harmless or actually helpful. Unfortunately Erasmus did not confine himself to considering the particular "allegorical" interpretations which may have been intended by Plato or Vergil; he opened the door to floods of arbitrary glosses and moral

---

[1] Basil's Letter was translated by Lionardo Bruni under the title *De legendis Gentilium libris*, one of the most popular tracts of early humanism. On Augustine, Eras. *Op*. x. 1731.

[2] Eras. *Op*. v. 856 E; iii. 251 E.

lessons such as the mediaevalists had applied to all departments of thought. On the other hand this should be said.
The allegorical method is the intermediate stage between a
conscious antinomy and its historical solution. Now the day
for the perception of evolution in knowledge, beliefs, or morals
was not yet: though we can trace certain partial recognitions
of it in Erasmus. A harmony between apparent contraries—
for example, the God of the Gospels and the Jehovah of the
Book of Judges—must be reached, for both concepts were
integral parts of the same belief. The historical attitude being
impossible, the Allegory was the only instrument of reconciliation. But such allegories rested upon no critical basis, they
were at the disposal of any ingenious mind, and could take any
form which the exigencies of the argument required. Hence
to the neutral enquirer, with no specific cause to advance, such
a method served to bring to light, rather than to solve, the
problem to which it was applied. In a review of Erasmus'
attitude to antiquity this illustration of it is of interest. For it
reveals, once more, his essential position—that the ancient
culture must be reconciled with the Christian ideal before it
can be assimilated by the modern man. To sum up, Erasmus
did not believe that the risk of paganising western Europe
through the classics was serious enough to be accounted an
argument against their study[1]. He was conscious, on the
other hand, that the "Ages of Faith," or as he regarded them
the "Ages of barbarism," were by no means guiltless of
moral degradation, of which unenlightened Christian Germany

---

[1] For the same common-sense point of view in English educators of the
Tudor time see W. Raleigh, Introduction to the *Book of the Courtier*,
p. xlvi.

As to danger to faith, positive anti-Christian feeling was very rare
amongst Italian or other humanists: though it came, of course, easily
enough to a controversialist to confuse indifference to, or criticism of,
received opinions with absolute disbelief. In this way Valla and Erasmus
were both "unbelievers."

afforded a contemporary example. To Erasmus or Melanchthon[1] there could be no alliance between religion and ignorance, no antagonism between Christianity and intelligence. A new body of organised wisdom had been revealed to the world: it stood in true affinity to sound religion. But only on certain conditions. First, the pre-eminence of the Christian—not the ascetic, but the self-respecting—type of personality must be assumed: next, the end of all wisdom is the service of God and the community, not the self-culture of the individual: thirdly, such practical ends are inconsistent with an ideal of mere imitation or reproduction of the letter of the past.

§ 3. ERASMUS AND THE CICERONIANS.

A chapter of much interest in the history of Latin scholarship is occupied by the development of the doctrine of Imitation. It may be accepted as generally true that the earlier humanists, Bruni, Poggio and Vittorino, aimed at a sound working Latin style, suited to the needs of the age, fit to be the medium of expression in affairs as well as in learning. The standard to be obeyed was indeed that of the best Roman period, but, so far as general classical usage in accidence and syntax allowed, the principle of elasticity and adaptability was observed. No one model was regarded as exclusively authoritative: nor was rigid adhesion to precedent for inflexional form or vocabulary imposed[2].

[1] Melanchthon in his inaugural address at Wittenberg in 1518 proclaims the impossibility of knowledge or moral advance without a fervent revival of Greek studies in Germany. Religion, above all, stood in need of their aid. *De Corrigendis Studiis*, 1518.

[2] "Scuole umanistiche l' Italia ne ebbe due: una grande e una piccola, quella degli eroi del quattrocentro e quella degli epigoni del cinquecento. I latinisti del quattrocento riproducevano tutte le forme letterarie della cultura romana per il bisogno di riprodurre, ma vi imprimevano la propria

With the elaboration of grammar and the closer study of style which date from Valla, the claims of special authors to pre-eminence were accepted. Before the end of the fifteenth century the theory of Imitation in Latinity was keenly discussed between scholars of weight, like Cortesius and Poliziano. Pico and Bembo carry on the controversy in 1512; Erasmus and Longolius discuss the subject eight years later; by 1526 the question has become a bitter dispute, and France and Italy are involved against German scholars. This issued (1528) in the *Dialogus Ciceronianus* of Erasmus. A year or two later Scaliger and Dolet joined the fray. Though Erasmus preserved a dignified silence under a storm of personal abuse, his friends took up his cause; and the argument was dying out when the great Muretus (1556) closed it once for all in the Erasmian sense.

The controversy is pertinent to a study of Erasmus but not on the issue of the special merit of Cicero's Latinity as against that of Livy or Tacitus. It concerns the present enquiry by reason of the light which is thrown thereby upon the attitude to the Revival of Letters which characterises Erasmus.

The arguments turn upon four points: first, the function of Latin, as understood in the age of the Revival; second, the determination of "perfection" in Latin literature; third, the relation of "imitation" to style; fourth, the broader implications which in Erasmus' belief were bound up with Ciceronianism.

It has been said that the founders of humanism had a clear concept of Latin as a *living language*. And it is of the essence of a living tongue that it has freedom to adapt itself,

---

personalità potente e viva, riuscendo nell' imitazione originali, dovechè i cinquecentisti non facevano che bamboleggiare ciceroneggiando." Sabbadini, *Prolusione*, p. 18. It may be stated perhaps as a principle that, in the first stage of every Revival, spirit rather than letter is seized and reproduced. The tendency to scholarly, and ultimately pedantic, imitation follows when the original impulse has died down. Cp. infra, p. 60, note.

to expand, to absorb and assimilate. A vigorous language will none the less preserve its special genius, its inflexional system, its syntax. On the other hand to restrain a language from enlarging vocabulary, from enriching its figures, metaphors, similes, by modern instances, from utilising its fullest in-flexional forms, in deference to the limitations of a past age, means only one thing—that the language is dying, or is dead. Now, the Ciceronian in disallowing a word, a compound, or an inflexion, absent, by accident or design, in the surviving works of Cicero proclaimed Latin to be just a toy or a specimen: the appanage of the *dilettante*, not the instrument of a living civilisation. Erasmus saw this clearly. "Times are changed: our instincts, needs, ideas, are not those of Cicero. Let us indeed take example from him. He was a borrower, an imitator, if you will; but he copied in order to assimilate, to bring what he found into the service of his own age. Through-out Cicero's letters,—what verve, what actuality, what life! How remote they are from the compositions of the pedant working in his study." He criticises certain orations of the Ciceronian Longolius. He finds them stuffed with artificiality: their author is as " a man walking in the land of make-believe : where by waving the Ciceronian's wand he calls up before an admiring world Senates and Consuls, 'colonies' and 'allies,' Quirites and Caesars, and persuades us that they are the actualities of to-day, alive and real, substances and not shadows." Why pretend that the antique virtue is restored by the trick of dubbing modern degeneracy by ancient names? Let us face realities as we know them and fit our Latin to these as the expression of a modern world of politics, thought and feeling. The Ciceronians deliberately ignored this prime condition of the function of Latinity, in their pursuit of a liberal, and formal reproduction of their model[1].

---

[1] Dolet, indeed, maintained that Cicero gave all that was necessary to the full demands of the present: " human character and social life are not variable quantities." But the limits imposed are such as to cramp

Secondly, the purists, as Burckhardt[1] rightly says, regarded the Ciceronian style as *Latein an sich*—the Absolute in Roman speech. Bembo describes Cicero as "unus scribendi magister": Dolet affirms that he is "purissimus linguae Latinae fons, flumen, oceanus," and adds that vocabulary, sentence forms, harmony of construction, all reach their highest conceivable pitch of refinement in him. If other writers may be read it can only be as examples of what must be avoided, as a sure means of bringing back the errant reader to the one attractive path[2]. Scaliger placed Cicero on the supreme pinnacle: his was the glory of literal inspiration, criticism of which was a form of profanity.

Now Erasmus was saved from such exaggerations partly by that instinct of proportion which was in the main his constant quality, partly by the width of his outlook upon classical antiquity. He points out that Cicero does not cover the whole ground even of Roman culture. Further he recognises in Cicero certain marked defects in style; so that Quintilian even had already found it necessary to deprecate an ignorant worship of his oratorical method. He goes further and bids the scholar follow Cicero in spirit, which will compel him to study the genius and not the letter of the language. In the *Dialogue* Erasmus wields the keenest weapons of his satire. "Woe," he says, "to the scholar who closes a Letter with a date of the

individuality of expression. "Qui in Cicerone versatur, *eadem semper verba* usurpet necesse est, sed ad rem susceptam ita diverse accommodata ut simul latine, pure, eleganter, proprie, apte, ornate, copiose, denique tulliane loquatur et varie, ut nihil repetitum aut plus semel dictum iudices." It is evident from this that Dolet in reality would force matter to comply with the requirements of Ciceronian style. There was to be no going outside of Cicero's precedents, until you were absolutely certain that these could not be twisted to the desired use. "Good Latin" thus became a mere matter of ingenuity.

[1] Cardinal Adriano, of Corneto, is the scholar to whom Burckhardt specially refers, *Civil. of Ren.*, p. 254 n.

[2] Bembo, *Ep. Fam.* v. 17: Dolet, *De Ciceroniana imitatione*, p. 62.

year as well as of the month : Cicero gives the month only ; or who opens it with *S. p. d.* : Cicero's practice is to omit the adjective. *Ferdinando Rege* has precedent : there is none in Cicero for *Rege Ferdinando.*" We can imagine the scorn which the broadly human scholar, the large-souled man of the world, poured out upon pre-occupation with such verbal criticism. Where was the hope of an universal culture, to be built upon all that was greatest in antiquity, if the men of the past were to be regarded as so many corpses for dissection? The Ciceronian superstition, therefore, meant the death of scholarship ; and Erasmus said so. For this he was denounced[1] as "the enemy of Cicero," "the destroyer of the Latin tongue," "monstrum," "carnifex."

Next, as the Ciceronian canon was slowly formulated, it was inevitable that, in an age when Oratory and Letter-writing held so large a place, scholars should debate the question of the limits of Imitation in composition. The true proportions of the problem first appear in the discussion between Poliziano and Cortesius. In writing to the latter Poliziano[2] states his own doctrine of style. "The truly learned writer is one whose style emerges from a continued process of erudite study, of comparison of styles, and of actual effort at composition." Fine expression, he means, is a sort of emana-tion from the equipped and practised writer, something intimate, personal and therefore inalienable. "On the other hand he whose method is that of direct imitation is hardly different from a parrot, which repeats what are to it but meaningless sounds. Hence," he goes on, "writing of this kind is without reality; it lacks the stamp of individuality, it leaves no impress; it has no nerve, no life; it arouses no emotion in others, no energy. Tear yourself away from that miserable superstition

[1] We must note that Bembo and Sadoleto recognising the distinction of Erasmus took no part in this abuse. Scaliger and Dolet were the real offenders.

[2] The letter of Poliziano in *Politiani opera*, Ed. Aldina, sig. I. III., Lib. viii.

which forces you to decry your own writing because it is not a copy of some one else's, and which bids you never withdraw your eyes from Cicero. Non exprimis, inquit aliquis, Ciceronem. Quid tum? Non enim sum Cicero: me tamen, ut opinor, exprimo."

The same argument was adopted by Pico[1] in his correspondence with Pietro Bembo. Accepting to the full the Renaissance doctrine of *virtù*, he maintains that every man must be something personal and individual, and that imitation of another is a mere substitute for personality. No one, therefore, can properly limit himself to one model of expression. Like a painter he will appropriate and combine what is best for his purpose from all schools. The variety of modern life makes it impossible for one writer to give us vocabulary or style equal to so far-reaching a demand. Admitting that a modern can "imitate" Cicero: what does this mean? He may adopt his vocabulary; but Cicero's handling of his vocabulary is not within any one else's power. An illustration: "You try to re-build *as it stood* a wall which has been thrown down. The material, we allow, is the same, but almost of a certainty the ordering of the bricks, and beyond all question, the cementing, will be new, and will be yours." You must admit therefore an original, self-directed element in every imitative style. An actual reproduction of Cicero could be nothing but a *tour de force*, ingenious but worthless. A "Ciceronian" Brief issued from the Chancery is an impossibility: for a *cento* of phrasings and passages would not rightly be called after Cicero's name.

Bembo[2] replies that an original style cannot now be produced. All conceivable styles have been exhausted by the ancients. An eclectic style would have no unity. He affirms as the final law of the writer: seek out the one supreme

---

[1] J. F. Picus *ad P. Bembum, de imitatione*, 1530. It was written 1512.
[2] P. Bembus *ad J. F. Picum, de imitatione*, in same volume as the Letter of Pico: cciiii.

stylist and imitate him, and him alone: so imitate him that
you may attain his excellence : so attain that you may even
surpass.   This unique master is, of course, Cicero, whom the
aspirant must so study that the whole being becomes saturated
with him.

Erasmus held with Poliziano, for whom he had a profound
respect, and with Pico.   In 1520 he writes to Longolius, the
purist, warning him against too scrupulous a choice of words
on the ground that this was incompatible with that higher
scholarship whose main interest must lie in the thing expressed.
A self-conscious style was to Erasmus as to Vittorino the mark
of a second-rate thinker.   The true disciple of Cicero is above
all things careful of the requirements of his subject-matter.
"No form of expression can be pronounced elegant which is
not both congruous to the artist and rightly fitted to the
subject."   "I will deny that name of true disciple to every
one who does not thoroughly understand that of which he
writes, who is not sincerely moved by what he understands, who
does not with exactitude convey what he has thus felt and
understood[1]."   Such is Erasmus' claim for individuality in expression and for the right subordination of style to thought.

In respect of his own Latinity, Erasmus whilst scrupulous
in respect of grammatical canons was by no means bound by
Augustan precedents.   His style is always in thorough accord
with the genius of Roman speech.   In its amplitude, elasticity,
copiousness of vocabulary and of figure, in its antithetical
skill, its entire freedom from mediaevalisms, and from Teutonic
modes of expression, it is worthy of high respect as an *original*
style[2].   It was this conscious freedom of movement within the
limits of the Latin tongue that made Erasmus peculiarly con-
temptuous of the smaller men who, to his seeming, were bent
on exhibiting Latin as henceforth a dead language.

[1] Eras. *Op*. i. 1026 A, B.
[2] Cp. Sabbadini, *Ciceronianismo*, p. 59: and M. Pattison in *Encycl.
Brit*. Art. "Erasmus" on the Latinity of Erasmus.

The *Dialogus Ciceronianus* (1527-8) is one of the best examples of the Erasmian method of illumination by the way of satire. It falls into two main divisions; a criticism partly satirical, partly serious, of the Ciceronian position, and a solemn gravamen against the quasi-paganism fostered under the cloak of stylistic purism. Nosoponus, the Ciceronian interlocutor, lies under a sad affliction. Once he was cheerful, handsome, well set-up. But for fourteen years he has been the prey of an obsession—a craving to be a new Cicero. For seven years he never read a line written by anyone but his great exemplar: he saturated his mind and his taste with Cicero: he never permitted himself to look upon the portrait even of anyone else. In his dreams also Cicero was always turning up. During this period he succeeded in compiling three weighty dictionaries: the first contained every word used by Cicero, its derivation, and a note of every inflexion sanctioned by his usage. The next included all phrases, figures, metaphors and similes occurring in Cicero; the third and the biggest was a compilation of the rhythmic tags and metric feet which the scholar had noticed in the Orations and elsewhere. Seven subsequent years were then spent in "imitation," relying on the dictionaries. Cicero, so these prove, used *amabam*, but not *amabatis*; *amor* but not *amores*; *ornatus* but not *ornatior*. In no emergency would Nosoponus employ these unauthorised inflections. By dint of most rigid seclusion from all distractions, *e.g.* by living always in a room without windows on to the street, by never marrying, by refusing all duties public or private, he had created for himself a purely Ciceronian atmosphere. Working very late he contrived in this manner to produce one fair-sized sentence a night. This is afterwards reviewed, filed down, or enriched, perhaps re-cast. Six such sentences make a letter worthy of Cicero. Nosoponus eschews conversation, for the risk of drifting out of the right atmosphere is too serious. People

said that this was hardly caricature after all : there were plenty
of scholars in Rome of whom it was a fair portrait[1].

This brings us to the fourth aspect of the Ciceronian
controversy as it concerns Erasmus. For such men were the
enemies of sound learning in a wider sense. Their affectation
of purism was, in not a few of them, bound up with a trick of
playing at paganism. "Paganitatem profiteri non audemus,
Ciceroniani cognomen obtendimus[2]." The Ciceronian was,
by virtue of his profession, obliged to eschew Christian nomen-
clature, and thus expended much ingenuity in expressing
sacred things in classical diction. *Jupiter Opt. Max.* was his
equivalent for *Deus Pater*, *Apollo* or *Aesculapius* for *Christus*,
Diana for *Maria* ; *diris devovere* for *excommunicare*. *Tinctura*
stood for baptism ; *victima* for the Mass[3]. Erasmus recalls an
incident of his stay in Rome (1509). He was present at a
Good Friday sermon preached before Pope Julius II. In
purest Ciceronian prose the orator quoted deeds of self-
sacrifice and patriotism from Greek and Roman myth and
history : Decius, Curtius, Iphigenia, Socrates were dwelt upon,
but the Crucifixion was all but forgotten. "As for religion,"
says Erasmus, "there was not a touch of it from beginning to
end—of sham Cicero more than enough[4]." To Erasmus the
sincere study of Letters had for its end the deepening of man's
hold upon realities. Antique culture, whether viewed as knowledge or as literature, found its value to the New Age in the aid
it rendered to life, service and religion. This is what he means
when he declares: "huc discuntur disciplinae, huc philosophia,
huc eloquentia, ut Christum intelligamus, ut Christi gloriam
celebremus. Hic est totius eruditionis et eloquentiae scopus[5]."

---

[1] Sabbadini, *op. cit.* p. 63.

[2] Eras. *Op.* i. 999 E.

[3] Pontanus, the Neapolitan scholar, uses *genii* for angels: *umbrae* for
the future life; *virgo capitolina* for Madonna, and that before Leo X.

[4] Nolhac, *Érasme*, p. 77.

[5] Eras. *Op.* i. 1026 B.

Thus does Erasmus in the field of pure style once more affirm his attitude to that problem of the Renaissance which concerns the relation of antiquity to the modern world. His was what Walter Pater[1] has called "the old true way of Renaissance" whereby ancient material is acted upon by a new principle, a modern need. So far, indeed, as language was concerned, this principle was in the event applied with more completeness than Erasmus imagined. Not in Erasmian Latinity—vigorous, individual, modern as it was—but in the language of Machiavelli and Castiglione, of Montaigne, of Shakespere, of the Authorised Version, was realised that union of the Old and the New for which, unknowing what he asked, Erasmus prayed[2].

§ 4.   ERASMUS AND THE VERNACULAR TONGUES.

It now becomes necessary to consider the attitude of Erasmus towards the vernacular tongues of his day. In doing so it will be impossible to confine our view to the question of language, which was to Erasmus, as it is to us, but one aspect of the larger problem of nationality. His relation to the

---

[1] Pater, *Marius the Epicurean*, ii. 99.

[2] The parallel between the Ciceronian in Letters and the Vitruvian in Architecture is both exact and instructive. The great builders, with Brunelleschi at their head, who were the first to come under the influence of the antique, correspond in their power of free assimilation to such scholars as Vergerius or Ambrogio Traversari. The purist Serlio in the 16th century insisted that every architect must observe "Vitruvius' rule and most certain and infallible directions," since " in every art there is one more learned than another to whom such authority is given that his words are fully accepted and without doubt believed." Hence " the writings of Vitruvius ought for their worthiness to be inviolably observed." But no sooner had this doctrine taken root than classicism as an architectural ideal suddenly crumbled, as a consequence of its divorce from constructive utility. Serlio is the Longolius of the building art; and the influence of the two men is precisely similar in their respective spheres.

position of the Italian humanists will also come up for consideration.

The knowledge of modern tongues which Erasmus possessed has often been discussed. It is curious, however, that his own allusions to it leave his biographers[1] still in doubt as to the extent of his ability to understand any native speech other than Dutch. We are, however, in no uncertainty concerning his unwillingness to *express* himself in anything but sound Latin. Dutch he could not fail both to understand and to speak. Until he was fourteen years of age, at least, it was the language of his home life. We have sufficient allusions to such a familiarity with it in later years as is implied in his ability to follow the preaching of a Friar or to take part in conversation.

As regards his acquaintance with the speech of Lower Germany it can be proved that he had a traveller's knowledge —easy enough to acquire for a native of the Netherlands. He writes to a correspondent at Lubeck with an apology for his Latin : "non fastidio linguae nostratis," but on the ground that his German would be a halting performance and might cause misunderstanding[2]. A student of the University of Paris for ten years and more, could hardly escape a working facility in French, even were he less interested in the manners and thoughts of his fellow-men than Erasmus. The evidence, however, is not copious, and it is mainly indirect. But it is impossible to read the letter describing his adventures on the road to Paris in February, 1500 (Nicholls, No. 122, Richter, No. 144) without concluding that Erasmus was fully competent to hold his own incisively with his inn-keeper. Indeed he expressly says that the burden of the wrangle fell to him as his travelling companion spoke no French. It may, however,

---

[1] Mr Mark Pattison for instance was certainly wrong in saying : "Erasmus had passed nearly all his life in England, France and Germany; he spoke not one of those three languages." *Encycl. Brit.* Art. "Erasmus."

[2] Eras. *Op.* iii. 16 D.

be gathered from a passage in the *De Pueris* that Erasmus had wrestled not happily with the pronunciation[1].

On the other hand he was much less at home with English. His first visit to this country was very short and was passed wholly in learned society. His later visits belong to a period when he had made abstention from modern tongues a principle. In the house of Sir Thomas More he found the conversational use of Latin, if not the normal practice, at least one gladly adopted in presence of so distinguished a guest. Warham, in presenting him to the living of Adlington, relieved him of residence expressly on grounds of his ignorance of the language of his parishioners. The same indifference marked his attitude to Italian. The learned environment in which he spent his Italian sojourn at Bologna, Venice or Rome precluded any need for facility in what he would have called the corrupt dialects of the peninsula. He rebuffed the grave Ruccellai with a blunt "Surdo loqueris" when the Florentine addressed him in the Tuscan speech which in his eyes was in no way less noble than its mother-Latin. Of Spanish he probably acquired some slight knowledge from intercourse with officials in the Netherlands, although the evidence of it is very sparse. To Charles V and his Court Spanish was the customary language and Erasmus was in an honorary sense a member of that Emperor's Council.

Such evidence, however, does not close the question. It is clear, for instance, that the author of the *Moriae Encomium* and of the *Colloquies* was one able to observe acutely by ear as well as by eye as he went on his quiet way through the world. Only sharp, clear-cut perception of what was passing could have afforded Erasmus that power of moving freely amidst the facts of common life, that insight into popular foibles and superstitions, which gave the edge to his satire. Again, Erasmus had something of the feeling of the philologist for parallel forms and for etymologies; he saw that the three

[1] Er. *Op.* i. 501 F. Infra, p. 199 s.f.

Romance tongues had grown out of Latin, and that as a consequence they might be, scientifically, not without interest to a scholar[1]. We find express allusion to the employment of the modern languages in this manner.

When, however, we turn to the use of the vernacular tongues for purposes of literature or education we are upon more definite ground. The popular speech has, and ought to have, no claim to be regarded as a fit instrument of literary expression. To the more rigorous humanists the mere suggestion of such a claim was a standing cause of irritation. It is one thing to accept as established facts the several dialects of the common people and to use them when need compels. But nothing justifies the abandonment of a universal, highly-developed and historic speech, such as is Latin, for a series of local, rudimentary and obscure jargons[2]. For these are as an Oscan or Umbrian dialect, or the parlance of the Suburra, to the finished diction of Cicero and Vergil. Nor can any beyond the most meagre employment be made of such in education. For beginners in Latin it is permitted to set the subject for composition in the vernacular[3]: but if a modern language *must* be learnt it can be picked up. The Strassburg School Ordinance of 1528—strictly Erasmian in spirit—affirms "Vernacula lingua loqui in ludo nostro piaculum est, atque non nisi plagis expiatur." A modern language is impossible as a school-subject in humanist eyes. To take one reason alone—a decisive one. Teaching demands before all things fixity, definiteness, uniformity in its material. In the department of language Latin and Greek provide precisely those qualities: orthography, accidence and syntax are determined. The modern dialects have none of these indispensable notes. It may be safely assumed that Erasmus never contemplated a day when English, French or German could attain the stage of

[1] *De Rat. Stud.*, infra, p. 167.
[2] Erasmus wonders why Albert Dürer wrote in German: *Op.* i. 928 c.
[3] *De Rat. Stud.*, infra, p. 170.

an organically developed speech, worthy of a true literary status, and that he viewed with distrust the efforts of Poliziano and Bembo to secure the recognition of a standard Italian tongue.

It is strictly pertinent to note, in the next place, the contempt which Erasmus avows for popular stories, folk-lore, and traditional tales of national heroes. He especially deprecates their use with young children who should rather find their imaginations satisfied with moralised stories from antiquity or the Old Testament. Erasmus thus again reveals his lack of concern for the elements of national life, and his ignorance of the true basis of national culture. He does not see[1] that the classical spirit implies a respect for the methods of antiquity, for to the Greek and to the Roman education was built on national traditions in their local setting. To Erasmus the Arthurian cycle, to take one instance, is but trivial nonsense. It is not true to fact, not morally edifying, and above all not clothed in notable language. In this important aspect of the phrase, the historic sense was lacking to every strict humanist : for to hardly one of them does the national history, unless it be identical with that of the classical ages, make any appeal. The attitude of Erasmus reminds us of that of Aeneas Sylvius to whom it seemed futile in a prince to waste time over the story of the nation whom he was called upon to govern. "Beware," he writes to Ladislas, the young king of Hungary, "of wasting time over such a subject as the history of Bohemia or the history of Hungary. For such would be but the productions of mere ignorant chroniclers, a farrago of nonsense and lies, destitute of attraction in form, in style, or in grave reflections." Vives, the friend and correspondent of Erasmus, is almost alone amongst humanists in finding a

---

[1] Yet Erasmus had realised this when, only a year earlier, he had urged in the *Ciceronianus* that true Ciceronian imitation implied obedience to the *spirit* of Cicero and to the methods which he himself pursued. Supra, p. 54.

place for Monstrelet, De Commines, and Froissart in historical study[1].

Yet Erasmus, as a man of practical sense, accepted the modern State as a fact, and service to the community as one of the main ends of Man, and therefore of education. Good government is the duty of prince, noble, and burgher alike. "The father who neglects the training of his son is guilty of offence against the fatherland." "Children are born for the State and for God": and all sound education will fit them for their place in Society and in the Family. The ultimate utility of the higher learning lies in the service which it enables a citizen to render to the country of his inheritance. But we must not interpret the claims of fatherland too strictly. "Love of fatherland is good, but it is more philosophic to regard things and human beings in such a way that this world may be looked upon as the common fatherland of all." We should ask "not *where*, but *how nobly* we spend our lives." This is conformable to his reply to the offer of the citizenship of Zurich, "I wish to be a citizen of the whole world, not of a single city[2]." The "Respublica Litteraria," as Hutten termed it, was his ideal.

The reconciliation of the practical aims of Erasmus with his indifference to the essential characteristics of the modern world, and with his positive rejection of the concept of nationalism in education, is not easy to find. Erasmus was of German stock, and was proud of it. Much as he admired Italian learning he had no yearnings for a life to be spent at Rome. But he was dominated by the ideal of a universal culture, within which racial differences would sink into due subordination. This ideal, as we have seen, was intimately bound up with the revival of antiquity. Now, for a hundred years, an extraordinary—almost inexplicable—restoration of the knowledge of the ancient world had been in progress.

---

[1] Vives, *De Disciplinis*, p. 385.
[2] Eras. *Op*. iii. 757 D.

Both in Art and in Literature the new time had absorbed the fashion and spirit of the old. Why should not the same transfer be possible in respect of Speech? The Gaul of "the Province," the Lombard, the Northman offer examples of acceptance of a new tongue. Given a common culture, in harmony with a common Church, a common speech might, nay must, follow, if the chiefs of learning were in earnest. The Church and the professions had proved that in specific regions of thought and activity such a step to universality was attainable. To Erasmus and those who thought with him the problem was of deepest moment in the interests of civilisation. On the other hand, Erasmus urges the use of the vernacular in preaching, for only thus can the faith stir the emotions and active impulses. It is, one may say, a point of Christian duty for a churchman, whose functions lie in that direction, to stoop to acquire the popular tongue. Yet he does not perceive the essential note of the Lutheran conflict—the yearnings of the Germanic self-consciousness, and the claim for the expression of it in language, and in ecclesiastical order and independence.

He is blind, also, to the fact that in Italy both a language and a literature, independent of Latin, were growing up and that this development was fostered by certain humanists of undoubted rank. The plea for Italian was urged by no less a scholar than Bembo, who, quite consistently, was at the same time the leader of the Ciceronian purists. On the other hand, the best statement of the case for the Latinists came from the pen of Franciscus Floridus[1], an intimate friend of Erasmus, and like him a keen anti-Ciceronian. It will be of interest to summarise his argument, as expressing the judgment of the group of scholars of whom Erasmus is chief. The date is 1537.

---

[1] On Floridus, cp. Sabbadini, in *Giornale Stor. d. Letteratura Ital.*, viii. p. 333. He had been ardently engaged in defence of Latin for some time before Erasmus' death. The passage here summarised is from his *Apologia*, p. 105.

Floridus deplores the apparently increasing use of the Italian language. Some scholars indeed profess to regard it as worthy of the same care and elaboration as that which the Greeks and Romans bestowed upon their own speech. Such a monstrous blindness to the light reminds us of the Scythian or the Mede, and renders Italy a derision in the eyes of Spaniards, Frenchmen, Englishmen, or Germans. For in all those countries men of learning prize ever more and more the inheritance of the ancient tongues. It is sheer perversity to compare, as some do, the lyrics of Petrarch to the hexameters of Vergil, or the light and easy style of Boccaccio to the grave periods of Cicero[1].

The chief argument which he finds for the adoption of the vernacular is this : the language of the home and the nursery must be the language of our subsequent life : for such a language, being our native speech, will be that of the majority of our fellows. Now the argument from the majority carries no weight with a wise man ; "for the custom or convenience of ten thousand hinds is not to be weighed against those of a single man of learning."

The pleas for the vulgar tongue—Floridus is an Italian and has the Italian language always in mind—are met by a series of arguments. First, the contention from usage is invalid when we consider the actual facts. There is no such thing as "the Italian language." A Florentine travels to Apulia or to Naples ; his Tuscan speech is to the natives of the Kingdom as the speech of a Tyrian or a Bedouin. In Sardinia or in Sicily he would run risk of being locked up as a lunatic at large. Let him go farther afield : if he speak Tuscan in Germany, France, or Spain he has a crowd after him, and is

---

[1] Cp. the attitude of certain humanists of the previous century towards the great Tuscans. Niccoli asks, "Quos tu mihi Dantes, inquit, quos Petrarcas, quos Boccatios ? Nam quid est in illis quod aut admirandum aut laudandum cuiquam videri debeat ?" L. Aretini, *Dialogus*, p. 60. Salutati regretted that Dante had not written in Latin. *Ibid.* p. 59.

asked if he has lost his dancing bear.   But Latin is of universal currency.   Apply the facts to literature instead of to travel.   On what grounds should "a nation's exploits be recorded in that nation's tongue"?   If facts are worth relating they should be narrated for all places and for all times: not through a medium which is current for some hundred square miles: Florence, Lucca, Arezzo, Siena each has its standard idiom.   How then is the vernacular to "save labour" to the learner?

Again, the Italian dialects are unfixed, imperfect, and unequal to the varied demands of a literature.   Consider the position of Dante.   He writes in a language still fluid and uncertain, in a style which cannot be called finished, in a word, in a medium unequal to the distinction of his subject. Boccaccio's prose for similar reasons is read without pleasure. Petrarch, on the other hand, seems to have reached the high-water mark in Italian verse, but he uses it only to handle trivial themes: whilst Ariosto—a first-rate Latinist, we must remember—cannot be said in his *Orlando* to equal even the second or third rank of Roman poets.   As to serious composition in history or oratory there is none in Italian (Machiavelli, Guicciardini, Castiglione notwithstanding). Floridus then criticises the vulgar tongue from the point of view of its origin.   Italian is the quintessence of barbarism, that barbarism which overthrew civilisation itself in our own land.   How prefer a language whose roots lie in the invasions of Goth, Vandal, and Lombard?   What elegance, what elaboration can be looked for from such a source?   To take but two instances: the contrast between classical metres and that which passes for metre in Italian; and the decay of inflections. The Scyth and Numidian may do without these aids to exact expression, can civilised man?   There are those who would drive out of language every word which cannot be traced back to the barbarous enemies of our race.   Language and literature are, both of them, works of human skill and not unconscious products of nature[1]. Further, Italian is avowedly poor in vocabulary, and needs to be copiously enriched. Why, if Latin has to be thus relied upon, not recognise the fact and use it as the current tongue as it stands?

If scholars who cultivate both the ancient and the modern tongues imagine that they gain repute thereby they are in error. They must know that their fame rests upon their skill in classical letters, and upon that alone. Perhaps, however, they only wish to prove to the world how easy it is for a truly learned man—who has spent twenty years in attaining eminence in Greek and Latin—to be an "Italian scholar" in a couple of months.

The points therefore upon which the humanist argument turns are these. The vernaculars lack fixity, elaboration, and universality—the latter even in a single country. They are not adaptable to the manifold needs of literature; they lack serious gravity; they demand no effort in acquisition, and that which can be picked up by mere use or instinct is hardly "human" so much as "animal." They are the products of barbarism, and are barbarous by nature. They are local, limited in range, without authority.

An argument which scarcely appears in the criticism of Floridus, but which was always of weight with the humanist, was that the vernacular lacks the element of "eternity[2]." It was a standing principle amongst scholars that nothing worthy of perpetuation might be expressed otherwise than in fine Latinity. And closely allied with this was the deep-rooted desire of the man of the Renaissance to find a place in the elect company of the great names of old. How was this

---

[1] It is important to note that the first grammar of the Italian tongue was published in 1516; the work of Giovanni Fortunio: *Regole Grammaticali della Volgar Lingua.*

[2] Filelfo, for instance, writing in 1477 says of Tuscan : "hoc scribendi more utimur iis in rebus quarum memoriam nolumus transferre ad posteros." Cp. Voigt, *Wiederbelebung,* ii. 422.

possible if men of Letters should permit uncouth, local dialects to supersede the dignity of the universal speech? That nationalism in politics as against the Empire, in religion as against the Church of Rome, in language and in literature as against the classics—one movement in several aspects—was the abiding note of the modern world—this was in no way realised by Erasmus.

But the most effective pleading for the new tongue was, notwithstanding, the production of one of the chief of the Latinists, Pietro Bembo. It need cause no surprise; for Bembo had done his best to relegate Latin to the category of the dead languages. His Dialogue on the *Lingua Volgare* was written in 1512. He turns the argument from dialectic variety by pleading for a standard or classical Italian to be established on the authority of Dante, Boccaccio, and Petrarch. The Dialogue contains also an alternative canon—viz., that the Italian tongue be accounted that which is accepted in the Court of Rome[1], the idiom, inflectional system and pronunciation commonly understood by ecclesiastics and men of affairs gathered at the Vatican from all parts of Italy. We here come upon the first deliberate effort to erect a rule of strictly classical Italian upon a norm against which no charge of provincialism could be raised. The Dialogue is in large part occupied by a critical study of the material out of which an authoritative grammar could be compiled. Bembo was wont to complain that Fortunio had pirated this matter—from MS. copies circulating in Rome—and issued it in his *Regole* as his own.

The substantial argument of Bembo is contained in the following passage[2], which may fitly close this chapter:

"Il Volgare è a noi piu vicino; quando si vede che nel Volgare tutti noi tutta la vita dimoriamo; il che non aviene del Latino: si come à Romani huomini era ne buoni tempi piu

---

[1] Bembo, *Della Volgar Lingua* (1525) f⁰. xii.
[2] Bembo, *op. cit.* f⁰. iiii.

vicina la Latina favella che la Greca; conciosia cosa che nella Latina essi tutti nascevano, et quella insieme col latte dalle nutrici loro beeano et in essa dimoravano tutti gli anni loro communemente, dove la Greca essi apprendevano per lo piu gia grandi et usavonla rade volte, et molti de loro peraventura ne l' usavano ne l' apprendevano giamai. Il che a noi aviene della Latina; che non dalle nutrici nelle culle, ma da maestri nelle Schuole, et non tutti, anzi pochi, l' apprendiamo, et presa non a ciascun hora la usiamo, ma di rado, et alcuna volta non mai. Cosi è...et questo anchora piu oltre; che a noi la Volgar lingua non solamente vicina si dee dire che ella sia ma natia et propria: et la Latina straniera. Che si come i Romani due lingue haveano, una propria et naturale, et questa era la Latina, l' altra straniera, et quella era la Greca; cosi noi due favelle possediamo altresi: l' una propria et naturale et domestica, che è la Volgare; istrana et non naturale l' altra, che è la Latina."

CHAPTER III.

THE EDUCATIONAL AIM OF ERASMUS.

§ 1. The General Purpose of Education.

It results from the considerations laid down in the last chapter that the ideal of culture as understood by Erasmus was ultimately social in trend. The uplifting of the standard of religion and conduct in the community was the motive which gave urgency to his plea for knowledge. He saw, moreover, that the cause of religion and conduct was intimately bound up with better political and social conditions. "Barbarism"—the term so common with him—implied not only superstition and ignorance of sound learning, but cruelty, reckless war, and bad government. The one remedy for this universal darkness was the union of enlightened Christianity and the wisdom of the ancients. Erasmus realised the mediaeval order as a firmly compacted whole, whose amelioration could be attained only by a force operating upon and transforming the entire fabric. That force was learning.

Now it is an invariable law that the accepted ideals of the adult generation shape its educational aims; that the school-master obeys and does not lead. It was inevitable, then, that wherever Humanism gave its impress to a community or to a group a speedy effect thereof would be manifested in the School. It was not enough for the citizens of Florence and

Venice to find themselves emancipated from darkness, their children must from the very first be saved from its shadow. In the belief in the importance of a cultural ideal is involved of necessity a corresponding conviction of the need of a new education.

The organised life of the civilised community is to Erasmus the only life worth living: his educational aim, therefore, is a social aim. It does not stop short with the perfection of the individual, the preparation of a self-contained life. When he speaks of the knowledge of Christ and His glory as "totius eruditionis scopus[1]," he by no means implies that the end of right training is personal salvation. He has given in the *De Civilitate Morum puerilium* his description of education in definite terms: "Sicut prima (pars), ita praecipua, est, ut tenellus animus imbibat pietatis seminaria, proxima ut liberales disciplinas et amet et perdiscat, tertia est, ut ad vitae officia instruatur, quarta est ut a primis statim aevi rudimentis civilitati morum adsuescat[2]." Now, as viewed by Erasmus, each of these aims is bound up with the rest, just as each points to a joint factor in social well-being. " Piety and Good Letters "—Sturm's *sapiens et eloquens pietas*—a union which adds wisdom to faith and reverence to learning, stand opposed to ignorance and wickedness. It can be amply shown from Erasmus' writings that he regarded all that supplies men with higher motives and worthier interests, that affords warnings and examples from the past, as a religious force. The religious end of education therefore was hardly viewed by him as a thing apart. Everything that enlightens ultimately raises the individual and purifies the social order. In spite of uninformed criticism, the classical

---

[1] From *Ciceronianus* (1528): *Op.* i. p. 1026 B.

[2] *De Civ. Morum* (1526): *Op.* i. p. 1033 B, C. Another definition is given in *Colloquia, Op.* i. p. 653: " Tria mihi curae sunt, ut proficiam in probitate morum. Dein, si quid nequeam, certe tuear illibatam innocentiam ac famam. Postremo paro mihi bonas literas ac disciplinas in quovis vitae genere usui futuras."

literatures, rightly handled, notably served this purpose. In the training of the young we find that Erasmus lays little stress on observances or on religious dogma, but much on personal piety and the elements of Christian faith and practice.

Next, Erasmus brings into prominence the claim of the State or Community to the services of its members, and for such service the child must be fitted by education. Such an end is strictly in accord with antique ideals. Parents are urged to be careful of their duty to the fatherland ; to neglect the right training of the child is to ignore this obligation. A brave and efficient citizen is the gift which a father owes to his own city. In the same way the prince and the noble are exhorted to qualify their sons by sound education for their grave responsibilities. Beyond this, when Erasmus dwells upon the need of courtesy and good manners he is considering a man as a member of Society—a dim reflex of that social distinction which is embodied by Castiglione in *Il Cortegiano*. In Germany, at least, this was of no slight importance amongst the ends of culture.

The family, again, has its claims. By education the boy must learn how to bear himself as a dutiful son, able and willing to take upon himself part of the burdens of his parents. His distinction brings joy and credit to the home ; just as its grace and charm are increased by the skill or learning of the daughters. Sir Thomas More's household and that of Pirckheimer are more than once quoted by Erasmus to prove his contention that a woman's life is made more useful, by serious education, in each of the capacities that may fall to her. The home, moreover, gains in dignity by the share which the father takes in the children's training. The Roman parents at the best period never resigned their direct concern for this to the exclusive charge of another.

Erasmus lays little stress on the professional aspect of education. But he knows that a churchman, a theological student, an administrator, a landed proprietor, a statesman are

all made more efficient in their own spheres by sound learning[1].
Erasmus particularly inveighs against a common type of parent
who will accumulate estate for a son with untiring zeal, but
who is wholly careless as to the education which alone can fit
him to govern it. It is, he urges, a profound mistake to suppose that training for practical life is to be won by actual
experience of life itself[2]. On the other hand he declares that
preparation for a career ought not to be made subordinate to
purely literary attainment. Here, however, he is referring to
adult life ; and the warning is just a protest against neglect of
duty for devotion to dilettantism and self-culture.

Yet it must be carefully noted that the social end is to be
attained by the way of development of individuality through
liberal training. There are not two educations : training regarded as preparation for social service does not differ in
substance or in method from the education of the individual.
The difference lies in the application. Up to a certain limit,
which Erasmus placed at the 18th year, and Elyot somewhat later,
education should be uniform for all. Then supervenes the period
of gradual specialisation. But not even then may literature be
wholly abandoned in favour of professional studies. What is
desirable is that such studies should take the form, partly at
least, of concentration upon those aspects of letters which sub-
serve each particular pursuit. Law, Theology, Teaching will
all acquire an element which is "liberal" from such a method
of enquiry.

[1] Strictly in Erasmus' vein is the claim for this effect of erudition made
in the *Privilegium* of the royal Printing-press granted by Francis I to
Robert Estienne. "We are persuaded that those sound studies will give
birth in our kingdom to theologians who shall teach the sacred doctrines
of religion ; to magistrates who shall administer justice without partiality
and in the spirit of public equity ; and finally to skilled administrators,
the lustre of a State, who will be capable of sacrificing their private interest
to affection for the public good....Such are among the benefits that may
reasonably be looked for from sound studies, and from them almost exclusively." Quoted from Miss Lowndes' translation, *Montaigne*, p. 24.

[2] This is in part the argument of the *De Pueris*: infra, p. 191, § 12.

We may perhaps doubt whether Erasmus had reached a clear reconciliation of social and individual aims in education. At one time he speaks as though the best way of rendering service to the community lies in developing one's own personality. At another, he is more conscious of the risks attaching to a bold claim for free individual expansion, and to the exclusive temper of the self-absorbed scholar. Yet this is certainly true. He felt, and he expressed, the full strength of the reaction against the mediaeval University training, which was primarily concerned with professions of Law, Medicine, and Theology. Erasmus has the distinctive note of the Humanist, that he is first of all a teacher of liberal disciplines, upon which when maturity is reached technical knowledge may be superimposed. Sir Thomas Elyot expresses this position, interpreting Erasmus, as he so often does, to Englishmen : "pure and excellent learning, if it be translated to another study of a more gross quality vanisheth and cometh to nothing." Wherefore, he goes on, "if children were continually retained in the right study of very (*i.e.* sound) philosophy"—which is the Humanist *sapientia*, or *eruditio*—"until they passed the age of 21 years, and were then set to the Laws......they should undoubtedly become men of so excellent wisdom that throughout all the world should be found in no commonweal more noble counsellors[1]." This is said in the truest spirit of Humanism.

It may be asked at this point whether the position thus defined is consistent with the overweening importance assigned to eloquence by Erasmus and all the other masters of the Revival? Was not "oratory" largely a professional aptitude— for Church, Court, or Diplomacy? In considering this it is necessary to recall the origin of that ideal of the completely educated man, the "orator." It reached the Italian Humanists mainly through Quintilian. It preceded, in the history of the Renaissance, the ideal of the "Courtier." As understood by Quintilian the perfect "Orator" was the noble type of

---

[1] *The Governour*, i. p. 141.

publicist, a combination of personal presence, of virtue, and of learning, as well as of eloquence. He was the good man, the highly-informed man, trained in oratory : each of these factors was essential to the complete product. Both " Orator " and " Courtier " came to signify to Italian society of the 15th and 16th centuries the full range of qualities which should mark in a modern community the perfect man of the world—scholar, man of affairs, man of courtesy. In this way it happened, in the 15th century as in the first, that what were, to begin with, the characteristics of the highest professional type were trans-ferred to the general ideal of higher education. So in ancient Rome the training of the " Orator " was the education of hundreds of young men who had no thought of becoming advocates or debaters : and in modern Italy or England the maxims of the " Courtier " were eagerly studied by young men who would never approach a Court. To Erasmus the training of a gentleman was identical with an education in learned eloquence.

§ 2. The Three Factors of Human Nature.

The great Italian educationalists of the Revival built up their curriculum upon a union of Roman precedents with the courtly education of the later Middle Age. They took account, therefore, of each side of human personality. Erasmus, how-ever, held a somewhat different position. In his view, that side of development which concerned *physical excellence* was wholly subordinate. The absorption in sport and arms which he notes as characteristic of the upper ranks of Teutonic society he regards as a serious hindrance to intellectual advance. 'Gross,' 'boorish,' 'cruel' are the epithets which seem to spring naturally to Erasmus' lips when he contemplates the average parent of the land-holding class in Germany. There was, to Erasmus, much risk in pressing the claims of the body in education. In Italy it was far otherwise. We know that feudalism had left but little impress on the society of the Renaissance ; and the climate and the conditions of town life there rendered vigorous physical activity a needful discipline.   Apart from which the social graces filled a large place in personal distinction.   But to Erasmus it is enough that children be kept in health, for the body is but a means, an instrument, and has no true excellence beyond that.   Erasmus, we do not forget, had been a monk ; neither by aptitude nor disposition had he any inclination to physical skill.

Passing to the second and third constituents of human personality, the *mind* and the *spirit*, the point of view of Erasmus has been already outlined.   *Ingenium* or *intellectus*, as the seat of *ratio*, or active reasoning, is the chief differentia of Man.   But the teacher may not regard this faculty as existing independently of the religious instinct.   For the term which expresses the highest product of *ingenium*, viz., *philosophia*, covers both knowledge, conduct, and religion.   *Philosophia* is wisdom applied to life : the opposite is *stultitia*, which is ignorance applied to life[1].   The borderland of *pietas* and *mores* is indefinable ; and the soundest forms of *eruditio* inevitably develop that *bonus animus* whose expression is *pietas*.   It is impossible to realise the Erasmian concept of the relation of wisdom to spiritual well-being unless we grasp clearly his notion of *eruditio* (or *sapientia*) as "learning in use," or "wisdom interpreted for living."   It was something quite other than "research" in our modern sense.   Hence (though the words are those of his intimate friend Sadoleto), "devotion to philosophy serves as the best preparation for all sides of honourable action, and at the same time brings man nearer to God."   The education of "the spirit," therefore, to the earnest humanist,

---

[1] *Op.* i. 497 E : "quid est hominis maxime proprium ? Juxta rationem vivere.   Quid est perniciosissimum ?   Stultitia."   On the other hand *ratio* may lead to harm, for *eruditio* without virtue as its end does hurt to the character.   But if the consensus of the wisdom of mankind is rightly applied—*i.e.* if education is sound—good and not evil may be counted upon as the result.

and so to Erasmus, was the natural crown of all sound training; it did not demand a special section of the curriculum to itself. That Erasmus was by nature practical rather than devotional in his concept of religion, that "in things of the spirit" conduct mattered more to him than dogmatic equipment, that mysticism meant little to him, are undeniable. But it is profoundly untrue to insinuate, as his opponents often did in his lifetime, and certain critics have done since, that his perception of the religious factor in personality, and consequently in education, was feeble in itself and insincerely held.

There remains to be considered the function of education in respect of this training of character and intellect. The psychology of Erasmus has never been very carefully examined. It was mainly identical with that of Plutarch, and has therefore much in common with the Aristotelian analysis. The three factors in mental activity are *Natura, ratio, usus sive exercitatio*[1]. By *natura* Erasmus understands an innate capacity, both moral and intellectual. These blank capacities are affected from outside by experience, notably by *disciplina* and by *institutio* or instruction. On the intellectual side such instruction is by the way of information orderly presented, or *scientia*. On the moral side it comes through example, warning, or advice, whether drawn from books or persons. *Ratio* is the thinking endowment—its organic relation to *natura* is never defined—by which the learner judges, orders, and stores up in memory, external knowledge, and by which the teacher exhibits his matter in right method. In education, therefore, *ratio* is at once the enlightened reasoning of the teacher operating

---

[1] *Christ. Matrim.*, *Op.* v. 710 D: "Naturam voco aptitudinem quandam ad discendum quod traditur. Ratio praeceptis judicat quid expetendum, quid fugiendum. Usus ducit in habitum id quod praescriptum est." Cp. *De Pueris*, infra, p. 191, § 11 s.f. On the Aristotelian doctrine which Erasmus has in mind in this analysis cp. *Ethics*, i. 7. 9, and Burnet, *Aristotle on Education*, p. 27; "the *practical* life of the rational part of us" is the differentiating function of man. Cp. Becher, *Erasmus*, p. 32.

upon the learner, and the active reason of the learner reaching out to meet it. The term is often used by Erasmus in either sense. But invariably it implies faculty *in act*. *Ratio* is the peculiar quality of Man : "ratio facit hominem," as he explains ; "ratio ducit naturam[1]." *Usus* is practice, at school or in life, in aptitudes acquired, and the application to circumstances of knowledge assimilated. A boy applies a rule of grammar in composition ; a statesman a lesson from history ; both by virtue of *usus*.

Such are the definitions of the principal terms employed. Now *natura*, the mental self, comes into existence with very few instincts, with no innate ideas, but with large capacities ; lower animals, on the other hand, possess sharply-defined and highly-developed instincts, but slight power of advance beyond these. This marks man's superiority and proves the overwhelming importance of education. The metaphors borrowed by Erasmus to express this abstract capacity for taking form are various : the ploughed but unsown field ; the twig pliant and as yet unshaped ; soft wax or clay, and others[2].

This capacity reveals at a very early stage certain tendencies, notably to memory, to activity, and to imitation : it is intensely receptive : its absorptive powers work upon good or evil material with equal avidity. Hence the need for profitable occupation from the very first, that room be not left for evil influences, always ready to encroach upon the empty chambers of child-nature[3]. It is the peculiar function of the mother to "shelter the nursling from wrong impression." Hence Erasmus acutely sets aside enquiries as to the age at which education

---

[1] It need not be pointed out how defective is the analysis of *ratio* presented by Erasmus, who leaves in obscurity his view of the place of the imagination and the emotions. However, Erasmus always moves more easily in the sphere of practical aims than in that of theory, so that in dealing directly with educational method his precepts are sounder than his psychology. *Ratio* may often be best translated by *Training*, cp. p. 197.

[2] Cp. Tögel, *Pädag. Ansch.*, p. 37.

[3] "Sapiens industria parentum occupat naturam." *Op.* i. 497 E.

should begin. From birth, nay before it, the manifold operation of nurture and environment is at work. It is not a question as to the 7th year or the 5th or the 3rd, as the authorities
propound it; from the first day of his existence the child's
education has begun.

But *Natura* includes another factor besides abstract general
capacity for development: it contains a special quality which
varies with each individual and constitutes the basis of personality[1]. This individual quality is originally but a capacity for
receiving a special bent from external forces: it may be due
to inheritance, but when once recognised it may respond in
marvellous fashion to careful education. Training, therefore,
is all important. Nature gives potentialities, education transforms them into realities. " Efficax res est natura, sed hanc
vincit efficacior institutio." " Homines, mihi crede, non nas-
cuntur sed finguntur[2]." Further, " Educatio superat omnia."
By training we may eradicate evil tendency due to heredity;
but bad education will extinguish a bent to higher things.
Moreover, and we here reach the climax of the Erasmian
optimistic view of Man, we have in *Natura* a capacity which
in virtue of its divine origin is " apt for reason," prone to
obedience, and therefore capable by training of indefinite
advance. Nay, by education, diligently and skilfully directed,
the *rudis massa* of the nursling may be moulded into the visible
image of God[3].

It is a sanguine view of the possibilities of education. But
we must remember, first, that the Erasmian concept includes
the Platonic view of the function of Nurture—that unconscious

---

[1] *De Pueris*, infra, § 16, § 29 s.f., and § 25 s.f. Just as an ox or an
ass is put to the plough or the pack-saddle, so the dullard must for his
own sake be treated as fit only for the farm or work-shop. Again, there
are children whose bent lies towards Music, Arithmetic or Geography.
"Nature" ought to be followed in such cases. In Discipline also the
same holds good: infra, p. 205, § 24.

[2] *Op.* i. 493 B, infra, pp. 184, 186, §§ 4 and 7.

[3] *De Pueris*, infra, p. 187, § 7 s.f. Cp. Becher, *Erasmus*, p. 12.

presentation and absorption of impressions, moral, intellectual and aesthetic, which is the true note of Greek culture, and the conspicuous absence of which is the crucial defect of popular educational opinion in modern England.   In the next place, it is abundantly clear that Erasmus did not identify education with literary instruction in a narrow sense.   There is much in his view of morality which presages Herbart's concept of the dependence of conduct upon the "circle of thought."   *Stultitia* is moral, not less than intellectual, shortcoming: just as a wide range of interests lifts the mind above unworthy preoccupations.   Hence instruction (*eruditio, institutio*) is a most comprehensive force, operating upon a free will, whose determinations are easily fixed in the direction of reasonable action.   This conviction of the influence of the human intelligence in moulding the character of men is not peculiar to the Humanist.   The typical man of the world of that age was Machiavelli: and he arrives, though from an opposite standpoint, at the same generalisation.   "All that have reasoned on civil government, and all history, prove that it is necessary that he who frames a Commonwealth and ordains laws in it should pre-suppose that all men have their bent to ill-doing: that they desire to practise the wickedness of their minds whenever opportunity serves."   Hence, he continues, follows the necessity of Laws: for Laws make men good, seeing that by laws Education is framed, and by Education men, though naturally evil, are gradually trained to set examples of virtue in the State.   Thus the man of Letters and the man of Affairs agree : innate goodness (Erasmus) or innate wickedness (Machiavelli), fostered (Erasmus), or checked (Machiavelli), by education, produces notable virtue.   That 'virtue' to each of the two thinkers meant a different ideal does not affect the argument: in both cases contribution to the well-being of the community is the prime content, and in both the determining force is Education[1].

---

[1] Cp. Machiavelli, *Discorsi*, i. 3.

§ 3. LIMITATIONS OF THE EDUCATIONAL IDEAL.

This broad and liberal view of the aim of Education represents the essential principle of humanism, and, except on the side of the culture of the body, does not differ in type from that of the great Italians from Vergerius to Sadoleto. But, in the process of application of ideals to practice, the limitations imposed by social and historical circumstance call for careful noting.

First, Erasmus laid it down, with ample reason, that his standard of efficiency demanded either a small school conducted by brilliant scholars or the method of home tuition. The latter alternative depended inevitably upon the nature of the home in question : where there is right example, and due respect for learning, private tutorial instruction may be the best choice. Under no circumstances was a Religious House a fit seminary for the young : *schola aut publica aut nulla*[1] was his doctrine. But endowed or civic schools competent to the lofty functions of liberal education scarcely existed. Colet's foundation excited his admiration, as at once civic, lay, and humanist. But the majority of local schools were prisons and torture-chambers, homes of darkness and barbarity. Further, Erasmus propounded a curriculum which should carry youth to the threshold of manhood, when, the stimulus of the teacher being withdrawn, the spontaneous interests of the pupil could be counted upon to carry onward the pursuit of learning into adult life. Now all this implies an education for the prosperous class : the gentry, the wealthy burgher, the state official. The poor man can only secure education by civic or private benevolence, a form of charity which he earnestly commends[2].

[1] *De Pueris*, infra, p. 204, § 23 s.f.

[2] *Op.* i. 508 E, infra, p. 209, § 26 : *Op.* v. 716 A. With Erasmus the education of the poorer class was the object of pious wish, a most suitable work of charity in individual cases of special talent. Erasmus, like his humanist—and other—contemporaries, has no consciousness of a problem

In the next place, the choice of *instrument* is rigidly conditioned : the classical literatures are alone admitted. This carried with it the elimination of purely national elements in education, and the substitution for them of a universal culture. This accounts for the fact that the influence of the Erasmian ideal in Germany was inferior to that of Melanchthon, with that Protestant Teutonism which coloured all his educational propaganda.   Perhaps it was in the Jesuit schools that the curriculum of Erasmus was most adequately presented.

That the new education found no place for instruction in natural phenomena is hardly to be set down to its disadvantage. There was as yet no science of nature available for teaching[1]. Astronomy was attaining fixity, it is true : but both geography and natural history still rested on unsound knowledge of facts and perfunctory classification.   The age of over-sea discovery was but dawning in Northern Europe.   "Cosmography," therefore, meant, even yet, Strabo and Mela.   Modern geography did not, could not, yet exist.   The life of plants and animals was, as in previous centuries, the sport of credulity and *à priori* hypothesis.   The vernacular was beneath consideration : it was a mere dialect.   Mathematics had no human interest.   Modern historians were but annalists.

to be faced.   He knew that on his own lines popular education was impossible ; and indeed he may be said to have emphasised the deep distinction between the educated and the uneducated classes.   It is, however, clear that he regarded training in rudiments of religion and duty as the fitting education for those who had to work with their hands. Preachers must use the vernacular, and so familiarise their congregations with Scripture and Church doctrine.   " I see no reason why the uneducated should be kept from the New Testament."   Instruction of this sort, Catechisms, Hymns, with private reading of Scripture will form a training which in its degree will be a compensation to those to whom learning is inaccessible.   Cp. Glöckner, *Bildung und Erziehung,* p. 97.

[1] In the *De Pueris,* §§ 10, 30, we have instances.   Topsell's *The Historie of Foure-Footed Beastes,* which in its original Latin form was perhaps the most popular Natural History throughout Europe in the century 1560—1660, will illustrate the same argument.

Briefly put, the only available material for instruction was that contained in the ancient writers. Partly, because through them alone could mind come into contact with mind. Partly, because subsequent enquiry had added nothing to the scientific wisdom therein contained. Partly, that outside of them there was no *organised* secular knowledge at all. And Erasmus knew that facts which, however interesting, are formless and unrelated, have no value for the education of the young. Finally, the doctrine that education can only follow opinion is clearly realised. Erasmus is for ever proclaiming that " opinion " both in clergy and laity must be reformed before scholars can effect their ends. Rulers, parents, nobles must move before instruction can be moulded upon new lines. The absence of state organisation throws the onus upon the Church and the governing classes. A new standard, a fresh subject of education is impossible without the strong impulse of social, or professional interest.

CHAPTER IV.

THE BEGINNINGS OF EDUCATION.

§ 1. EARLIEST CARE.

THE first responsibilities towards the young[1] are of much concern to Erasmus, as indeed they are to most humanists who write upon Education.   Erasmus realised that heredity has a certain influence, which a man of intelligence will recognise in choosing his wife.   It is often possible to affirm that the wrong bent of a child is congenital and may, therefore, prove to be ineradicable.   But the mother may do much to secure that her child be born with a nature apt to good impressions by diligent care for her own health, by maintaining equability of temper and moderation in all things.   The nursling must be the mother's exclusive care.   The custom of putting the new-born child to nurse is condemned—on the best classical precedents[2].

---

[1] Erasmus treats of this subject in the *De Pueris* and *De Chr. Matrim.* It has often been said that the humanists had no message to offer concerning the education of young children.   This is, as a fact, wholly untrue. They had of course an imperfect concept of what was necessary.   But the essential point is that they realised that there *was* a problem.   The Middle Age had neither a view upon the beginnings of teaching nor a sense that a view of any kind was needed.

[2] Plutarch's tract περὶ παίδων ἀγωγῆς was appealed to in this matter, as in so many other precepts upon the training of the young.   Erasmus follows Plutarch very closely, as did most humanists.   It was one of the earliest Greek treatises to be translated into Latin (by Lionardo Bruni d' Arezzo) in the course of the Revival.

Children acquire through unconscious imitation much, even at this earliest stage, which abides for life. Hence the importance of the right education of women. Cornelia and other Roman mothers are a standing proof of this. Feminine influence is specially enduring in the beginnings of speech. In this respect the danger arising from contact with ignorant women servants is hard to overrate. In physical care, in manners, in the simple duties of truth and reverence, the responsibility during the early stage falls wholly upon the mother.

It is a grave question at what period this oversight of women should be superseded. There is beyond doubt a reminiscence of the celibate ecclesiastic in the view of Erasmus and of Sadoleto that the mother's place should be taken by the father or tutor about the fifth year. Both depre-cate the influence of women even at the first stages of boy life. Erasmus thinks that they lack self-restraint, are indulgent and cruel by caprice, a consequence, no doubt, of vicious train-ing which precluded all serious thinking upon life and duty.

Yet Erasmus affirms constantly that no force for good can surpass the child's home atmosphere. Nurture and example are the stimulus to the formation of an unconscious standard of conduct, intelligence and taste. In a pious household it is customary for the child to see food sent from table to the home of a suffering poor neighbour ; the walls will have illus-trations of virtuous and brave actions. Interest in religious truths will be aroused. " Nec fere impii liberi nisi parentum culpa."

§ 2.   HEALTH AND PHYSICAL WELL-BEING OF YOUNG
CHILDREN.

Erasmus, like Locke, had learnt from his own experience the importance of health as a condition of efficient intellectual life. His view of the relation of mind and body was derived from Aristotle. It is of no great concern to Erasmus whether that view was or was not scriptural : the body may be a prison, or a temple, or a garment; in any case these are metaphors only. He is solely concerned with the practical question : its abstract, philosophical formulation has no concern for him. This at least is clear to him : the relation of body and mind is organic, whence a constant interaction between the two. Just as spiritual character is reflected in face and bearing, so anger, envy, desires, are closely bound up with bodily states. Thus he sees the whole question on more than one side. As an end in itself bodily culture makes little or no appeal to him. The soul is the end : it is enough that the body fulfil reasonably its behests. In this he differs from the earliest humanists, and from ancient ideals. We must not forget that the "cult of the body" in Germany meant a warlike ferocity of unparalleled coarseness, not the grace of Apollo or of the *Ephebi* of Athens.

Yet during the earlier years of childhood—to the seventh at least—much care is needed. In this the mother's action is of chief importance. Erasmus enters into some detail[1]. Too much, or too rich, food, spices, wine, are all forbidden ; the mind, not less than the body, suffers from such indulgences. Too much sleep is equally injurious. Exercise, he expressly urges, should be free and spontaneous. Dress should always allow of such activity. Girls suffer more than boys from custom and from parental vanity. Smart, cramping dress, with sleeves and trains and collars, not only hampers them physically but begets childish conceit. If parents must have an object for foolish pride of this kind let them buy a monkey and work off their vanity by dressing it up instead. Moreover, it is of great importance under what conditions of air and

---

[1] Eras. *Op.* v. 710 E—711 A. Erasmus has in mind advice given by Aristotle, *De Generatione*. All is to be done and allowed by way of the Mean. See also *Op.* i. 447 A, B.

climate children are nurtured. Foul air and warm temperatures are injurious. The Germans, he often records, are grievous offenders in this regard. Yet the hardening by exposure—thin dress, bare legs, no hat, has a critic in Erasmus. Baths are good, in moderation. Sadoleto deprecates the idea of washing as often as once a day, "in northern fashion."

Erasmus has observed the effects of the imitative instinct in bodily affections. Hence the care which must be exercised as respects companionship. Contagion, bodily and mental, is a risk to which "the moist and tender bodies of the very young" are particularly liable. Stammering, some eye-affections, and nervous tricks are readily acquired from others. And he warns against allowing intercourse with crying, peevish and irritable companions. The dangers involved reveal themselves only gradually, but they are very hard to eradicate in later years. Games, fresh air, regular habits, no fasting, no night-work are his prescriptions for the health of the young boy or girl: "ut corpore bene composito animus sit ad institutionem habilior[1]." It was objected to Erasmus that he was exceeding the Christian norm in his concern for the body; a judgment which he scornfully rejected. He has, however, wholly outgrown the mediaeval concept of the need of depressing the body in the interests of the spirit.

None the less he is careful always to say that he will not regard the vigour of an athlete as a compensation for lack of learning. A grown man needs just enough health to go along with. The "Orator"—the man of affairs and society—will need no doubt a training in gesture and bearing: such outward aptitudes are the complement of the inner aesthetic results of polite letters.

[1] *Op.* v. 712 B. Quintilian advises gymnastic exercises for an orator, to enable him to cultivate gesture. So Erasmus, *Op.* v. 963.

§ 3. HOME INSTRUCTION.

Erasmus would prefer that the foundations of instruction should be laid at home and that the mother and father should, in this respect also, qualify themselves to guide the growing mind. Systematic teaching will hardly begin before the seventh year. But before that certain rudiments may well be imparted. In religion, for example, the sacred name of the Father and of the Redeemer will be taught : the reverence due to Scripture : the simple meaning of Baptism : the protecting presence of the Guardian Angel. Such teaching will be associated with regular observance of Christian worship. In intimate dependence on religion stands the elementary morality of childhood : obedience, respect, and, above all, truthfulness. Lying is the worst vice of childhood. Tales and proverbs, read from ancient history and Old Testament Scripture alike, form the material for such instruction. But parents must remember that all such training is nullified by examples of coarseness or indulgence on their part. As to knowledge— the most important duty is to impart the first facility in Latin Grammar. Here Erasmus touches " praeludia quaedam " of education. For instance the alphabet and the first steps in reading and writing should be learnt always by way of play. Then good articulation and pronunciation must be insisted on. Following this may come the naming of objects, in the con- crete or in picture. But objects are clearly valued, at this stage at least, only as aids to linguistic advance. There is to be no use of the vernacular : Latin has become the natural means of communication. Hence the necessity of keeping menials at arm's length. We are reminded of Montaigne's ex- perience, although every humanist, Vives, Melanchthon, Sturm, prescribed the same rule. But the note of this stage is this : " usque ad annum septimum tantum novalis praeparatur ad sementum[1]." Aristotle had fixed the fifth year as the earliest at which compulsory exercises might begin.

Erasmus had much to say respecting discipline during this period. He insists that the method of training must be " per lusum "—by way of pleasant device, and by kindly interest. He quotes the case of a mother who ruined her little daughter's nature by sheer cruelty. " The child could as yet hardly speak properly when she took her in hand to train her as a lady of society." The process involved beating a little girl of six until she fainted : yet the mother was not yet 26 years of age. " I for my part," says Erasmus, " would gladly have seen this tyrant thrashed in the child's stead. For, you see, it was really an aggravated case. Supposing that the 'instruction' in question was genuinely worth giving, even so it was a wicked way of going to work. But here was some trivial nonsense of conventional manners—and for that she tortured her own child[2]." No, all discipline and all method for the young has as its aim to win and not to drive. Undoubtedly the content of the instruction in this stage is slight, but the genius of Erasmus is shown in his insistence that the teaching of such young children is a problem worth solving[3].

[1] Eras. *Op.* v. 710 D, Arist. *Polit.* vii. 17; his objection is that premature intellectual work might interfere with physical excellence. Cp. Burnet, *Aristotle on Education*, p. 103, 5. Elyot fixes seven years; Sturm between six and seven; Quintilian, and many humanists, refused to state a limit.

[2] Eras. *Op.* v. 712 D : a very important passage.

[3] Erasmus is almost alone in urging the importance of careful observation of temperament and capacity in the very young : " non mediocris artis est instituere primam aetatem." *Op.* v. 715 B. There are not a few parents who can make no allowance for childhood and wish their children to be born grown up. The " petty school " in England of the 16th and 17th centuries was a deplorable institution : even Brinsley could propose that " to teach them (little children) would help some poor man or woman who knew not how to live otherwise." Cp. Foster Watson, *Curriculum*, p. 6. Erasmus, in his sense of the importance of the foundations of education, strikes a most modern note.

§ 4.   School-life and Home Instruction.

A momentous decision has now to be made.   Shall the boy remain at home or shall he go to school?   Erasmus would ideally prefer that a boy at the age of seven should attend a day school from his own home, and work after school hours under direction of a tutor.

At this age the child's special bent of mind and temper is in great part revealed.   He is able to endure systematic mental work and is benefited by social intercourse with his equals.

A wise parent will have already followed a well-considered scheme of training, which leads directly to the stage of school-life : and thus will be competent to decide the question which now confronts him.   Erasmus is not able to lay down a uniform procedure, though some points are clear.   The father is the best educator, if only he be duly qualified.   First he has nothing but denunciation for the monastic boarding school removed from public observation and control : education is a matter of civic responsibility[1].   Aristotle and Plato advocated a 'public' school in preference to private ventures.   Yet (*a*) the existing schools are thoroughly unsatisfactory (he is referring to the local grammar schools, the Cathedral schools, &c.), their staffs are worthless ; the head-masters are there by the favour of careless and ignorant governors.   "Drunken, broken down, imbecile, they teach in miserable hovels : as though they turn out pigs instead of citizens.   Such is the seed-plot of the State[2]!"   There is (*b*) further the risk of herding a large gathering of boys together ; for inevitably in such a mingling of characters evil has an undue chance.

Again individual instruction is out of the question where classes are large and parents have no control over the type of

---

[1] Eras. *Op*. i. 504 D.   Infra, p. 209.   For the reference to Plato and Aristotle, *Op*. v. 713 C.

[2] *Op*. v. 713 C, D.

master engaged. In collegiate or higher schools language teaching is thoroughly bad ; and the more ambitious boys are by the time they are 15 or 16 hankering after freedom, or university courses, and degrees which will—save the mark !—give them the status of teachers themselves. So that Erasmus feels driven to propose that one tutor be engaged to teach five or six boys[1], who then enjoy the benefits of companionship, emulation and personal interests, whilst not losing the stimulus that home-life supplies. The parent, indeed, has no right to disown his responsibility at any time during the education of his son. The choice of the tutor or the school by no means implies that the father has abdicated. How valuable wise supervision may be was recognised in ancient Rome : it was common in Athens.

§ 5.   The Qualifications of the Master.

The Tutor must be, first of all, a man of high character, worthy of fullest confidence. He must be active, vigorous and of healthy habit. His age should be such as to secure experience, but not such as to remove him from sympathy with active youth. His great aim will be to kindle spontaneous interest. Manner is of importance ; he must not be gloomy in appearance, nor passionate ; he must be serious, indeed, but patient, remembering that he too was once a boy. He will be on thoroughly frank and friendly terms with the parents and will be trusted by them. But there will be " liberalis quaedam reverentia " withal. Learned he must be ; indeed, without a high qualification as a student he has no right to his post. Erasmus is dismayed at the low estimate which most parents form of the tutor's functions. His pay is less than that of a cook, and his selection a matter of far less thought. A man will often give away the appointment—to oblige a friend ; a

[1] *Op.* v. 716 A.

mother is often more careful of her pet dog[1].   The essential
marks of his erudition are his knowledge of Latin and Greek,
his breadth of reading and his mastery of sound conversational
Latin.   A university degree is never named as a qualification,
which is evidence of the divorce still subsisting between
humanist study and the northern university.   Erasmus sets
undoubtedly a very lofty standard of attainment before his
ideal master.   Admitting that his functions as a teacher will
have a comparatively narrow range, he should, notwithstanding,
have covered the whole field of learning as contained in
classical literature ; and in any case have acquaintance with
the principal subjects therein treated of.   Writers are to be
read not merely as stylists, but as authorities on the various
arts and sciences.   History, geography, astronomy, mythology,
philosophy and theology ; the arts of war, agriculture, of
architecture ; the accounts given of trees, plants, animals, of
customs and antiquities—these are to be known, and the whole
fabric of ancient culture realised in living fashion by the
perfect scholar.   A right grasp of the Erasmian concept of
scholarship will save us from much shallow criticism of the
Renaissance ideal of knowledge and of education.   Naturally
a man of such erudition may find it difficult to adapt his
teaching to the child-mind.   Here comes the third qualification required of the master ; his insight into the moral and
intellectual disposition of the pupil, and his ability to order
discipline and instruction accordingly.   Erasmus shows a most
remarkable power of observation on his own part in regard to
personal bent, capacity and disposition in boys.   He insists
that such insight is as easy to acquire as it is essential.   Looks,
expression, gesture, degree of self-control, facial conformation,
personal habits in respect of dress and speech, temper in

[1] No woman is competent : "praeter naturam est feminam in masculos
habere imperium." Cp. i. 504 C, and Becher, *Die Ansichten*, p. 8.   For
the denunciation of similar indifference by Italian humanists cp. Woodward,
Vittorino, p. 201.

games, all carry their message to a skilful observer. Intellectual taste and capacity are, he affirmed, always purely individual; ready perception of such special endowments is the first step towards adapting instruction to the pupil. The master must be competent to adjust means to ends[1]. Young boys entering upon new and, at first stages, unattractive subject-matter must be won by patience, by incentives of rivalry and reward, by devices such as pictures, stories and moral lessons. The tutor will welcome the presence and co-operation of the father in stimulating the desire to excel. Excess of preparatory work, undue stress on learning by heart, ill-judged themes for composition, all imply that the master forgets what a boy is. The teacher must never take his own mental interests and capacities as his guide either in discipline or instruction. " Remember that your pupil is a boy still, and that you were a boy yourself not so long ago." Then the master will show himself at once reasonable and humane.

Erasmus regarded the creation of a new type of master, private or public, as the first condition of educational reform. That he himself set forth an ideal hard to attain, he was well aware. To provide for this pressing need is the urgent duty of an enlightened Prince. The rightly equipped master ranks with wise kingship, upright officials and a devoted clergy, as one of the four pillars of national well-being. He elaborated his first picture of a modern master for Colet's school. He would have found it, had he known, realised in the person of Vittorino da Feltre, in the famous school of Mantua nearly a century before.

[1] *Op.* i. 513 A. The place of interest in learning was thoroughly realised by Erasmus. The order of its development is not very consistently worked out, but it is somewhat as follows: spontaneous interest in play; love and respect for teacher; derived love for knowledge following upon the personal bond; fear of blame and of falling below proper self-respect; desire for praise, which is identical with the man's love of Fame. *Op.* i.

§ 6. THE BEGINNINGS OF SYSTEMATIC INSTRUCTION.

The Erasmian education began, as we saw, unconsciously. Speech, *i.e.* Latin speech, must be acquired as early as the home conditions admit. In some cases a child might, like Montaigne, be so fortunate as to acquire good conversational Latin before the end of the fifth year. This, indeed, is the natural method of learning Latin. In this way articulation, pronunciation and expression will be cultivated. Vocabulary will be derived from object teaching, and the *Colloquies* are full of instances of this use of external things in instruction. As word-forms come gradually into use, arrangement of simple inflections will follow : but of systematic grammar there will be at first very little. Ancient stories, historical and mythical, and descriptions of animal and plant life, all illustrated by pictures [1], will be told, and conversation leading up to moral truths built upon them. Travellers bring stories of wonder, modern history also narrates incidents which are of interest, and which when remembered may be helpful later on. It is remarkable to note the important place which teaching of this kind occupies in Erasmus' ideal ; and how elaborately he has worked it out as an element of home education. Undoubtedly it was instruction *about* objects rather than *through* objects, and it had a dual aim : linguistic as well as quasi-realist. Still it was devised on true grounds of child interests and went as far, perhaps, as the state of scientific knowledge then allowed. For the school can only adapt such knowledge as its age provides. The *Colloquies* were as a whole lessons in the concrete, although their objects are social life, daily experience, and humanity rather than Nature. These are, however, " nature study " in as genuine a sense as demonstrations in natural history : for their actuality is not limited to human character, but extends to environment and setting. Their

[1] Infra, p. 226 : the *Colloquy* upon " A serious Entertainment."

intent is to arouse observation, criticism and ethical selection; the method is an approach, at least, to direct handling of facts. It is evident in this connection that, although Erasmus would refuse a place to the vernacular in the school, a working acquaintance with the mother tongue was assumed as the means of acquiring such general knowledge of common facts as is here indicated.

Reading[1] follows. It must be taught early: "Sonare primum est, proximum legere." That is the order. Letters are taught and recognised: this by the method of the biscuit letters of Horace, or by ivory tablets, or by pictures; and there was a game of Scaci in which Greek and Latin letters were employed in a sort of competition. Letters are named, written and pronounced; then syllables, words and sentences. Reading matter must be intelligible and attractive, though we should be glad to know the type of book contemplated. Nothing very attractive has come down to us. Probably extracts were written, or later on dictated, for temporary use. Consecutive reading should be practised on some author worth studying. The *Colloquies* of Erasmus were the most popular "Reader" of the 16th and 17th centuries.

Writing, in turn, is of later introduction than reading. In its beginnings it is a form of drawing. Handwriting, says Erasmus, like one's voice, is a part of our personality and should be cultivated accordingly. This is not exclusively a mere utility. A start is made with simplest capitals of Roman, not Gothic, type. The best examples are the letters to be found upon the coin inscriptions of the sestertii of the early empire—a very remarkable bit of true artistic perception of Erasmus[2]. He describes carefully the formation of letters to be followed in writing-copies. Simpler capitals first, then the more complex ones, lastly groups and abbreviations. Before

---

[1] *Dialog. De Pronun., Op.* i. 929 A.
[2] Cp. the *Dialog. De Pronun., Op.* i. 925, 6.

the age of seven this will be taught by a teacher of sense
"by way of play." The Greek and Latin alphabets ought if
possible to be learnt side by side[1]. Let all headlines be
sensible and useful. Drawing is attractive to boys, in that
every child is delighted to express in this way what he has
seen : at a later stage it will be found helpful to add manual
dexterity in painting, modelling and architecture : we need not
fear the reproach of the rigid humanist, "for we cannot forget
that our Lord was not only the son of a craftsman, but was
one Himself[2]."

§ 7.   Discipline.

Erasmus has two charges to make against the schoolmasters
of his day : they are ignorant and they are brutal. He con-
nects the two by proving that brutality is the resource of the
master who has either no method of teaching or nothing to
teach[3].

The insight into child nature which Erasmus displayed was
accompanied by a definite concept of the conditions of right
discipline, which he properly understood as including both
stimulus and restraint.   This psychological theory implied that
the growing mind is by nature curious, imitative and tenacious;
and that it is by nature amenable to right guidance.   Hence
the boy may be counted upon to obey suitable incentives.
These are in part personal to the teacher, in part they belong
to his instruction.

The first step is to secure the respect and the affection of
the pupil for the master, an affection which will not be allowed
to degenerate into familiarity.   This leads to the second stage :
the affection for the subject taught.   But this will not be maintained unless interest is aroused.   Now interest in the subject-

---

[1] *Op.* v. 712 c : this before the 7th year, and always " per lusum."
[2] *Op.* v. 716 b, c.
[3] The *De Pueris* should be read in illustration of this section.

matter may not be at first strong enough to survive: it must be nourished by associating pleasure with the actual teaching process. This is secured by wise devices, which Erasmus describes " per lusum discere " ; by encouragement of ambition ; by emulation ; by alternation of subjects, and intervals for relaxation. The *Colloquies* as a means of learning Latin in lieu of the method of logical grammar are a standing instance with Erasmus. Moreover he sees that clearness in exposition and arrangement, variety of illustration, of contrast and of parallel, are essential factors in retaining attention. Exercises, for instance, in speaking Latin, should be carefully adapted to the boy's own interests, his play and social life. The choice of such material was, no doubt, less easy than it appeared to be to Erasmus. He had himself no competing interests outside his life of a student ; and had never experienced the sweeping tide of physical energy with its imperious demands for bodily activity and achievement. He admits that to some boys intellectual pursuits make no appeal, and for those he urges a wholly different training, though one in which he can take little concern.

The desire of fame and fear of dispraise or of ridicule become with Erasmus an educational motive. These indeed have in them something of the nature of instinct. But whilst backward boys may be thus encouraged, good scholars are not to be over-praised. For though despondency is to be avoided, conceit and contempt for others are not less objectionable.

Strictly in harmony with this view of the forces which make for interest is Erasmus' position respecting punishments. He contrasts the method of Christ with his disciples with the habit of the teacher of his own day. Erasmus draws a repulsive picture of the customary discipline of the grammar school. Petrarch had done the same before him : but whilst he had stood amazed that any one should undertake so trying a trade as that of school teaching, Erasmus glorified it as amongst the highest of Christian duties, and the noblest of intellectual careers. For he did not admit that harsh discipline was a necessity. If there are boys who may only be controlled by flogging, let them be sent away from school as being incapable of liberal education, and find industrial occupation. In reality cruelty was in those days a common vice, and re-acted inevitably upon school-life. Parents—widowed mothers in particular—were not seldom given to violence towards their children. They forget that offences are often due to mere thoughtlessness and excusable ignorance. No woman ought to be allowed to strike a child ; she has not the self-control required. Harshness drives boys to enlist or to take monastic vows. Girls are broken in spirit. Corporal punishment must not be such as offends self-respect and modesty, and is unsuited for any but moral faults. But he roundly declares that the boy who is not influenced by the fear of God, by regard for his parents, by shame, by conscience, is not likely to be moulded aright by mere physical pain. The stories which he relates from his own experience in the tract *De Pueris*[1] are very significant ; and throw into strong relief Erasmus' enlightened attitude on the question. There is obvious relation between that attitude and his optimistic view of human nature, just as the mediaeval and Lutheran conviction of depravity might suggest a sterner need for repression. It must not be forgotten moreover that Erasmus had never been a schoolmaster.

[1] Infra, pp. 205—7.

CHAPTER V.

THE LIBERAL STUDIES.

§ 1. THE TEACHING OF GRAMMAR.

IT is important to understand the attitude of Erasmus to the subject of Grammar in education. It need not be said, perhaps, that by "Grammar" is meant that of the Latin and Greek languages, and not of German or Dutch. We shall find that Erasmus holds opinions upon this branch of instruction which alone would entitle him to a notable place in the history of teaching.

The content of the term Grammar has varied in the history of scholarship. To Quintilian it implies not only accidence and syntax, and the art of reading aloud, but also the study of the poets, historians, philosophers and orators. It is a pursuit which demands the highest intelligence ; it corresponds in fact to our concept of the study of Literature. The professional grammarians, on the other hand, of later date, Donatus, Priscian, and Servius, mean by the term the authoritative accidence, syntax, and prosody of Latin and Greek. They were in principle followed by the mediaevalists from Isidore down to the eleventh century. But from 1150, or so, onwards we trace the rapid intrusion of dialectic into the province of grammar, which ceased to be the formulation of usage of expression, and became concerned with the laws under which thought was held.

This tendency became more pronounced as the reign of dialectic throughout all branches of knowledge was gradually established. Whilst in Italy the humanists were busily engaged in restoring the antique conception of grammar, in the north of France, in England and in Germany, it had sunk into complete subjection to logic. The following is a definition of the function of the Pronoun from a grammar for beginners printed in 1499. " Pronomen...significat substantiam seu entitatem sub modo conceptus intrinseco permanentis seu habitus et quietis sub determinate apprehensionis formalitate[1]." Or we may illustrate the mediaevalist idea from the discussions upon the Absolute case. It was not enough for the scholar to know that Latin usage constructed this in the ablative : the special "ablativity" of the "absolute" concept[2] was really what interested the grammarian. In the same way the usages of the participle, of the genitive of possession, of the passive voice, were of far less concern than their *modi significandi* or underlying dialectic conceptions. Hence came the endless gloss and comment which, like those of Petrus Helias, overlay the texts of Priscian and Donatus, and which became the substitute for grammatical treatises outside the circles of humanism in the fourteenth and fifteenth centuries. The same confusion is witnessed in the Dictionaries, where etymologies and explanations of words pass very often into a dialectical or ethical region. Papias, for instance, the chief of the vocabularists, gives under *Homo* definitions of Man, in logical shape and completeness, instead of a description or synonym : under *Aetas* we find religious admonitions. Elsewhere *pronomen* is thus explained : homo est tuum nomen, peccator est tuum pronomen. In fact no grammarian could resist the temptation to digression and homily. For the true limits of grammar had been lost to sight. It had lost its objective character as the

---

[1] Thurot, *Extraits*, p. 490. This is taken from a printed grammar dated 1499.

[2] Cp. Thurot, *l.c.*, pp. 311 seqq.

formulation of inflection and construction as determined by right choice of authorities[1]. It had abandoned its independent status, and having become a function of logic shared the futilities of the current word-spinning of the day[2]. Its relation to style and to literary interpretation was understood in Italy alone. Humanists were undoubtedly right in ascribing to the dialectic method of handling grammar the stagnation of Latin learning which marked the later Middle Age[3].

---

[1] There was always a current of opposition to the prevalent confusion of grammar and dialectic during the middle age. But the scholars who urged the authority of classical writers were very few, and the Universities were against them. Chartres and Tours held out against the dominant influence of Paris; but the point is that they could not influence educational opinion. Cp. Clerval, *Écoles de Chartres*, p. 230; Sandys, *Classical Scholarship*, p. 516.

[2] The following is from Helias: "Consideremus *Vergilium vivere bonum est: Vergilium* accusativus *vivere* infinitivo regitur. Quare? Quoniam infinitivus accusativum regit ex vi infinitivi." Thurot, *Not. et Extraits*, p. 245. This, a very common type, shows to what dialectical grammar could sink. The mediaeval position is clearly stated, *l.c.* p. 102: "cum Priscianus non docuerit grammaticam per omnem modum sciendi possibilem, in eo sua doctrina est valde diminuta. Unde constructiones multas dicit, quarum tamen causas non assignat, sed *solum eas declarat per auctoritates antiquorum grammaticorum*. Propter quod non docet, quia illi tantum docent qui causas suorum dictorum assignant."

[3] Cp. Eras. *Op.* i. 892, iii. pp. 3, 68, 930. Infra, p. 221. The mediaeval grammarians, against whom Erasmus specially protests, are these: Johannes de Garlandia, an Englishman who resided chiefly in France (circ. 1230). His *Synonima* and *Vocabulorum aequivocorum interpretatio* were very much used: one or other of these is referred to by Erasmus as used by him at school: supra, p. 3. Both were sufficiently in demand to be printed by W. de Worde (1499, 1500), and later by Pynson. They are both in metre. Michael de Marbais, known as Modista from his book *de modis significandi* (circ. 1220). Ebrardus (circ. 1212), known as Graecista from his metrical work on grammar, which contains some speculative etymologies from the Greek. Ludolphus, called Florista from his metrical syntax, much used in the Netherlands. Papias (circ. 1050) and Hugutio (circ. 1200) produced dictionaries which sorely offended by reason of their indifference to classical authority and to classical quotation. The most

The revolt against the mediaevalist grammarian, begun by
Petrarch, found its distinguished champion in Lorenzo Valla
(1415—1465). Himself a scholar of the first rank in his day
he waged relentless war against the depravers of Latin. His
cardinal principle was the exact opposite to theirs. " Ego pro
lege accipio quidquid magnis auctoribus placuit[1]." To him
language was a body of phenomena whose laws were ascertain-
able from the study of the given facts, and were, once arrived
at, available for use in speech and in interpretation. All
à priori, subjective, or allegorical intrusions into this region of
plain authoritative usage were to be rigorously barred out. All
humanist scholars followed Valla. The first systematic Latin
grammar upon the new method was that of N. Perotti, a pupil
of Vittorino da Feltre, which was printed in 1473.

The position affirmed by scholars was in reality the precursor
of the Baconian doctrine, applied thus early to one special
department of Nature, viz., organised speech. In their respect
for actual facts, and their aversion to dialectic speculation, a
profound spiritual kinship links the great minds of the Revival,
such as Valla and Erasmus, with that of the famous elaborator
of method.

popular of all grammarians at the beginning of the Revival was Alexander de
Villa Dei (circ. 1200), whose hexameter poem (ed. Reichling, 1893) treating
of accidence, syntax and prosody, was regarded less unfavourably by humanists, and was edited by Sintheim of Deventer (supra, p. 3). It rested upon
Donatus and Priscian ; though the glosses added by later commentators
were of the usual dialectic sort. The best of the Dictionaries was the
Vocabularius Breviloquus, often ascribed to Guarino, or to Reuchlin ; both
wrongly. It grew from an anonymous production which saw the light at
Basel about 1400 ; but its inclusion of much theological and legal terminology
shows that it was not a scholar's handbook but one for professional use.
In the form of the Strassburg edition of 1491 it was probably the commonest
dictionary of Erasmus' day. A review of the relation of the *Doctrinale*
of Alexander de Villa Dei to earlier humanist grammars is given by Sabbadini, *La Scuola e gli studi di Guarino*, pp. 38 seqq. In its treatment of
irregular inflections and of syntax it was held to be sound.

[1] Valla, *Eleg. Ling. Lat.* iii. 17.

The reverence which Erasmus entertained for Valla's scholarship has been already noticed. He shared his view of the function of grammar as generalised usage, in inflection and in construction, formulated as a guide in interpretation and composition. It is true that, like nearly all humanists, Erasmus occasionally extends the term to cover the study of Literature, in imitation of Quintilian. But as a rule he limits the use of the word "Grammatica" to accidence, syntax, and prosody, as does Sadoleto in his tract on Education, and our own Sir Thomas Elyot[1]: "grammar being but the introduction to the understanding of authors."

The view of grammatical method held by Erasmus is instructive. Its philosophical basis is never very clearly exhibited, for it is characteristic of him to work intuitively towards right methods whose psychological validity he had no means of proving. But it is obvious that, however unconsciously, he accepted those principles of language-teaching which have been regarded as a peculiar discovery of our own day. We must remember that Latin was understood by Erasmus, and was to be taught, as a living language in the sense that French and German are "living" languages in a modern school-course.

We can distinguish three stages of grammatical instruction, each of which has its phase of *natural acquisition*, of *generalisation* or systematic grammar, and of *practice*, whereby the pupil fixes and applies rules formally learnt. The *earliest* stage is that already touched upon[2]. The first steps are taken by way of naming, conversation and description : these steps are accomplished in the home, if possible in the nursery, where as we know Montaigne learnt to speak Latin and that only. It is to secure this natural method that Erasmus is so insistent on the choice of attendants and companions, and on the engagement of a learned tutor. For the same reason Erasmus

[1] Sadoleto, *Op.* iii. 105.   Elyot, *Governour*, i. 55.
[2] Supra, pp. 90, 96.

debars the use of folk-lore and national stories. Parents and friends of the child should keep up their conversational Latin and read aloud in the language to further this introductory stage[1]. When the child can understand and take part in such conversation he should be taught the first rudiments of grammar. This is confined carefully to the regular forms of Noun and Verb which are detached and learnt by heart. These in turn are to be brought into exercise and applied by further conversation, so that they may become thoroughly familiar.

At the *second* stage, that of earliest school instruction, which corresponds to the seventh year of age, the boy will make the practice thus gained the basis of a more systematic study of grammar. He will now have the advantage of more extended power of conversation and of simple reading such as we find in some of the easier *Colloquies*, in tales from Aesop, and especially in such carefully devised aids to naming and description as are set out in the Colloquy *Convivium Religiosum*[2]. Here a garden laid out with terraces and shaded walks is furnished with specimens of all common plants, and with an aviary ; each object is accurately named, and mottoes are added. The walls bear frescoes of strange animals and trees, also appropriately named. The head of the house converses about all these and calls attention to their characteristics. It is at once instruction in natural objects and in language. Thus a vocabulary is formed without books, the Latin name is derived *directly from the object*, not by translation from a vernacular word. So epithets, verbs, adverbs, are acquired in the same way. Thus a store of words and of rudimentary sentence-forms is accumulated, and Latin is associated with common life. Such preparation leads in appropriate sequence to further grammatical acquisition. But at this stage also

---

[1] Eras. *Op.* i. 509 F : and infra, p. 212 ; this section of the *De Pueris* refers wholly to the first stage of teaching language.

[2] The *Colloquies* in Bailey's translation, i. 21—120 (*Op.* i. 630—672), esp. Bailey, i. 156 (*Op.* i. 672), are excellent examples for reference.

systematic grammar is strictly limited in amount. Such portions only of accidence and syntax are to be learnt as are needed for use in easy reading and composition. There is as yet no thought of a complete grammar to be taught in its logical order. The treatment is determined by the *pupil's* needs and power of assimilation, not by the requirements of the *subject* regarded as an organised whole. Hence the Master will be most careful in his choice of material, which must be stated in the simplest fashion and illustrated by intelligible and attractive quotations. Unusual and anomalous forms are, so far as may be, ignored ; and no word out of ordinary use may be included. Such a text-book serves as verification and as clear definition of usages already partly perceived from reading and conversation. For the standing principle is always : from reading to perception of usage, from usage to authoritative rule. The mediaevalist had completely inverted the order ; and the 18th century revived the same inversion.

In the *De Constructione*[1] Erasmus has left us his idea of a Syntax for boys at this second stage of Latin instruction. It was originally drafted by W. Lily, and was at his request revised by Erasmus for the use of St Paul's School. The selection and order of the material is interesting : the contents are as follows :

1. The cases required by different classes of verbs.
2. The simple uses of the Infinitive, Supine, Gerund and Participle.
3. Certain common case constructions other than those with the Verb.

---

[1] *Libellus de octo orationis partium constructione, correctus ab Erasmo, cum praefat. J. Coleti.* Basil. Aug. 1515. Upon the history of this grammar see Lupton in *Notes and Queries*, Series vi, vol. ii. pp. 441—2, 461—2. In the form which it had assumed by 1540 Lily's *Grammar*, as revised by Erasmus, was by royal proclamation "authorised" for exclusive use in Grammar Schools. See Foster Watson, *Curriculum and Text-books*, p. 28.

4. The concords of noun and adjective: relative and antecedent.

5. The construction of degrees of comparison, and of certain groups of adjectives and numerals with case.

6. Certain constructions of Dative, Accusative and Ablative with noun and adjective.

7. The adverb in construction with a noun.

8. Conjunctions and Interjections.

9. Prepositions and their cases.

The whole occupies about 25 pages of the size of the present volume. Its gradual development into the Eton Latin Grammar is a curious proof of the remarkable survivals which characterise school books.

The criticism has often been made that in this outline Erasmus shows himself arbitrary and illogical in arrangement. But the answer is that his method is the express antithesis to a systematic teaching of grammar. For he handles the subject in the order and with just so much complexity as are adapted to the learner beginning to construe; to the end that he may find his accumulating knowledge of language—empirically arrived at—best codified. Grammar follows speech. It is by conversation and by reading that a boy must hope to acquire the laws of expression, not by learning grammar[1]. Elyot, who in so many ways interpreted Erasmus to England, in the true spirit of his master, "would advise not to detain the child too long in that tedious labour" of grammar, which if "made too long or too exquisite to the learner, it in a manner mortifieth his courage....The spark of the fervent desire of learning is extinct with the burden of grammar[2]."

Memory work is thus reduced to small limits, but within

---

[1] *De Rat. Stud.* 521 C: infra, p. 164. For an example of inductive treatment of a construction cp. Eras. *Op.* i. 667 D—668 D: the instance chosen is "constat."

[2] Elyot, *Governour, l.c.*

these it must be exact. Its place is taken by practice. Herein lies the value of the *Colloquies*, which were devised originally to aid conversation by bringing daily life and school topics within the circle of Latin instruction. The method long survived, as we know from such text-books as the *Dialogues* of Mathurin Cordier[1] and the later *Janua* of the Jesuits and of Comenius.

Two defects in the current grammars of mediaeval origin were specially noted by Erasmus. The first was that the rules were never illustrated by quotations from classical authors. The Erasmian method made this essential. He further urges that such examples should be in themselves likely to interest children, should be of moral worth, or of poetic charm. The second was that the mediaeval teacher did nothing for vocabulary. Young men grew up under such a master, and after years of his instruction knew nothing of names of common animals, plants, geographical facts, or objects of daily life. Hence Latin meant nothing to them as a practical aptitude[2]. But to Erasmus Latin was either a working tool for life or nothing.

The *third*, or higher, stage of Latin study required, however, a much more thorough mastery of grammar. It is now systematic—"per locos et ordines." Practice upon the basis of the previous stage is extended. But text-books such as Valla's *Elegantiae* and Perotti's *Rudimenta* are to be in the pupil's hands. Reading will still have for one of its ends the verification and amplification of rules : and care will always be taken to remember that grammar is never an end in itself[3].

---

[1] M. Cordier, a famous school-master in Paris and Geneva. Calvin was a pupil of his. His *Colloquies* was a popular school book in the second half of the 17th century, and was edited by C. Hoole in 1657 for English pupils.

[2] The first part of the *De Rat. Stud.*, infra, p. 162, should be read in conjunction with this passage.

[3] *De Rat. Stud.*, infra, p. 169, § 6.

The principle applies to Greek as well as to Latin. Gaza's grammar, which Erasmus edited, he quotes as an example of a sound systematic treatment. Lascaris, Urbanus, and Chalcondylas are also available. The parallel study of the two languages is strongly advised ; and Erasmus is not blind to the use which can be made of Romance languages and modern Greek on the comparative method[1]. The former device is common to most humanist masters, the latter is quite unusual.

It is evident that in laying down this enlightened method of teaching language Erasmus relies upon two conditions. The first is, that from the beginning the learner is reared in a home in which Latin is a standing factor of daily intercourse : the second, that the master is not only a scholar of wide reading, but a teacher of insight, and of special capacity for evoking interest. It is not easy for us to-day to judge of the success of such a method owing to our unfamiliarity with Latin as a living language. But if we substitute French for Latin, we can perceive the psychological soundness of its principle. The progress is from (*a*) practice, whereby eye and ear are early accustomed to word and sentence, through (*b*) systematisation by which phenomena of usage are reduced to rule and paradigm, to (*c*) application of such formulae to extended and more certain practice : this, in turn, forming the starting-point for what becomes ultimately the stage of logically complete grammar, which serves as the standard authority in composition and in reading.

One word may be said upon the attitude which Erasmus

[1] *De Rat. Stud.*, infra, p. 167, § 5. Upon the parallel teaching of Greek and Latin Erasmus is not very definite. He implies distinctly that at the age of five Greek and Latin letters may be learnt, *Op.* v. 712 C. The first steps in grammar should be taken in both tongues, *De Rat. Stud.*, infra, p. 163, § 2. But it is obvious that the conversational method was impossible, so that the general lines of teaching Greek must have been conceived mainly on grammatical lines. At Cambridge Erasmus began with the *Erotemata* of Chrysoloras.

adopted towards the mediaevalist. He is, no doubt, entirely in the right in basing grammar for beginners upon usage alone. None the less the learner gains something from the habit of seeking in self-analysis the underlying principles of all syntax. Our method of grammatical analysis rests upon such practice. Usage in language, though in a true sense objective and authoritative, is by no means an arbitrary phenomenon. In another sense, not less true, speech takes its usage from thought. The mediaevalist, passionately anxious to "explain" the universe, was not illogical in including human speech among its factors, and he was right in seeking his clues in the laws of thought[1]. None the less Erasmus, as a teacher, was justified in his contention that speculation about facts is by no means identical with a wide and a firm grasp of such facts ; and that for the purpose of literature and of practical life it is only the latter that is of importance.

§ 2. THE CHOICE OF AUTHORS IN GENERAL.

The principal contribution of Erasmus is contained in the *De Ratione Studii*, which must be consulted throughout this and the following sections. His criticisms of authors from the standpoint of education is less suggestive than those recorded by the Italian humanists[2]. In the main he reproduces Quintilian's choice of writers[3].

The earliest books to be attempted will be the Proverbs and the Gospels in the Vulgate. These should be supplemented by portions (in Latin) of Plutarch's *Apophthegmata* and *Moralia*, "quibus nihil sanctius inveniri potest." To these he adds Seneca "qui lectoris animum a sordidis curis in sublime

---

[1] On mediaeval scholarship generally, and in particular upon the eve of the Revival, Dr Sandys' *History of Classical Scholarship* must be in future carefully consulted.

[2] Cp. Woodward, *Vittorino*, p. 212.

[3] Quintilian, *Instit. Orat.* x. 1.

subvehit[1]." The foundations of moral teaching as well as practice in Latin are hereby secured, and specially is this of importance in the training of a prince. Aesop may profitably be chosen as the first Greek author. The immense range of school editions of the *Fables*, often illustrated, dating from the middle of the 16th century, proves how widely this advice was accepted. Erasmus indicates from the outset that he has regard to interest and edification in his method of language-teaching.

The general list of writers named by Erasmus for school use is the following. In Greek, Lucian, Demosthenes, Herodotus; Aristophanes, Homer, and Euripides. In Latin, Terence and Plautus, Vergil, Horace; Cicero, Caesar, Sallust. Quintilian gives less prominence to Lucian and Sallust than does Erasmus. The note of this selection is the value of the writers as aids to the formation of the conversational and rhetorical styles. It is important to remember how intimately Erasmus knits together reading and composition both in respect of form and of matter. Lucian's *Dialogues* had, as we have seen, peculiar attraction for Erasmus, who learnt Greek through them. In the parallel acquisition of Greek and Latin Terence took place side by side with Lucian[2]. Both serve as models for conversational style, and present ancient speech in living form. Regarding Terence it is well known how highly he was esteemed by all humanists: the German protestant scholars not less than the Italian masters gave him the chief place among junior texts. The taste, wit and grace displayed

---

[1] *Instit. Princip. Chr.*, in *Op.* iv. 587: in *Op.* ix. 92 B Erasmus brackets together Cicero, Quintilian and Seneca as authors wholly blameless in the eyes of the most strict Christian educators: he speaks thus of these three authors, "qui non solum absunt ab obscenitate verum etiam saluberrimis praeceptis vitam instituunt."

[2] "Graecitatem ex Luciano discendam": ix. 92 B. He has an elaborate defence of his suitability for this purpose. On Terence, Sabbadini, *Guarino*, p. 147.

in the Comedies, the purity of their diction, make them so helpful to the young scholar that he should be called upon to learn whole scenes by heart. Further, they are "interesting": and only a mind already evil will take harm from their reading. Guarino considered Terence a profound teacher of morals. In the same way, Erasmus commends his Comedies as a reflection of the morals and habits of his age, as a picture which "in right hands not only does no harm to morality but is of immense service in improving it[1]." He admits that the power of drawing out moral lessons from plot and character varies with every teacher. Quintilian, Jerome, Augustine, and Ambrose studied Terence in their youth and enjoyed him in manhood. In short, only barbarians fail to appreciate him. Perhaps the best critical work done by Erasmus in Latin scholarship was his edition of Terence. Plautus was less favourably viewed for school purposes on moral grounds, and selections only can be admitted[2].

We may be surprised at the place given to Aristophanes, considering the demand which his plays make for a knowledge of Athenian life and politics possessed by no scholar of the century of Erasmus. But he brings the student face to face with living figures and colloquial speech. Demosthenes is there for his eloquence, and Herodotus, perhaps, as being attractive in matter and of utility for his moral instances. The inclusion of Homer needs no explanation. Euripides closes the list. Next to Lucian he was Erasmus' first choice when he himself was learning Greek. He then found the choruses lacking in true feeling; and would like to have re-written them in a worthier fashion[3]. But Erasmus, like most humanists, has nothing of the poet in his composition.

Amongst Latins, Caesar and Sallust, to whom Livy and Tacitus[4] are elsewhere added, have as historians special claims.

---

[1] Eras. *Op*. iii. 1457 E and 1886 D, E.
[2] *De Rat. Stud.*, infra, p. 163, § 3.   [3] Supra, p. 38.
[4] Eras. *Op*. iii. 971 D.   Infra, p. 128, on teaching of history.

Cicero attracted every humanist on the three sides of orator,
letter-writer and moralist.   Vergil is, in virtue of his elaboration, chief of all poets, Horace ranks next.   Erasmus says of
these: "when I read this I can scarcely refrain my petition,
'Holy Socrates, pray for us.'   Similarly I can hardly restrain
myself from wishing happiness and salvation to the holy soul
of Maro and Flaccus."   As Raumer says, there is room for
surprise at this sentiment[1].

It is noticeable that Erasmus will have nothing to do with
Latin versions of Romances[2].   It is more worthy of attention
that he rules out even of the higher stage of education
Christian writers, in prose or verse, and the great Greek
philosophers.   He laid down two canons on this head: (1) all
writings that demand theological knowledge[3], (2) all writings
involving the young learner in abstract speculation[4], are
unsuited to education.   Thus he differs from most early
humanist masters, and from Wimpheling, Nausea, Vives, and
Colet in excluding such writers as Lactantius or Cyprian[5]: and
the poets Juvencus or Prudentius.   Elyot, also, otherwise his
disciple, is anxious to turn boys of 17 on to the *Ethics*[6],
and Sadoleto has the deepest respect for Aristotle and Plato[7]
as instruments of teaching youth.   Erasmus, however, takes
his own line.   *Sermo Latinus* being the aim, the best only
should be studied[8]; as to content, the ancient world in its

[1] Raumer, *Gesch. der Päd.* i. 79 n.

[2] Eras. *Op.* iv. 587 "fabulae stultae et aniles": he expressly mentions "Arthurs and Lancelots." The judgment of Montaigne is as severe. *Ess.* i. 25.

[3] Eras. *Op.* ix. 93 C. Prudentius can only be understood by a theological scholar; and "who would dream of forming anyone's style on Juvencus?"

[4] *Id.* i. 522 B.

[5] *Id.* ix. 93 C.

[6] Elyot, *Governour*, i. 91. When a boy has reached the age of 17, "to the intent his courage be bridled with reason" he must study Aristotle's *Ethics* i. and ii. These would be followed by Plato.

[7] Sadoleto, *De Instit. liber.*, *Op.* iii. 125.

[8] Supra, p. 47.

classic perfection can afford moral instruction of wholly adequate type.

Such a range of reading Erasmus regards as sufficient for the ordinary student who is to prepare for a professional life. But those who pursue the classical course in order to qualify themselves as masters must pursue a far wider range. Upon this he lays down a comprehensive programme in the *De Ratione Studii* (§ 5). Now he has no scruple as to the moral problem, nor does he exclude Christian writers, nor philosophers. But he is, even here, averse from a study of Renaissance Latinists, as substitutes for the great writers of antiquity : although he makes one exception in admitting Poliziano as a valuable model for the Epistolary style. In this exclusiveness he differed from most of his contemporaries[1].

§ 3.   Method of Reading an Author.

This may be considered under three divisions : aim, procedure, devices.

In the first place it is necessary to disentangle the various *aims* with which a given author may be read with a class. The master will always use his author for the purpose of verifying and amplifying grammatical rule. Accidence, syntax and prosody will be constantly illustrated and practised through this medium. Next, vocabulary, the range of sentence-forms, of figures and metaphors, of similes, and enrichment generally, — the rhetorical aptitudes — are strengthened by properly directed construing ; and this accumulation of actual material for composition is one of the main ends of school reading. In the third place, style in the finer sense, the adaptation of

---

[1] Nausea, *De puer. lit. inst.*, pp. 24, 27; Vives, *De Trad. Discip.*, iii. 313, 318. Wimpheling at the end of the fifteenth century included Petrarch, L. Bruni, and Filelfo amongst prose Latinists to be read in schools: also Baptista Mantuanus, the poet. Cp. Paulsen, p. 37.

expression to theme, is acquired by reading and by reading only. The learner perceives through Cicero or Demosthenes the spirit of oratory; in Vergil he finds the picturesque elaboration of poesy; the incisiveness of Tacitus, the narrative powers of Livy, learnt at first hand, teach a student the essentials of a historical style. For such qualities as these must be felt, and absorbed; they cannot be imparted by precept. Again, the ancient literatures embrace the whole of attainable knowledge in the secular sphere. It is only by reading that a modern can enter into the true significance of antiquity: the way lies alone through the gateway of the famous writers. Erasmus is anxious that the learner should penetrate into the actual personality of each author studied; of this personality his literary expression is an inseparable part, and demands therefore intimate analysis. There may, there will, be much in any ancient book which for some time will remain hidden even from the most industrious. But the moral temper, the aesthetic form, the worldly wisdom which a great work reveals, the student will in part realise, and will thereby enter into a new possession : by such reading he will acquire an insight into a civilisation. Finally, the master will remember the individuality of his pupils, and will direct the aim of a lesson accordingly. For example, a masterful boy will not be left to browse upon the Homeric stories of the wayward Achilles, whilst he may well take warning from the fate of Xerxes. Moreover, if another has before him a career which demands a high sense of responsibility—as for example a young noble or prince—the teacher will call his attention to the lessons of philosophy and of history, and select authors from that point of view.

Regarding *procedure*, the master will from the outset base his method upon the principle that learning depends upon interest. The subject or the text must be introduced in whatever way may best stimulate this. The wise teacher will spare no pains in learning how to create an atmosphere favourable to the assimilation of new matter. This principle is worked out with much clearness in the *De Ratione Studii*, § 10, where Erasmus exhibits the essential condition of all good teaching in relation to lessons on Terence and Vergil. "You begin by offering an appreciation of the author, and state what is necessary concerning his life and surroundings, his talent and the characteristics of his style....Next you proceed to treat briefly and clearly the argument of the play, taking each situation in due course." The passage which follows in the same paragraph, upon the best manner of opening the study of the second Eclogue deserves careful attention. A Herbartian might well seize upon these examples to prove Erasmus a prophet of "apperception."

After a preliminary construe, to gain a knowledge of the general sense, which may presumably be given by the master, serious application to the text is first directed to the grammatical structure, prosody, and vocabulary, with particular reference to parallel word-forms in Greek. The teacher notes any conspicuous elegance in choice of words, or such peculiarities as "archaism, novel usage, Graecisms." Orthography has a place here, and etymology. The rhetorical factor at the same time falls to be considered. This is of great importance. For sound expression, as an acquirement of our own, is dependent upon close regard to the style of the great models of antiquity. The differences of the various literary forms—the oratorical and historical style, the satyric and the epic, for example—are now dealt with. It is necessary thereupon to treat style analytically. Metaphors, similes ; the artifices of poetical prose, and of oratorical poetry ; the accepted formulae of the letter-writer, or the orator ; the vast complex of amplification which forms the material of the *De Copia* ; the authoritative structure of the political or the forensic oration— all these are dissected, compared with other known instances, criticised and made available for future use. Nor will the rhetorical factor be regarded by the master in its purely technical aspect. For he will analyse the sources of the

pleasurable emotion aroused by any special passage through
its manner of expression.

Thirdly, the lesson will allot a large space to subject-matter.
As this is the chief end of the study of authors, so it must
constitute the real core of every lesson.   It is a characteristic
instruction to the master : "postremo ad philosophiam veniat
et poetarum fabulas apte trahat ad mores[1]."

The *Eclogue* referred to is handled by way of example as a
lesson on the conditions of true friendship.   For it is by
observing examples of conduct set forth in literature, and
especially in history treated after a literary manner, that we
learn to distinguish between good and bad actions, between
disgrace and honourable repute.   In the same spirit the master
will seize upon all matter which may be used as a basis for
moral suasion.   It was thus that Erasmus turned the attack
upon the devotion of the scholar to pagan Letters by per-
petually forcing to the front the doctrine of the " ethical end "
of the new education.

But the subject-matter of authors includes much besides.
The humour of the satyrist or the comic poet will be brought
clearly to view.   It will be shown how Comedy treats of the
less strenuous emotions ; while Tragedy appeals to the deeper
currents of human feeling.   Nor will the logical fence of
dramatic dialogue pass unnoticed.   Further, descriptions of
places, of physical features, of animals, plants and natural
phenomena, will be called for.   Allusions to myth, tradition,
and to history will be explained, and political and social conditions of antiquity referred to.   Erasmus admits that only
few scholars will follow so far : and that the competent master
is rarely to be found.   He adds a caution against undue
digression : " ne taedio graventur ingenia discentium."

Upon what have been alluded to as *devices* not much can be
said.   First, it should be noticed that very often the text itself
of the author was, in the absence of cheap editions, *dictated*,

---

[1] The right method of reading is laid down with precision in *Op.* i. 447,
which passage is printed, infra, p. 223.

either as work to be prepared in advance or during the lesson itself. Melanchthon had to provide Greek extracts for his class at Wittenberg. The increasing activity of the presses at Venice, Florence, and Lyons rendered this less necessary before the date of Erasmus' death. But everything beyond the bare text was of necessity dictated : as school-boys certainly would not use a costly *Vocabularius*. Next, Erasmus discourages literal *note-taking* as a habit injurious to memory and to the power of selection. Such as were taken were to be reduced to order, and arranged under headings in manuscript books. Charts and lists of words might be wisely hung on the schoolroom walls. Thirdly, if *questions* were asked these would be mainly catechetical, to test memory. Yet there is in the *Colloquies* much questioning which is of a Socratic sort, but it is not possible to claim for anything that we have of Erasmus that it has a so-called " heuristic " aim. The humanist believed that instruction meant the imparting of knowledge which the learner could not possibly acquire apart from a teacher. However, seeing the great importance attached to spoken Latin, there is no doubt that large opportunity for question and answer and for conversational teaching was provided.

Erasmus clearly intends that, both in respect of choice of subject-matter and of procedure, teaching shall conform to the "law of interest." He is, of course, far from attaining a method consciously based upon psychology. Sound principles, indeed, he has, but they are reached empirically : they are partial, and often enough fail him. His analysis, as has been said before, is rarely deep. So we find him always assuming that his own studious and, so to say, adult, interests constitute the only rational rule of life. He is thus led to overlook completely the physical energy and its accompanying activities, which forbid the average boy to accept a standard of attraction which consists, all but exclusively, in absorption in purely passive instruction.

None the less the general method of treatment of a classical lesson reveals a remarkable touch of modern practice. It exhibits systematic progress from the initial rousing of interest and preparation of the ground, through exposition and varied treatment of the material, to careful welding of new acquisition to knowledge already held, and finally to application first, to practice in composition, and then, more broadly, to thought and conduct.

§ 4.   ORATORS AND ORATORY.

The first place amongst classical writers was undoubtedly given by the humanists to the orators and the writers upon rhetoric. This is closely connected with the position accorded to oratory in the society of the Renaissance.

In a previous chapter attention was drawn to the characteristic of the Revival which consists in the assertion of *personality* as a determinate aim in contrast to the mediaeval spirit, whose achievements, for example, in art, architecture, science or Church order, strike us as corporate and impersonal. Petrarch, however, struck the dominant note of the new age in an exuberant self-consciousness. Thenceforward the essence of Italian *virtù* was that it *recognised* its own distinction. Now, although this characteristic is stamped upon all forms of humanist production, oratory lent itself most readily to the infection of this spirit. In the eloquence of the Renaissance the personality of the speaker wholly dominates his subject, which is often merely a vehicle for the exhibition of learning, taste or flattery. There was in Italy in the Quattrocento a remarkable demand for Latin speeches of a formal sort—a demand due, in part, to the inexhaustible supply. "Every government, and large municipality, even private families of position, employed their official Orator," says Villari[1]. A Latin oration held at a festival

---

[1] Villari, *Machiavelli*, i. 93.

the place which music does to-day. In a land of multifarious sovereignties like Italy, diplomatic commissions, dynastic celebrations, academic functions, apart from civic and semi-private festivals, provided countless ceremonial opportunities for "eloquence." It was inevitable that the lack of substantial content compelled attention to rhetorical display[1].

This was, however, the perversion of an effort which otherwise had ample justification. Latin was unavoidably the language of affairs; its cultivation on the oratorical side was, therefore, wholly desirable. As an educational instrument Roman and Greek oratory was deserving of close study and imitation. But we may doubt whether it would have received the enthusiastic regard which all humanists accorded to it but for two facts, the space filled by his *Orations* amongst the extant works of Cicero, and the accident that the one practical and systematic treatise upon Education left from antiquity treats of the education of the Orator. It is indispensable to any proper understanding of humanism to realise the position filled by Quintilian in the world of fifteenth century scholarship. From the date of the circulation of the complete codex of his work, about 1418—21, his fame grew rapidly and overshadowed that of all Roman prose writers, Cicero alone excepted. Every humanist tract upon education or upon rhetoric is largely a reproduction of Quintilian: words, phrases, illustrations, criticisms, principles, are often merely copied from the Roman master. Typical examples are Aeneas Sylvius *on Education*, and the *De Copia* of Erasmus[2].

In presence then of the demand and the apparatus for rhetorical training it is not surprising that oratory filled a large

---

[1] Burckhardt, *Renaissance*, p. 240, for examples: "Filelfo begins a speech at a betrothal with the words 'Aristotle, the Peripatetic'." "Most of his speeches are an atrocious patchwork of classical and biblical quotations tacked on to a string of commonplaces."

[2] The former in Woodward, *Vittorino*, p. 136: Quintilian was reduced to epitome by F. Patrizi, about 1460—70. Bod. Lib., *Can. MSS.* 285.

place in the curriculum of the Italian schools. It was from them in due course transferred to the schools of Germany, France and England. Erasmus, therefore, is but typical of humanist masters in his view of the importance of the subject in education. It will be understood that the relation between the study of ancient orators and the corresponding art of rhetorical composition is an intimate one, more intimate than in any other branch of humanist instruction, not excepting Letter-writing. The rule that an author must be read as a model for imitation, and not only as literature, applies, therefore, particularly to Cicero and Demosthenes.

The concept of oratory as it was derived from the Roman masters was one of much distinction. The orator, in the first place, is defined as "the good citizen skilled in speaking." Quintilian's words are "quum bene dicere non possit nisi vir bonus." He supports this from the *Gorgias*—"ἀνάγκη τὸν ῥητορικὸν δίκαιον εἶναι." Thus the education of an orator implied that a high moral standard was aimed at. For the noble expression of noble thought must be the product of a noble personality. Next, oratory implies wide knowledge, indeed the ideal orator will be an omnivorous reader. Lastly, he will have a corresponding command of language. The function of eloquence in stimulating virtuous ideas and actions was tacitly accepted in spite of much of what to us seems disappointing experience in the Italy of Lorenzo and of Rodrigo Borgia—a period when the country reeked with oratory.

It is not necessary to discuss the selection of models for study. Cicero and Demosthenes stand out above all. Yet Erasmus is in accord with Quintilian in refusing to limit the learner to these. Quintilian is the great master of technique; though the *De Oratore* of Cicero is to be closely followed. The speeches of Livy and Sallust are of great service : Tacitus is less useful. Lucan, as a rhetorical poet, is worth study. Isocrates is referred to. Unlike Sturm, who says of Luther's

German eloquence, "Lutherus quasi magister extitit nostri sermonis, sive puritatem consideres, sive copiam," Erasmus has not one word to show that he recognises vernacular oratory as other than a self-denying condescension of the preacher.

§ 5. COMPOSITION IN LATIN PROSE.

It will be convenient to consider here the subject of Composition, since its climax is reached in an oration. The study of eloquent Latinity in Germany rested on sanctions somewhat different from those of the Italian world. There also, however, Latin was the tongue of educated and professional life, of administration, law, medicine, the teaching profession, the Church. It has been shown that of books circulating in Germany, even as late as the middle of the sixteenth century, 70 per cent. are written in Latin : in the lifetime of Erasmus the proportion was no doubt larger still. For we must remember that in distinction to Italy there was as yet no literature, in German, of scholarly type, whether serious or "polite," to correspond to the work of Poliziano, Bembo, or Machiavelli, at least until the Reformation. Latin composition, therefore, was a necessary aptitude. This explains how it was that humanist masters were able to retain public assent to the leading place which they claimed for Latin prose. There was a practical demand for Latin, and Erasmus, Melanchthon and Sturm insisted that this should be classical Latin. It was no question of an "accomplishment" : the business-like Luther, with his strong German bias, was not less clear upon the point than the humanist.

That oratory was the chief force in affairs was a conviction based upon the precedents of Greek and Roman history, as the humanists understood it. It was their tendency to view all prose writing, and even poetry, through the glamour of rhetoric.

" My greatest approbation," says Erasmus, " is reserved for a rhetorical poem and poetical oratory...the rhetorical art should transpire through the poem." This is the evil influence of Lucan[1]. The Epistolary style became artificial and inflated, and was the subject of endless hand-books upon the form and diction of various classes of Letters. Further, "the mysteries of the Faith," so Erasmus contends, "owe their power over the minds and conduct of men, in large degree, to the grace and eloquence of their presentation[2]." For thus the Fathers of the best age qualified themselves to be the teachers of the Church by their training in rhetoric and style. Eloquence, therefore, in the mind of Erasmus has, as a practical art, a wide range: it covers forensic, didactic, hortatory, complimentary, and other forms of address; historical, narrative and descriptive composition; argument, dialogue and correspondence. Indirectly it affects poetical art. It is evident then that systematic teaching of Latin Composition will largely concern itself with the oratorical style as that form which has something common to all styles[3].

On the other hand Erasmus affirmed with iteration his protest against absorption in the art of expression. Professional aims and breadth of culture alike come before style. His general position on Imitation has been referred to. In the dialogue *De Recta Pronunciatione* he realises that reaction against mediaeval " barbarism " has gone too far in the direction of stylistic display[4]. In Christian education ostentation

---

[1] Eras. *Op*. iii. 104 D.

[2] *Op*. v. 30 A, iii. 1275 D, E.

[3] So Colet requires "eloquence" as the characteristic product of scholarship for St Paul's: Lupton, *Colet*, p. 169.

[4] His words are: " This is apparently a law of human progress, that on attaining a certain point in its course a movement only escapes harmful exaggeration by a violent rebound in the opposite direction, whereby the evil tendency is corrected by its contrary." *Op*. i. 923 C, E. This is an interesting recognition of the law of re-action, and implies a historical perception which is unusual in Erasmus.

in speech, which strives to display personal qualities, will be
discouraged[1]. Hence, "it is good to speak Attic Greek, but
it should not be too ostentatiously Attic[2]." The old authorities, he affirms, always insisted upon appropriateness,
naturalness, sincerity: the subject first, with expression in
strict harmony.

Yet, though such a position is didactically sound, in practice
Erasmus is not always consistent. For in discourse appropriateness needs to be enhanced by fulness (*copia*) and elegance,
which follow very closely in degree of importance. Expression
cannot be truly "simple" or perfectly "adapted" unless it
emanates from mastery of all the resources of the art[3]. The
best equipped scholar moves most easily within the rudiments
of his subject. Thus it still remains true that the teacher of
composition will find it necessary to lay stress upon training
in the whole range of rhetoric. Redundancy, embellishment,
copia rerum et verborum, carried even to excess, are not faults
in a learner[4]: oratory must be taught as a conscious art, to
serve as an equipment, whose superfluities will be cast off as
taste and judgment mature. Nay, it is defensible to accustom
the scholar to argue the Unjust Cause for the sake of practice in
setting out every side of a question. Hence what is objectionable as a habit of style is allowable or necessary as a stage in
education, when the entire apparatus of Cicero and Quintilian
is to be employed.

The epistolary style, for obvious reasons, ranked next in
importance. The function of correspondence in the life of the
Renaissance was to serve as the organ of cosmopolitan criticism. It was so recognised by scholars, in spite of the fact
that it degenerated into a vehicle of ostentation on the one
hand, and of shameless flattery or slander on the other.
Erasmus protested that the ancients respected the limits of
right criticism, whilst Christians had forgotten them. Letters

[1] Woodward, *Vittorino*, p. 233, n. 3.   [2] Eras. *Op*. iii. 10 D.
[3] *Op*. iii. 726 C, D.   [4] *Op*. i. 5 B, iii. 197 C.

were written to be kept and were often collected by their writers[1]. Immortal fame might be expected for one who numbered several fine Latinists among his correspondents.

As regards *Methods*, the beginnings of composition arose by natural process from the first efforts at conversation, that "daily intercourse with those accustomed to express themselves with exactness and refinement" to which Erasmus attached so great importance. The master amplified this by dictating formulas (preserved in the earlier Colloquies) for use in play, intercourse, entertainments and school. At this stage rules of syntax were learnt as described above[2]. The order of exercises in composition is not systematically set out. But simple original compositions (with full directions for treatment), by way of expansion of conversation, may be begun very early. Subjects will be chosen with due regard to the intelligence and interest of the pupil : say, a theme from an incident of ancient history, with a moral reflection ; an apologue, or a simple myth. General knowledge will provide a topic : the powers of a magnet, or "mirum polypi ingenium." Such exercises will demand only grammatical accuracy within the forms of the simple sentence, with a gradually enlarging vocabulary. The learner will acquire the art of making a lexicon of his own, arranging his words not alphabetically, but under subject-headings[3].

A second stage is reached when the close study of easier authors, as models, is possible ; such aids as *De Copia*, *De Conscribendis Epistolis*, and the *Colloquies* are introduced. Greek and Latin prose exercises may with advantage be worked together. The exercises now available are apparently

---

[1] The letter of Poggio to Vittorino (cp. *Vittorino*, p. 83) is an excellent example of the humanist letter of the "self-conscious" sort.

[2] *De Rat. Stud.*, infra, p. 163, § 3. Cp. p. 106.

[3] *De Copia*; *Op.* i. 11. So Nausea, *De Puero litt. inst.*, p. 52, urges indices for "nobiliores sententias, quas Graeci γνώμας dicunt," so that they are readily available for composition. The *De Rat. Stud.*, § 8 onwards, should be read as the text of what follows.

the following : (*a*) paraphrase of poetry, (*b*) duplicate treatment of one theme after differing models, (*c*) exposition of one
argument upon divergent lines, (*d*) imitation of an easy Letter
of Cicero or Pliny, (*e*) the most important exercise of all,
version from Greek into Latin. It has the authority of Quintilian ; and Erasmus would, we know, not admit as a qualification that to Quintilian Latin was a vernacular tongue. This
practice will be found to involve three valuable processes : the
analysis of Greek construction ; the comparison of the genius
of each language in respect of sentence structure ; exercise in
moving rapidly through sentence forms and vocabulary of Latin
for the purpose of reaching equivalent expression.

The third stage, corresponding to that of systematic grammatical study, is that of full freedom on the part of the pupil,
when theme alone is suggested with occasional hints as to
models to be observed. There are four forms of Composition
for general use : the Epistle, the Oration, the Declamation
upon a historical or general subject, the Defence of a just or
an unjust Cause. The study of the entire art of the rhetori-
cian as laid down by Cicero and Quintilian is now begun.
Seven or eight carefully devised and corrected exercises will
be a sufficient introduction to the art of laying out subject-
matter for original composition. Much stress is now laid
upon *correction* : the master criticising in turn (*a*) selection,
(*b*) treatment, (*c*) imitation. He will censure omission or bad
arrangement of matter, exaggeration, carelessness, awkwardness
of expression. He will then ask for a re-written copy.

The chief aids to composition were, besides the great
classic masters, the *Elegantiae* of Valla, with typical letters of
Aeneas Sylvius, and Poliziano. Perotti, *De conscribendis Epistolis*, Trapezuntius, and Barzizza were in constant use in
schools organised under Melanchthon's advice, but neither
Erasmus nor Sturm utilised such text-books[1]. The *De Copia*

[1] Erasmus' own work *De Conscr. Epist.* was largely used. Cp. Paulsen
Class. Unter. p. 107—8.

Verborum et Rerum is the elaborate aid to Latin prose prepared by Erasmus for the use of students, and issued from Cambridge. It is a manual of "enrichment" and "variation," based mainly upon Quintilian viii, with modern examples. He defines the purpose of "copia": "brevity does not consist in saying *as little* as possible, but in saying *the best* that can be said *in the shortest way*." "Copia" implies *right* selection of words, figures, ideas: examples to the point, judgments clear-cut, digressions rigidly in hand, figures obviously appropriate. It is by no means identical with "indigesta turba" of illustration, or with tedious repetition: but variety, brightness, movement, are of the essence of "copia." A student of the classical Renaissance, desirous to make a first-hand acquaintance with the art of expression as understood by humanist writers, cannot do better than make a careful analysis of the *De Copia*, reading side by side the *De Oratore* and the fourth and eighth books of the *Institutio Oratoria*[1].

§ 6.   History and Historians.

Erasmus has himself admitted that he is no historian. We may with confidence accept his disclaimer. But in this respect he has the company of well-nigh every humanist.

It has just been said that oratory and orators constituted the true literary interest of the men of Letters of the earlier Renaissance. Now there is, has always been, and, it must be confessed, cannot but be, a sharp line of division between the real historian and the professed stylist. The great orators knew it. Cicero and Quintilian, for example, are at one in regarding Thucydides as a man apart, from whom the orator can learn hardly anything. Xenophon on the other hand,

---

[1] On the purpose and value of the *De Copia* cp. Benoist, *De Puer.* p. 101. Formal as it was in method, there is no doubt that it imparted excellent training in systematic observation of, and practice in, style.

"cuius sermo est melle dulcior," is most attractive. Livy and Sallust, as *historians*, are by reason of their measured judgments alien from the oratorical ideal. They may, indeed, be pressed into service, like any other store-houses of instances, for purposes of argument, of parallel, of illustration, of example. But Quintilian perceived that the orator whose function it is to convince an auditory has little in common with one who writes "ad memoriam posteritatis et ingenii famam[1]." The humanist was, undoubtedly, drawn to the historians, and Erasmus lays stress on the need of studying them. He specifically advises Livy, Plutarch, Tacitus, Sallust and Herodotus. In one of his letters he urges that a youth preparing for public service should add to this reading the moral treatises of Cicero: and from the course thus sketched "the practical wisdom so essential to a man taking his part in public affairs will be most surely attained[2]." Yet in spite of this, it is quite certain that all humanists, with the conspicuous exception of Flavio Biondo, honoured the historians for that very quality which as historians was most perilous to them, namely, their rhetoric. This then is the first use which Erasmus would make of a classical historian—he is a model of rhetorical treatment of narrative or debate. The closer the affinity he reveals to the orator, the greater his attraction. For instance, Erasmus, writing it is true in his early days, demands from a modern writer of histories correctness of style, "elegantia Sallustiana," "felicitas Liviana," clearness in presentation, inspiring variety, artistic completeness, and so on[3]. We recognise at once the artifices of the stylist. But, writing in the maturity of his powers, in the *De Ratione Studii*, he propounds historical themes,

---

[1] For the humanist view Aeneas Sylvius, *De Liber. Educ.* (in Woodward, *Vittorino da Feltre*) may be read. "It is peculiar to eloquence to depend on admiration," Quint. x. 7. 17.

[2] *Op.* iii. 971 D. But we should particularly have liked to find Erasmus explaining in what manner such reading would mould the judgment of the student.

[3] *Op.* i. 1817.

suggested by reading, which are purely formal, and reveal an entire absence of historical perception[1].

In the second place, the historian is to be valued in that he provides us with a stock of facts for the illustration of our arguments. Here "the rarer and more marvellous the instance, the greater will be the interest evoked....From old stories and annals, and also from modern history, we should learn by heart, and so have in readiness, examples of virtue and vice, of remarkable occurrences of any kind. Now such facts may be drawn from the history of every nation—from the company of great historians of Greece and Rome, from the Hebrew Scriptures; from the events handed down to memory from the story of the Egyptian, the Persian, the French, the British nations; from the stories of Sparta, of Thebes and Athens, even from the traditions of the Scythian. For every people has its remarkable occurrences, its customs and institutions[2]." This "spice of antiquarian knowledge," as he calls it elsewhere, is in no true sense historical equipment. It is all a mere matter of "copia," oratorical and stylistic embellishment, which indeed is evident from the fact that Erasmus very rarely refers to historical reading, except from the point of view of composition.

Thirdly, a literary history is to the humanist a gallery of moral example. Perhaps this is the highest function of history in the hands of the teacher: to illustrate moral law by recorded "cases." This is what Sadoleto[3] means when he vaguely puts forward the ancient historians as full of warnings against evil policy, and as such, of high value in training the young. It would be interesting to know how the Cardinal Secretary himself interpreted such moral guidance in handling the politics of Leo X. Now this method of application to

---

[1] Infra, p. 173. "Historians should enrich their narrative with fictitious speeches, than which nothing is better suited to their purpose." *De Copia*, i. 106 D.

[2] Eras. *Op.* i. 389 F, x. 1733 E.

[3] Sadoleto, *De Puer. Instit.* iii. 109.

immediate edification undoubtedly prejudiced humanist history as a serious subject, either of enquiry or of instruction. History became fragmentary, artificial, a *cento* of examples, of commonplaces, of biographical idealisations. Critical study tended to be shirked, as spoiling good illustrations; and the art of the historical writer was limited to clothing accepted versions of facts in novel and ingenious form. Bruni and Poggio, in their Italian histories, left models of imitation in its most barren form[1]. History, consequently, took but a poor place in education. Even a Prince, who is to be nourished on the *Politics* and the *De Officiis*, may be content with a modest review of the historians; the mode and extent of such interest being left quite vague[2]. The view of the function of history as edification is most instructive to the student of the Revival. For it is in entire harmony with the prevailing concept of the power of ethical teaching to mould life. The virtue of the antique world might easily be restored—so the scholar held—if only examples of ancient virtue were persuasively expressed and sufficiently forced upon attention. A belief that the impulse to imitate could be produced by passive contemplation of artificially selected situations was the bane of the literary educator. Erasmus himself knew better, but in respect of history he did not rise above the conventional attitudes of his day.

We must not forget, however, that the biographical treatment of history was in part the result of the conviction—largely justified by facts—of the influence of the Individual in the Italy of the Renaissance: and in part, of the large place filled by the passion for Fame[3]. Now this is by no means a merely

[1] An accessible account of humanist historians is to be found in Villari, *Machiavelli*, ii. 404. Cp. also Voigt, *Wiederbelebung*, ii. 482.

[2] Eras. *Op.* iv. 587.

[3] On the subject of the Individual and of Fame in the Renaissance cp. Burckhardt, *The Renaissance*, p. 134, Gaspary, *Letteratura*, iii. 14. The classic expression of the ideal is Petrarch's *De Viris Illustribus*.

humanist weakness. Machiavelli is more keenly individualist than Bruni or Bembo, for he had watched the forces of Italian politics at first hand.

And thus we understand the reason why the humanist left no direct impress in the department of history: *direct*, advisedly, for indirectly he made a broad treatment of national phenomena possible by revealing to enquirers a completed civilisation. Machiavelli complains that the study of histories is divorced from affairs, that there is no working-in of what is learnt into modern polity. In the organisation of the State, in administration, in military science, in expansion, the lessons of the past are not realised for purposes of the present. In other words, the scholar's view of history was purely literary[1].

The modern concept of history arose, in actual fact, amongst men of action, or at least amongst men in direct contact with affairs. The diplomatist, administrator, politician, not the scholars, were the authors of the political science, of which, in a different sense to that which Erasmus conceived, History was in truth the expression. Machiavelli and Guicciardini were the first to understand History as the record and analysis of the inner and outer determinations of national life. Yet these great Masters, as has been said, could not have been, had not the Roman world stood revealed to them by the same scholars whom in their own region they superseded[2]. They, too, were children of the humanist Revival.

---

[1] *Discorsi*: the Preface.

[2] Elyot's views of the aims of history teaching are of interest: *Governour* i. 82. Mr Foster Watson has pointed out how low a place the teaching of the subject held in English schools, even in the early part of the 17th century. The first school-book of *English* history known to me is a Latin metrical narrative of battles: Ockland's *Anglorum Praelia*, 1582. This was commanded to be read in Grammar schools. See Foster Watson, *The Curriculum*, p. 25.

§ 7.   LOGIC AND PHILOSOPHY.

This is the convenient point at which to estimate the functions of logic in education.   It has already been shown that the mediaevalist viewed "dialectica" in immediate relation to "grammatica[1]."   This led to a revolt on the part of the humanists against the entire method which then obtained of teaching these subjects.   The scholar, however, by no means banished the study of Logic from education : but he connected it, not with grammar, but with rhetoric.   To Aeneas Sylvius for instance, rhetoric and dialectic are almost convertible terms[2].   The whole apparatus of rhetoric as elaborated by Cicero and Quintilian was recognised as so much illustration of logical method.   Hence from an educational point of view Erasmus lays down that logical aid in ordering of subject-matter in composition is indispensable.   The pupil must understand by dialectic "quo pacto alia propositio ex alia pendeat : quot rationibus unaquaeque propositio fulciri debet, quot confirmationibus unaquaeque ratio[3]."   But this is the only end to which logic can be profitably studied.   As a substantial subject of enquiry or a self-contained discipline, Erasmus refused to consider its claims.   "I would not," he says, "have a boy wholly ignorant of logical rules, but I certainly decline to have him trained to exhibit those preposterous feats of dialectical juggling and tumbling so much belauded[4]."   Erasmus, indeed, doubts whether a boy should be urged to read much logic, or whether a grown man should carry forward the study of it beyond the mere stage of application: " ne tanquam ad Sirenaeos scopulos consenescat[5]."   Vives, Melanchthon, and

---

[1] Supra, p. 101.
[2] Aen. Sylv. *Op.* p. 989: based upon Quint. *Inst. Orat.* xii. 2. 13.
[3] Eras. *Op.* i. 526 B and v. 850 A.
[4] *Op.* i. 922–3.
[5] *De Rat. Stud.*, infra, p. 165, § 4.

Sadoleto speak with precisely the same voice, which was that of all the Italian scholars since Petrarch. Dialectic then is an aid to effective style. The protest was by no means otiose, for there was no school book more common in Germany on the eve of the humanist movement than the repulsive "Summulae Logicae" of Petrus Hispanus, afterwards Pope John XXII[1].

That Erasmus was by temperament averse to philosophical speculation has been already pointed out. His conception of philosophy excluded dialectic or metaphysic, whether ancient or mediaeval. He does not, indeed, hesitate to speak of Socrates as of one sharing divine inspiration: "Sancte Socrates, ora pro nobis," he is tempted to cry. But that has reference only to the moral wisdom which he finds ascribed to him in Xenophon and Plato. It may be said that of *ethical theory* Erasmus has as little perception as the mediaevalists had. Hence the didactic side of ethics alone affects him, and for this he recommends Hesiod, Horace, and Terence as hardly less valuable than the *De Officiis*, Seneca, and Plutarch's *Moralia*. The "philosophical" lessons to be drawn from any authors must be carefully shown by the master who will set themes for composition from Valerius Maximus or Plutarch, in part at least from the ethical point of view. Political philosophy is hardly alluded to ; however sound Erasmus' judgments upon government and royal responsibility, it was wholly alien from his temper to see them in the light of theoretic generalisations. Hence the great bulk of mediaeval philosophical speculation has no interest for him. He admits, however, that Scotus and Thomas may have had a message for their own ages, and where they derived their ideas from antiquity, may still serve some useful purpose[2]. In the region of "natural philosophy" he writes sarcastically of the men who talked as if they were peculiarly admitted into the secrets of the "Architect of the

[1] Cp. Paulsen, *Class. Unterricht*, p. 107, 110, for the popularity of this text-book in German schools at the beginning of the 16th cent.

[2] *Op*. iii. 704–5.

Universe," discoursing of the causes "obviously inexplicable," of the motions of the heavenly bodies, of the origin of thunder, of the winds, of eclipses, or go on further still to "primae materiae quidditates, ecceitates, phenomena so fine and so intangible that Lynceus himself would hardly detect their presence[1]." All this, of course, is merely evidence of speculative interests and of his unwillingness to make the necessary effort to go below the surface of a subject *prima facie* repellent to his genius. He refers to Aristotle, Plato, and Plutarch as philosophers to be read upon education; but apart from his debt to the latter writer he has in reality drawn very little from Greek sources upon the subject[2].

§ 8. Greek Studies, and the Argument for them.

It was, perhaps, amongst the more important results of his first visit to England that Erasmus returned to Paris with the single determination to qualify himself to read the Greek authors at first hand. It is at that time that we find him using such expressions as this: "Sine quibus (sc. literis graecis) caeca est omnis eruditio"; "hoc unum expertus video, nullis in literis nos esse aliquid sine Graecitate. Aliud enim est conjicere, aliud judicare, aliud tuis, aliud alienis, oculis credere[3]." A few years later he has no doubt that, "ex instituto omnis fere rerum scientia a Graecis auctoribus petenda est," and that: "imprimis ad fontes ipsos properandum, id est Graecos et antiquos[4]." It is impossible for a teacher, there-

[1] *Op.* iv. 462, 3.

[2] *De Christ. Matrim., Op.* v. 713 C. The *Republic*, and the *Laws*, of Plato, the *Politics*, vii. and viii. of Aristotle, are the works named. There are in reality no traces of any influence of the *Republic* upon Erasmus; Sadoleto, on the other hand, has seized certain salient characteristics of the Platonic education with some precision.

[3] *Op.* iii. 968 D, 96 B.

[4] *De Rat. Stud.*, infra, § 3. The specific authors to be used in education have been enumerated above, p. 112.

fore, to attain competency in his profession without a working knowledge of Greek. The argument for Greek is two-fold. In the first place the Greek literature contains the fullest know-ledge in all departments of human learning yet available. Melanchthon made this claim for the study of Greek in his address upon Studies at Wittenberg in 1518[1]. If we consider the level of political, mathematical, and scientific knowledge attained at this date, it is probably quite true to fact that the Greek world, say in the Augustan period, had reached a degree of enlightenment wholly in advance of anything which northern Europe could show. But the humanist had a second argument. The Roman of the great age had based higher education upon the interdependence of Greek and Roman letters. Cicero urges his son Marcus when at Athens never to separate the study of the two languages[2]. Quintilian presses the same advice upon the student of oratory. The Latin Fathers, Jerome at their head, are witnesses to the educational importance of a knowledge of Greek, whether in respect of learning or of expression. The dependence of literary form, of mythology, of vocabulary, as developed in Rome, upon Greek sources, revealed itself to the humanist scholar in the first steps that he made in the acquisition of the Greek tongue.

Professional studies, notably theology and medicine, have,

---

[1] Melanchthon, *De Corrigendis Adolescentium Studiis* (Aug. 1518): in *Corpus Reformatorum* xi. 15—25. Not only for proper understanding of Grammar and Rhetoric, but for Philosophy, Natural Science, History and Theology, is Greek indispensable. The reputation for coarseness under which Germany suffers can best be removed by the civilising influence of Greek learning. Cp. Eras. *De Rat. Stud.*, infra, p. 164, § 3. "I affirm that with slight qualification the whole of attainable knowledge lies enclosed within the literary monuments of ancient Greece."

[2] Upon the relation of Greek to Roman education in the Augustan age, see Rossignol, *L'éducation chez les anciens*, pp. 170 and 234. Quint. *Instit. Orat.* I. i. 12. Cp. Eras. *Op.* i. 922 F : Utriusque linguae peritiam exacte perdiscat teneris statim annis.

says Erasmus, suffered grievously from the lack of knowledge
of Greek on part of the experts. The same is true of mathematics. Hence not only must the Greek Testament be read
in the original, but Origen and Chrysostom ; the Paduan and
Salernitan masters of medicine must be corrected by a first-
hand acquaintance with Galen, Hippocrates, and the physical
writings of Aristotle. Indeed, he hopes that the time will
soon be come when a medical man will be disqualified by
ignorance of Greek[1].

There were many practical difficulties in the school teaching
of Greek. Texts were still scarce ; elementary readers and
grammars hardly existed at all. Reuchlin and Melanchthon
had to procure a printer who would issue for their use short
extracts from Xenophon or Demosthenes : or a printer was
subsidised to purchase a Greek fount[2]. Otherwise the entire
texts for beginners were of necessity dictated before being
construed. Melanchthon complains that he could only teach a
few lines at a time for this reason. It is probable that in good
German schools, Strassburg or Nuremberg, from two to four
hours weekly were given to the subject. The upper class
under Sturm, however, spent a much longer time upon Greek.
In most Protestant schools the Greek Testament formed the
chief reading book. Melanchthon proposed to take Homer as
the poet, and the *Epistle to Titus* as the prose work, in his first
year at Wittenberg.

Reference has been made to the somewhat restricted range
of Erasmus' reading in Greek, and to his defective power of
textual criticism. There is a vagueness in his allusions to
the scope and method of Greek studies[3] which is in marked

[1] *Op.* ix. 84 A. Cp. Glöckner, *Erasmus*, p. 46.

[2] The school-texts of the 16th cent. were printed, outside of Italy, at
Lyons, by Gryphius; at Antwerp, by Plantin; at Paris, by R. Estienne
and, to less extent, at Basel, Louvain and Deventer.

[3] For example it is doubtful whether Erasmus proposed that Greek
should be taught colloquially. In any case such a method could not be
defended on the same grounds as conversational Latin.

contrast to the precision of his injunctions upon the subject of
Latin teaching.   Erasmus, we must remember, began late, and
laboured under grave disadvantages as a student of Greek.
He probably always found Latin scholarship more congenial.
It is beyond doubt that he never attained the eminence in
Greek which characterised his contemporary Budaeus.   Indeed,
the real home of this branch of humanist study was neither
Italy, Germany, nor England, but France.   Guarino and
Aurispa, Linacre and Aldus, were but pioneers, and Erasmus'
place is with them.   French scholars of the sixteenth century
took over their task, and built up that elaborate apparatus of
grammar and lexicon, of textual criticism and of research in
the broad field of " Realien," which will always stand forth as
the notable contribution of France to the cause of Letters.

§ 9.   Mathematics and Nature Knowledge.

The opening sentence of the *De Ratione Studii*, "principio
duplex omnino videtur cognitio, rerum ac verborum.   Verborum prior, rerum potior," must not be taken to imply that
Erasmus was an advocate of "real" studies in education.
The opposing terms are drawn from Quintilian[1] who uses
"res" in the sense of "ideas," or νοήματα, in distinction to
names, "verba."   The expression no doubt includes facts of
nature, but it includes also such a "fact" as the versatility of
the god Mercury, or that "friendship between equals is the
more durable."

The study of facts is by Erasmus not differentiated into
systematic branches of knowledge.   Natural science, descriptions, travellers' tales, traditional lore, mathematics, astrology,

[1] *Inst. Orat.* x.   It has been well remarked by Bassi that Quintilian's
authority became almost pontifical for Italian and German humanists.   To
differ from him needed high moral courage.   *Rivista di Filol. e d' Instr.
Class.*, xxii. 7—9.

geography, medical rules, tend to merge into one another, and are classed under the common term "res." Their understanding is wholly dependent upon thorough training in language— for without vocabulary neither names nor epithets can be appropriately given : without arts of exposition and description neither due appreciation nor record of facts is possible. Hence language study must precede any attempt at "eruditio." For lack of Letters knowledge has wholly decayed : without a highly developed language the enquirer is deprived of the only means of (*a*) acquisition, (*b*) expression, (*c*) analysis, (*d*) exposition, of learning.

Concerning the function of "eruditio" (*Sachkenntnis*) Erasmus holds a somewhat uncertain position. He is, in the first place, fully alive to the importance of "information" as part of the equipment for life. But he is of opinion that this must be secured after the liberal education proper is completed, and the wide outlook of adult life reached. Yet he sees the importance of a judicious intermingling of teaching concerning plants, animals, geographical and other natural phenomena, with classical instruction. Pictures, charts, maps, even real objects, as in gardens, are of great help in such lessons, which arouse interest and impart a perception of the varied content of learning to which language affords the key. Nowhere, however, does Erasmus hint that observation or intercourse can serve as a substitute for ancient authorities in any subject, although occasionally a traveller or a modern writer may supplement what has been handed down ; and in archaeology, inscriptions, statues, coins and ruins may appropriately be worked in. Erasmus has given a list of the authors in whose writings such knowledge of "res" can be found, though he admits that the list is not complete. It will serve to indicate the scope of real studies as understood by Erasmus. The writers are Pliny, Macrobius, Eratosthenes, Athenaeus, and Gellius, in respect of general subject-matter. In connection with Geography or Cosmography, Pliny,

Ptolemy, Pomponius Mela, and Strabo; with Mythology,
Homer, Hesiod, Ovid eked out with Boccaccio *de Genealogia
Deorum*.   Philosophy will be read in Plato, Aristotle, Theophrastus, Plotinus; Theology in Origen, Chrysostom, Basil,
Ambrose, and Jerome[1].   Augustine takes a subordinate place
with Erasmus.   It is curious that in the *De Ratione Studii* he
makes no reference to historical study in this connection.
Whatever his conception of the end of *eruditio*, it is obvious
that the means to it are purely literary.

A passage written towards the end of his life upon the
effect of right religious instruction might lead us to believe that
Erasmus realised the emotional value of a study of Nature for
the young.   "Let the boy learn to consider the glory of the
heavens, the rich harvest of the earth, the hidden fountains of
rivers and their courses hurrying to the sea, the illimitable
ocean, the countless families of living creatures, all created
expressly to serve the needs of men[2]."   But we must not take
this very seriously.   In his Letters Erasmus has hardly a
reference to the impression made upon him by scenery;
neither the Alps nor the bay of Naples move him.   On the
other hand, he records a remarkable criticism on a well-known
passage from Bernard of Clairvaux: "Thou shalt find many
things in the woods that are not written in any book, and trees
and rocks will teach thee what thou canst learn of no Master[3]."
And he adds that he himself talks, to his vast profit, with the
trees of the forest.   "These," says Erasmus, "must in truth
have been wise trees which could produce so wise a scholar:
they deserve to sit in the professorial seat of the theologian, or
perhaps to be transformed into nymphs, instead of falling
prone upon the hills, or serving to fatten swine.   What can
men learn from *trees*?...Perhaps these are descendants of the
Tree of Knowledge, or of those which followed Orpheus; are

[1] *De Rat. Stud.*, infra, p. 167, § 5, and elsewhere.
[2] *Op.* v. 714 A.   [3] Bernard, *Epist.* cvi.

they perchance philosophers imprisoned by some god in woodland guise? But, joking apart, I am astonished that Bernard should have turned to trees rather than to men in his search for wisdom...Socrates would make his home in the city in preference to the loveliest spot which Greece could offer him, just because he could learn nothing from fields and trees. Does France then rejoice in trees more learned than any Greece could show?" There is only one way in which Bernard's words make sense : "he prayed under the trees, read there, pondered there; there he wrote, and thought." He sought solitude and peace for purposes of learned reflection, just as a poet may seek retreat in the silence of the woods[1]. But the true end of "scientia rerum" in the judgment of the humanist is its use as an aid to the proper understanding of ancient authors. Facts are to be derived from literary sources, and in turn they are to be employed in the illustration of literature. Erasmus, indeed, has a philosophy of speech of his own, suggested by the *Cratylus*, but very imperfectly worked out, by which the relation of words to the things signified was inherent and fixed[2]. Onomatopoeic words are by no means the only group which illustrates this hidden truth. "If there be not a traceable likeness between the word and the object or action which it symbolises, then there is some *invisible* reason why such object or action is named by the word which expresses it...Words which express *softness* or *slowness* prefer an *L* sound, *lenis* and *labi* are examples; size, on the other hand, appropriates the *M* sound, for that of all letters takes up most room (*Magnus*, μέγας)." Which only shows that Erasmus could take rank with the most whimsical of mediaevalist grammarians when he chose. But he stands on wholly different ground when he insists upon the importance of accurate and extensive knowledge of names and epithets in the understanding of things[3]. Modern grammarians, he says,

[1] *Op.* x. 1742 E—1743 B. [2] *Op.* i. 930 C.
[3] *Op.* v. 958 D.

ignore this ; and their pupils grow up wholly deficient in vocabulary for use.   Wherefore Erasmus urged the value of direct object-teaching, as in the famous instance of the *Convivium Religiosum*[1], where the garden, the aviary, and the walls of the terrace walks are used to impart nature knowledge. There each plant had its right name, with fitting motto or proverb attached, and strange beasts were depicted for the instruction of the household and its guests.   The same method was advised by him also in the teaching of children in school ; we have an illustration in the picture of the fight between the elephant and the dragon, "the large Indian variety," described in the *De Pueris*[2].   But the aim of such methods is not the imparting of facts, of the real knowledge of the things concerned, to serve as the material for reflection upon, and generalisation from, phenomena, and as the foundation of powers of framing concepts of natural law.   What is primarily sought is the acquisition of exact terminology, in accord with current popular knowledge.   Such general information served its main purpose in enabling the learner to appreciate intelligently the similes or metaphors of an ancient poet.   This is the argument proposed for " eruditio " in the *De Ratione Studii*.   " Astrology is futile in itself, but is the key to many allusions.   History explains many references in other writings.   Indeed, a genuine student ought to be able to grasp the meaning of every fact and idea which he meets with in his reading, otherwise their literary treatment through epithet or figure will prove obscure or confused.   There is no discipline, no field of study—music, architecture, agriculture, war—which may not prove of use to the Master in the exposition of the poets and orators of antiquity[3]."   So even right naming would appear to be chiefly of value in a literary sense. A sound acquaintance with phenomena for their own sake is

---

[1] *Op.* i. 673 seqq.   Infra, p. 226.   [2] Infra, p. 213, § 30.
[3] *De Rat. Stud.*, infra, p. 168, § 5.

not esteemed : indeed, actual contact with realities is only of use as enforcing what has been said about them by an approved author.

The use to be made of general knowledge in *composition* is treated of in the same tract. Quintilian[1] has a long section upon the relation of "eruditio" to the Orator. From this the Italian humanists drew their ideal of a liberal education, as oratorical skill adorning a many-sided learning. The educated man will be careful to have readily available for oratory or description[2] "all that varied mass of material which the curiosity of antiquity has handed down to us. To such belongs, first, the natural history of birds, quadrupeds, wild animals, serpents, insects, fishes ; this will be chiefly derived from ancient writers, with additions from our own observation. Next, we shall prize the accounts of singular adventures handed down to us by trustworthy authorities, such as the story of Arion and the dolphin, of the dragon who rescued his deliverer from danger, of the lion who returned kindness for kindness, and others which Pliny vouches for. There is also, in the third place, a vast body of facts concerning geographical phenomena, some of which are extraordinary, and these are of peculiar value to the scholar ; though even the usual occurrences of nature are not to be passed over. These, again, are partly drawn from antiquity, partly are within our own experience. I refer to rivers, springs, oceans, mountains, precious stones, trees, plants, flowers : concerning all of which comparisons should be derived and stored away in memory for prompt use in description or argument. Now, as certain of the illustrations which we may adduce from either of the three sources named are likely to be challenged as to their credibility, we must prepare ourselves to defend them, by careful noting of the authority on which each rests, and must give them the

[1] *Inst. Orat.* i. 10.
[2] *Op.* i. 389 c, d (*De Conscribendis Epistolis*). Erasmus is treating of 'exempla.'

air of reality by the style in which we clothe them. But, in the fourth place, we shall find by far our largest supply of instances for the embellishment of discourse in the sphere of human life and history[1]. Examples of virtue and vice, and of signal action, drawn from the annals of every nation, will be watched for, learnt by heart, and thrown into suitable literary form. So also rites and ceremonies, customs, wonders, institutions, all that is instructive will be pressed into use, and where the case demands will be arranged in order of climax that the effect may be the more striking." He adds that merchants and sailors can often supply the enquirer with attractive tales of strange lands for similar use[2]. In this department of instruction the ideal is a well-ordered and many-sided learning, which, in addition to other subjects, possesses a spice of antiquarian knowledge[3].

Thus so soon as Erasmus attempts to come to close quarters with real studies he finds himself unable to abandon a purely literary attitude. He gives the first place amongst them, perhaps, to *Cosmographia*—a better term than *Geographia*, as it embraces also the study of the heavenly bodies. We see no trace of any interest in recent over-sea discovery. The subject ranks as one of the mathematical disciplines, amongst which "vix alia vel jucundior vel magis necessaria[4]." It is "subtilior" than grammar, and appeals to some children—he thinks them abnormal—more directly than linguistic studies. Probably by "subtilior" he means "recondite," "abstract"; and implies his own ignorance of the subject. But a boy with a taste for it should not be debarred from pursuing the subject by aid of Ptolemy and the rest[5]. It is very doubtful if Erasmus had the faintest idea of the use to which an educated man would put

---

[1] Upon this method of regarding history as a series of striking incidents and characters, cf. supra, p. 131, and Woodward, *Vittorino*, p. 216.

[2] *Op.* i. 390 A.   [3] *Op.* x. 1735 E.

[4] *Op.* i. 923 A "prius perdiscat accurate," *Op.* iii. 1461 E.

[5] *Op.* i. 510 C.

geographical knowledge if he had it, excepting always as illustration of classical monuments. In the disturbed and perilous condition of the age the study of a map will serve as a useful substitute for travel[1].

There is, however, from the literary standpoint much to be said for Geography. It is of great use in reading histories, hardly less in reading poets[2]. The geography of the Holy Land and Asia Minor has the added interest of association with Scripture[3]. What is learnt, especially all ancient names, must be learnt accurately. The writers to be relied upon are Mela, Pliny, and Ptolemy; the latter is "the most learned of all geographers[4]."

The remaining mathematical disciplines are very briefly dismissed by Erasmus. "Arithmeticen, Musicam et Astrologiam degustasse sat erit[5]." As regards the first, Arithmetic was invariably excluded by humanists from the liberal arts. It was in a most rudimentary stage, and the effect of the adoption of Arabic notation had not made itself generally felt. The mercantile use of numbers was merely empirical, whilst the Roman notation was incompatible with any but the simplest processes of calculation.

Upon Music in education Erasmus had formed no settled opinion. He is aware, of course, that the Greeks regarded singing and playing as liberal arts; that they distinguished between various Modes, and that the Dorian approved itself to Plato. In a purely objective way he recognises the Greek theory of the relation of musical tones to character: and

[1] *Op.* i. 735 A. Elyot, *Governour* i. 76, should be read for a more serious view of the function of Geography, which he would have taught "by material figures and instruments."

[2] Infra, p. 167, § 5.

[3] *Op.* v. 79 (*De Rat. Theologiae*).

[4] Erasmus expended much sarcasm upon certain professors of the University of Louvain who refused to allow lectures upon Pomponius Mela, *Op.* iii. 535 etc. (to Vives, 1519).

[5] *Op.* i. 923 A.

records that there were writers who thought it an offence against the law to introduce a new mode not in accord with the temper of the State.   In considering the popular music of his own day Erasmus finds grave fault with the new songs which were being turned out, in Flanders, in great numbers, and caught the ear of the uneducated.   These are, he complains, bad in motive, in composition, and in allusions.   Girls even learn to sing these unworthy and corrupting airs : and there are fathers who encourage their children in the practice.   He would like to see authors and printers of such songs punished by law.

Erasmus is not only concerned at the words : the action which accompanies the air is indelicate and—here he is nearer the Platonic principle—the very music itself is trivial and debasing.   He objects particularly to 'tibiae Corybanticae,' and banging cymbals, to the sound of which young girls are made to dance by parents who are too dense to see the moral danger incurred.   He deplores also the intrusion of worthless music into the services of the Church, where solemn and dignified melodies alone are in place.   This barren treatment of the subject contrasts with the serious consideration of the place of music in education given to it by the Italian educators from Vittorino down to Sadoleto[1].

Astrology was in itself a futile study ; the point of view which characterised nearly every humanist from Petrarch downwards.   But, like Aeneas Sylvius, Erasmus thinks that the student should have some acquaintance with it, Aeneas because political adventures often turn on some "conjunction," Erasmus because astrological facts crop up in the poets.

Concerning Geometry in education there is nothing to be said.   In the *De Copia*[2] we have allusion to a knowledge of the square and the circle, which the scholar is advised to

---

[1] *Op.* v. 717 F etc. ; Sadoleto, *Op.* iii. 112.
[2] *Op.* i. 101 E.

understand, as these make an excellent comparison in describing "a man independent of the variations of fortune." In this respect also Erasmus falls below the practice of the earlier schools of the Revival. To him a purely abstract, non-human, subject could make no appeal.

Upon the natural sciences Erasmus has, as we have seen, hardly more to say, so far at least as regards their educational function. He does not recognise them as *organised knowledge*. The nearest approach which he makes to such admission is this[1]: "nonnullus et Physices praebebitur gustus, non tantum eius quae de principiis, de prima materia, de infinito ambitiose disputat, sed quae rerum naturas demonstrat. Quae res agitur in libris de anima, de meteoris, de plantis, de animalibus." No doubt he is referring to Aristotle as the source of all physical knowledge: the rudiments of it are to be carefully reduced to compendia, and acquired before the eighteenth year. The context (the *Dialogus De Pronunciatione*) renders it highly probable that he has in mind the literary utility of such information. It was the subject of two of the *Colloquies*[2]. These, however, treat of "physica" from the point of view of instructive amusement. One turns upon the "amicitiae et inimicitiae rerum" by which all phenomena are governed. Empedocles and Pliny are pressed into service, with tales from ancient sources concerning dolphins, crocodiles and ichneumons. The second dialogue discourses of the gravity of bodies, in a spirit characteristic rather of the mediaeval philosopher. "There is nothing in nature so heavy as that which is solid enough to depress beings, compacted of light and air, from the summit of all things to the uttermost depths." "Presumably; and what is that called?" "Sin, which dragged down Satan to the abyss." Next to their value as literary adornment, natural phenomena had interest for Erasmus as

[1] *Op.* i. 923 A.
[2] The Colloquies entitled *Amicitia* and *Problema*: in Bailey's Translation, ii. 300, 316.

analogies and parables for moral edification. "Nightingales[1] sing with such exuberance of spirit that they die competing with one another, and prefer death to relinquishing their song. Let men take warning from them, lest in an inordinate desire to excel they sacrifice their health and even life itself."

In truth, studies based on natural science in the fifteenth and sixteenth centuries lacked the indispensable qualifications of instruments of instruction for the young. They had in most cases neither certainty, nor precision, nor organisation as teaching material. Apart from the mathematical basis upon which certain of them rested, they were but collections of "interesting information," or "useful knowledge." In no way were they comparable, as apparatus for teaching, with the rigid and highly elaborated subjects of grammar and rhetoric.

One further allusion to an educational instrument, technical in nature, may here be quoted[2]. "It will be of advantage to the boy of expectations and of station to learn something of the mechanic arts upon their less undignified side, for example, painting, sculpture, modelling, architecture. The philosophers would not approve: but we Christians cannot scorn manual activities when we recollect that our Lord Himself, the Son of a carpenter, was brought up as a carpenter Himself. Such crafts as I refer to fill up leisure, and in case of need they may afford a livelihood." From the tone of the passage we may doubt whether Erasmus had much more feeling for Art than he has for Poetry.

§ 10. THE EDUCATION OF GIRLS.

In the republic of Letters neither nationality, age, nor sex constituted a bar to the rights of citizenship. The Italian humanists had effectively claimed for women the right to education in liberal studies, and had established thereby their status

---

[1] From the *Similia*, *Op.* i. 614 D. Cp. infra, p. 189.   [2] *Op.* v. 716 B.

in cultivated society. A woman, not less than a man, could in the Italy of the Renaissance stand forth independently in right of *virtù* or personal distinction[1]. Erasmus records that he was won over to this view by his intercourse with Thomas More and his household[2]. Thereafter he fought strenuously in defence of the educated woman. He thus took a further and most significant step forwards in his progress from mediaevalism. It is characteristic of Erasmus that he should pillory the antagonists of enlightenment for women in the person of a certain Abbot Antronius. "Women," so he opines, "have nothing to do with wisdom ; it is their one business to be pleasing.... I should be very sorry to see the brethren of *my* House showing interest in books[3]."

No doubt Erasmus—here again obeying his usual instinct— was moved to adopt a new point of view as the result of actual experience of the falsity of "the universal opinion that learning detracts from the repute and good manners of a woman." Observation showed him, on the contrary, that there is no such foe to moral fibre, whether in boy or girl, as idleness or triviality of interest. Absorption in learned studies is the remedy against both in a far greater degree than needlework —the approved pursuit for a girl—which mostly leaves the intelligence unoccupied. Character in fact is only rightly

[1] Burckhardt, *Civilisation of the Renaissance*, p. 396 (Eng. trans.) : "The Education given to women in the upper classes was essentially the same as that given to men. The Italian, at the time of the Renaissance, felt no scruple in putting sons and daughters alike under the same course of literary and even philological instruction....The educated woman, no less than the man, strove naturally after a characteristic and complete individuality." The entire chapter deserves careful study. Cp. *La Vita Italiana nel Rinascimento*, p. 98, "La donna Fiorentina," by Del Lungo; Mrs Abdy's *Isabella D'Este*; and the tract by L. Bruni in Woodward, *Vittorino da Feltre*, p. 119. In any study of the education of women in modern times the Italian ideal of the Quattrocento must be the starting-point.

[2] *Op.* iii. 769 D. For More's influence, cp. supra, p. 45.

[3] *Op.* i. 745 F; the Colloquy *Erudita Puella*.

ensured when it is based upon thought and free power of judgment, and for such intellectual exercise serious culture provides the material. It is preposterous to imagine that idleness and seclusion are the right prescription to secure virtue ; the full and effective education of a girl is not a merely negative thing[1]. Does anyone think that a girl can be "cooped up with foolish and empty-headed women" and not learn mischief? a knowledge of evil will come to her more surely so than by healthy human converse in society. Only a man who is himself an ignoramus will affirm that "a learned woman is twice a fool[2]." The position taken by Erasmus, with his customary practical sense, is that all must accept the argument that a woman should be trained to fill her natural place in society, as daughter, wife, and mother. It is evident, then, that an educated young woman is an ornament to her father's home. The daughters of Sir Thomas More[3], in whose house Erasmus was a welcome guest, and of Paumgarten, and the sisters of Bilbald Pirckheimer, are conspicuous examples. Such studious women remind us of Paulla, Marcella, and Eustochium, the lights of the circle which gathered round St Jerome. The well-educated wife, again, can safely claim : "et conjugem mihi et me illi cariorem reddit eruditio[4]." It is obvious to Erasmus that durable affection must be based upon such equality of interests : "it is real happiness for a man to live with a cultured and intelligent spouse." A wife honours her husband more sincerely when her training has rendered her capable of appreciating and imitating his true excellence. Without a head well-skilled to keep her home in order, and to respond to her husband's higher tastes, she will, in spite of good intentions, fail as a wife. On the other side, a woman of sound intelligence—so the husband will discover—is easier to guide ; for there is nothing so hard to control as ignorance, in

[1] *Op.* v. 744 E.
[2] Ibid. 746 B.
[3] *Op.* iii. 678 E ; iii. 1482 F ; iii. 196 E.
[4] *Op.* i. 746 A.

dealing with which reason and argument are of no avail. "'A wonderful sermon,' says the average woman, as she comes out of church : voice and gesture are all that she thinks about ; whether the preacher had anything to say does not interest her." Then Erasmus is concerned with the relation of girls' education to their subsequent efficiency in the bringing up of their children. It is clear that the intense distrust which he felt in respect of female influence is directly due to his contempt for the ordinary training of the women of his day. That same lack of serious interests and discipline, which he elsewhere remarks, must react with most disastrous effect upon their function as the guardians of the young. Capriciousness, hasty temper, childish vanity, are the results of a frivolous up-bringing, and produce like effects upon the next generation. The only resource in such a case is that the father shall decisively take the whole responsibility of the children out of hands so unfitted for it. The lot of girl-children, unfortunately, is less easily settled by such a method[1].

How Erasmus treats of early care for health, good manners, character and religion, has been discussed already. When he comes to speak of the actual content of a girl's education upon its literary side, he is unable to lay down any rule because, as he says, circumstances, individual and social, are much varied[2]. We may, perhaps, add as another reason, that Erasmus had no knowledge of the actual conditions of the problem. He was a celibate, a monk, with extremely few opportunities of seeing or sharing in young society. Hence his advice is largely negative. But even so it is that of a shrewd mind. He denounces fashionable society-education for girls. The ideal set before women was a poor thing, just subservience to convention. But the first duty of the educator is to train every

[1] Cf. supra, p. 91.
[2] *Op.* v. 716 D. But he has no doubt that "nothing is more conducive to true refinement and moral integrity of disposition than a classical education."

one to exercise their free will, and to make rational choice in the affairs of life. Again, such an unworthy aim in education, as that alluded to, is in practice quite compatible with acquaintance with evil, gained from vulgar humour or conversation at home. "In an ordinary town-house of well-to-do people the day begins with hair-dressing and rouging; formal attendance at public worship follows, for the sake of seeing and being seen: then comes breakfast. Gossip and the lightest of 'literature' fill up the morning until dinner. The afternoon is occupied by promenades, and, for the young people, games sadly lacking in decorum. Then more gossip and supper. It is no better when the family moves to the country, where amid idle days, the crowd of retainers, lackeys, and serving-girls, is a standing influence for evil. How different is such an environment for a young girl from that careful supervision which Aristotle commands[1]."

Erasmus is anxious that the home surroundings of children should invariably be cheerful, full of affection, according wise liberty. But he reminds parents that the "reverentia" due to boys is doubly due to their sisters. A lack of respect for divine things, avowed contempt for all that is lofty and serious in life, above all questionable humour and personal self-indulgence, are the worst of examples to girls. Erasmus was not unaware at first hand of the coarseness of manners which marked the average German household, especially in the landed class.

He offers one serious warning upon a habit, to which fathers are prone, of enforcing their views as to their children's future. In particular the conventual life ought not to be pressed upon a boy or girl just because such a vocation would fall in conveniently with the interests of the family[2]. The right principle

---

[1] *Loc. cit.*

[2] *Op.* v. 722 E. He says that his example of the conventual life is only by way of illustration. The warning is equally true of matrimony or of a scholar's career, 724 B.

is to follow the child's bent in determining his or her future career.

In conclusion, the nature of the references which Erasmus makes to the whole subject indicates that he has in mind the education of the daughters of the leisured class, such education to be carried out in the home, and certainly not under the control of a religious Order. In this he is in line with the Italian humanists, who, however, had before them a far more cultivated type of society. They were consequently in a position to work out a curriculum for girls with more precision, in that they had clearer and more extended views of the status and social function for which women should be prepared. It may help us to realise the gulf between the society of a cultured circle in Italy and that of a smaller Court in Germany if we try to imagine *Il Cortegiano* in a contemporary northern setting. Yet the *Book of the Courtier* was composed some ten years before the work in which Erasmus sets out his plea for a higher education for women[1].

[1] Elyot's *Defence of Good Women* was published two years before Erasmus died. He carries out the contention of Erasmus concerning the advantage of liberal learning to a wife. Zenobia of Palmyra declares that she spent the four years from 16 to 20 in the study of Letters, and specially of Philosophy; this she found most useful in bringing up her own children. She advises every maiden to devote herself before marriage to the earnest pursuit of learning. For "women being well and virtuously brought up do not only with men participate in reason, but some also in fidelity and constancy be equal to them." Vives, the tutor to Mary, daughter of Henry VIII, writes in much detail upon a curriculum for a girl. He has a particular aversion to the romances *Amadis de Gaule*, *Lancelot of the Lake*, etc., "qui non minus aversandi sunt quam vipera et scorpio." He urges the use of the Christian poets: and an "exigua cognitio naturae," such as may be useful in life. But grammar and composition in Latin are to be fully taught. In addition, he bestows attention on "res domestica": "discet ergo simul literas, simul lanam et linum tractare, et quaecumque ad tuendam et regendam domum spectant." His *De Institutione feminae* and *De Officio mariti* are important authorities on the education of girls as advocated in the first half of the 16th century in England.

§ 11. Moral Training: Character as the Supreme End of Education.

The rudiments of moral training as set out by Erasmus were considered in an earlier section. The discipline of home life and the example there set are the vital forces making for religion and character in the young. No overt teaching of duty can effect its purpose if the prime motive and sanction of conduct which the home supplies be lacking.

It is in the family life that the foundations of belief and reverence must be laid. No school kept by professed "religious" has like advantage in this respect. In the treatise *Upon Christian Marriage* (1526) he summarises the elements of Christian doctrine which may be profitably taught to children under the age of fourteen[1]. The characteristic note of this important passage is the sense of the intimate personal relation of the child to the Divine Father. The world of Nature and of human life is intelligible only in light of the beneficent Creator upon whom the Christian child must rest in conscious dependence. Upon this trust in the divine Fatherhood must be built up a corresponding faith in that "cognatio arctissima" within which all Christians ought to feel themselves united. Erasmus touches here one of his warmest aspirations, which was to see an end put to those internecine feuds by which the dynastic ambitions of his age kept Europe in constant unrest, and by which the day of enlightenment, and of the human well-being dependent upon it, were pushed into a dim future. This conviction of the divine sanction of human brotherhood is, in education, the connecting link between religious faith and social duty. For the child will now readily understand the conduct due towards parents, towards elders, equals, inferiors, and towards the poor. In the home, scripture will be set forth

---

[1] *Op.* v. 713 E—714 C.

as a gallery of characters, by the pattern of whose excellence conduct must be guided. Especially will the vices of lying, which Erasmus held in peculiar abhorrence, loss of temper, malice, self-indulgence, be stamped with condemnation as the worst of all faults in the young. If a boy is brought up at home, with such precepts enforced by right example, before he has completed his fourteenth year the solid foundations of character will have been securely laid. His nature—that primitive human "Natura[1]"—will have received its definite bent towards the Good, both in knowledge and in action. Hence the father will use his utmost endeavour to see that such a beginning shall have ample opportunity of subsequent development by aid of sound learning and wise discipline. Again does Erasmus affirm with all earnestness his standing principle—which runs also throughout the whole of the *De Pueris*—that such progress is initially dependent upon the condition that the home atmosphere be conducive to the best. That implies a high standard of interests in conjunction with a dignified, temperate manner of life. "Monita non multa adjuvabunt, si puer viderit aliud in vita parentum quam praescripserant. Imitandi vis peculiariter inest pueris[2]."

Nothing, indeed, is more significant of the modern spirit in which Erasmus approaches the problem of education than his determination to regard it as centring in the home. If it be true that a characteristic mark of a sound and progressive culture is the place accorded to the care of children, then we must recognise that the humanists set out a notably high type of social well-being. At no time in modern history was care for, and interest in, the young so striking a fact of society as in the Italy of the Quattrocento. The sense of duty towards the child in respect of discipline, example, and instruction is expressed on every hand. Then the rights of the child to a due place in the family were recognised to the full. Under

---

[1] Supra, p. 80–2.   [2] *Op.* v. 714 D, E.

the influence of home guidance obedience to the outer law was gradually resolved into an inner harmony, a conscious self-reliance, which in its course was developed as a free individuality. This was effected by admitting the child to the normal intercourse of the family. It was never accepted that a child should be confined to the society of other children; it was his acknowledged claim to share the interests of his elders, as theirs to take concern for him. Probably there was in the Italy of that great epoch no force so potent for the restraint of too exuberant exercise of *virtù* as this deep sense of responsibility for the up-growth of the children[1].

Erasmus has seized this truth. A celibate, a wanderer, a man owning no family ties, without one single relative to give him welcome, he has yet understood the significance of the home as a positive factor in education. That he saw in it a factor also making for the good not of the child alone we can clearly perceive. It was well thought, that in a new sense of duty towards the son or the daughter of the house Erasmus should find his most hopeful remedy for the " barbarism " in which he saw the German people sunk in his day.

Something may here be said concerning the little book of manners, which he published at Basel in 1526, under the title *De Civilitate Morum puerilium*. It had great vogue in the schools of the 16th century. In England it was translated before 1532, and many small manuals of behaviour were founded upon it[2]. We have evidence that between 1547—58 no work of Erasmus was more in demand in the great book mart of Germany, Leipzig[3]. The manual is thoroughly simple

[1] It should be noticed that the schools in England founded under the humanist impulse were, in contradistinction to the pre-Renaissance foundations, almost exclusively day schools.

[2] See Watson, *Curriculum*, pp. 8, 12. For the title of this and other English versions of Erasmus' educational books see infra, p. 235.

[3] "Kirchhoff, in his book *Leipziger Sortimentshändler im 16 Jahrhundert*, shows that in three years, 1547, 1551, 1558, not less than 654

n style; it was expressly written for boys' use, probably it was often learnt by heart. It contains the following chapters: upon Physical Training and Personal Carriage; upon Dress; upon Behaviour in Church; at Table; in Company; at Play; in the Dormitory. The temper of the book is admirable; it is never trivial, in spite of the intimate personal details into which the writer enters. Erasmus desires to set up a standard of manners to correspond to, and be the expression of, inward culture. He is fully aware of the advantage which Italy has, as against Germany, in this respect. But the moral ground-work is always in evidence: cleanliness, without and within, orderliness, truthfulness, frankness, self-respect, inbred courtesy to elders, to women and to companions, are the central points of the teaching which the book conveys. He ends by a monition to the young Prince Henry of Burgundy, to whom he addresses the treatise, a monition characteristic of the true humanist: "I would by way of epilogue add this piece of advice. Do not, in spite of what I have written, think un-worthily of a school-fellow who may haply fall short of your own standard of manners. For there are many who nobly compensate for such defects—due mostly to circumstance—by their excellence in more weighty virtues. Do not for a moment persuade yourself that a person cannot merit respect because he may lack something of the courtesies. A deficiency on this score you will wisely meet at most by friendly advice; never by superior airs of reproof[1]."

In connection with school influences we may recall what Erasmus laid down upon the choice of Masters. The example and stimulus begun in the home must be further maintained in the school-room by the Tutor. One ground for the bitter criticism passed by Erasmus upon the average master was the

copies (some with commentary) of the *De Civilitate* were in stock in Leipzig. No other of Erasmus' books is to be found in such lists in equal number." Glöckner, *Erasmus*, p. 28 n.

[1] *De Civil. Mor. Pueril., Op.* i. 1044 A.

too common fact of his moral worthlessness. Ignorance, doubt less, had much to do with the cruelty that so often marked his rule ; but there were moral offences to be complained of, such as drunkenness, neglect, and carelessness as to his whole function as a maker of character.

We see, therefore, that Erasmus bases moral training upon personal religion, home example and intercourse[1], and school influence. It is characteristic of him that he has so little to say of the direct value of Church ceremonies, confession, the influence of the clergy, or of theological studies, in the building up of character. On the other hand, upon the basis of wholesome obedience thus established at home Erasmus builds up an edifice of moral education through literature, which it is important now to consider. It has been already shown that in the reading of the classical authors a prominent place will be given to setting forth the moral drift of the passage studied. Worthy example will be carefully drawn out, with parallel and illustration, and with application to modern instance. But if the passage in hand treat of evil motive or action the Master will so explain it, so emphasise the warning called for, that the class will be in no danger of carrying away a false standard of conduct. Erasmus is at pains to point out that one special reading of each lesson-portion should, if the passage lend itself thereto, be confined to the noting of, and comment upon, the moral teaching involved[2]. How frequently does an author offer opportunity for such didactic review ! And how striking the effect of clear-cut pictures of virtue or vice drawn from the great authorities of the past ! Such "literary" exhortation is described by Erasmus as "exempla,"

[1] *Op.* iii. 1483 A. "Tenera aetas domi formatur ad omnem probitatem atque innocentiam."

[2] *Op.* i. 448 C : "releges igitur quarto, ac quae ad philosophiam, maxime vero ethicen, referri posse videantur circumspicies, si quod exemplum quod moribus accommodari possit. Quid autem est ex quo non vel exemplum vivendi, vel imago quaedam, vel occasio, sumi queat?

i.e. concrete cases, although of rhetorical shape. The *De Ratione Studii* contains instances of this method, which is applicable also to composition in Latin and Greek. In one of the Colloquies (the *Sober Feast*) Erasmus handles the question of moral worth as descried in the writings of antiquity. He has no difficulty in showing that ancient literature can produce types of character "of the very pattern of Christian goodness." He compiled also a collection of ancient moral wisdom, the *Apophthegmata* (1531), whereby he "brings forward the great figures of the past to celebrate the eternal laws of right." Special classical authors are advised for their excellence as aids to moral training. Plutarch stands first; indeed he ranks next to the Gospels; as a moral stimulus to youth he will prove more attractive than any of the Christian Fathers[1]. Basil and Chrysostom learnt much from Plutarch. Then follow Cicero, Seneca, Terence, Demosthenes, Vergil and Tacitus. It is noticeable that Erasmus warns the Master against turning moral teaching into teaching *about* morals : discussions "de summo bono," or the sanctions of Ethics, are otiose. The Master is concerned to give the stimulus to action and to enforce it by precedents; he will fail in this duty if he allows the youthful mind to wander off to mere speculation.

This literary treatment of morality, so objective and didactic, lends itself easily to depreciatory criticism, which, however, fails of effectiveness when we remember that Erasmus intends it as illustration, for intelligent youth, of precepts imbibed in the home. Further, it will be reinforced, as the threshold of manhood is reached, by a more intimate intercourse with elders. The young man entering upon direct preparation for professional life must be allowed free choice of career; a wholly modern concept, in which, however, Erasmus sees the crown of all right education. The development of individuality must

---

[1] *Op.* v. 856. Cp. Benoist, *Quid de pueris*, p. 131.

be watched from the very first years of life. Erasmus constantly warns parents against forcing all children through the same course[1], and when bent is fully in evidence in later boyhood, they and the Master must recognise it as decisive. Such freedom of personality is fully consistent with a uniform sense of public duty, which should mark every cultivated intelligence. The narrowing influence of a certain type of literary education, in the direction, he means, of disqualifying the studious for active 'interests in life, he much deprecates[2]. For "action" is the end of education, with Erasmus not less than with the great Italian Masters of the Quattrocento. The life of scholarship is only one small part of the career open to highly educated youth. To be a citizen of the world, marked by a due consciousness of obligation to the community in which we are placed, is the highest aim. Thomas More, Colet, and Paumgarten are instances. Erasmus is reminded in his allusions to the Paumgarten family of the value of Travel in education : "adolescentia prima statim ab aedibus paternis ablegatur in Italiam aut in Galliam, quo simul et linguis et moribus alienis assuescant, nihil enim fere morosius iis qui in patria consenuerunt ; oderunt exteros, ac damnant quicquid a vernaculis ritibus diversum est[3]." In this way the consciousness of an "international solidarity of learning" was strengthened. Finally, the higher end of humanism was attained when the sense of duty to self, to the community, and to God, was realised as the triple aspect of one and the same ideal.

[1] *Op.* v. 722 D ; i. 502.   Infra, p. 196.   [2] *Op.* iii. 1482 F.
[3] Ibid. 1485 A.

PART II.

NOTE.

THE works of Erasmus here presented include the two treatises which best express the ordered views of their author upon Education. These, with a portion of one of the *Colloquies*, are given in English. A short chapter from the *De Conscribendis Epistolis* is printed in the original Latin with English headings.

The tract *De Ratione Studii* has not, I believe, appeared before in an English version. The *De Pueris* was translated by 'Rychard Sherry, Londoner,' head-master of Magdalen College School, and published in or about 1550 by John Day, under the title 'A declamacion *That chyldren even strayt fro' their infancie should be well and gently broughte up in learnynge.* Written fyrst in Latin by the most excellent and famous Clearke, Erasmus of Roterodame.' This was issued in one volume, of which it forms the second part, with a *Treatise of Schemes and Tropes* (*i.e.* figures of Rhetoric). The volume is exceedingly rare. The *Colloquies* were translated by N. Bailey in 1725. Any compressions noticeable in the versions as printed below are only by way of restraint of Erasmian redundancy of illustration.

In addition to these four works the student of the subject will perhaps find the following next in order of interest: *Christiani Matrimonii Institutio, Op.* v. 708 B—724. *De Civilitate Morum Puerilium*, i. 1033—1044. *De Rerum Copia*, i. 75—110.

CHAPTER VI.

THE TREATISE OF ERASMUS *DE RATIONE STUDII*, THAT IS, *UPON THE RIGHT METHOD OF IN-STRUCTION*, 1511.

§ 1. Thought and Expression form the Two-fold Material of Instruction. 521 A—B.

ALL knowledge falls into one of two divisions: the knowledge of "truths" and the knowledge of "words": and if the former is first in importance the latter is acquired first in order of time. They are not to be commended who, in their anxiety to increase their store of truths, neglect the necessary art of expressing them. For ideas are only intelligible to us by means of the words which describe them; wherefore defective knowledge of language reacts upon our apprehension of the truths expressed. We often find that no one is so apt to lose himself in verbal arguments as the man who boasts that facts, not words, are the only things that interest him. This goes to prove that true education includes what is *best* in both kinds of knowledge, taught, I must add, under the *best* guidance. For, remembering how difficult it is to eradicate early impressions, we should aim from the first at learning what need never be unlearnt, and that only.

§ 2. EXPRESSION CLAIMS THE FIRST PLACE IN POINT OF TIME.
BOTH THE GREEK AND LATIN LANGUAGES NEEDFUL TO
THE EDUCATED MAN, 521 B—C.

Language thus claims the first place in the order of studies
and from the outset should include both Greek and Latin.
The argument for this is two-fold.   First, that within these two
literatures are contained all the knowledge which we recognise
as of vital importance to mankind.   Secondly, that the natural
affinity of the two tongues renders it more profitable to study
them side by side than apart.   Latin particularly gains by this
method.   Quintilian advised that a beginning should be made
with Greek before systematic work in Latin is taken in hand.
Of course he regarded proficiency in both as essential.   The
elements, therefore, of Greek and Latin should be acquired
early, and should a thoroughly skilled master not be available,
then—but only then—let the learner fall back upon self-teaching
by means of the study of classical masterpieces.

§ 3. THE RIGHT METHOD OF ACQUIRING GRAMMAR RESTS
UPON READING AND NOT UPON DEFINITIONS AND RULES.
521 C—522 A.

Amongst Greek Grammars that of Theodore Gaza stands
admittedly first, next to it I rank that of Constantine Lascaris.
Of the old Latin Grammarians Diomedes is the soundest;
whilst the *Rudimenta* of Nicholas Perotti strikes me as the
most thorough and most comprehensive of modern works.
But I must make my conviction clear that, whilst a knowledge
of the rules of accidence and syntax is most necessary to every
student, still they should be as few, as simple, and as carefully
framed as possible.   I have no patience with the stupidity of
the average teacher of grammar who wastes precious years in

hammering rules into children's heads. For it is not by learning rules that we acquire the power of speaking a language, but by daily intercourse with those accustomed to express themselves with exactness and refinement, and by the copious reading of the best authors.

Upon this latter point we do well to choose such works as are not only sound models of style but are instructive by reason of their subject-matter. The Greek prose-writers whom I advise are, in order, Lucian, Demosthenes, Herodotus : the poets, Aristophanes, Homer, Euripides ; Menander, if we possessed his works, would take precedence of all three. Amongst Roman writers, in prose and verse, Terence, for pure, terse Latinity has no rival, and his plays are never dull. I see no objection to adding carefully chosen comedies of Plautus. Next, I place Vergil, then Horace ; Cicero and Caesar follow closely ; and Sallust after these. These authors provide, in my judgment, sufficient reading to enable the young student to acquire a working knowledge of the two great classical tongues. It is not necessary for this purpose to cover the whole range of ancient literature ; we are not to be dubbed " beginners " because we have not yet mastered the whole of the *Fragmenta*.

Some proficiency in expression being thus attained the student devotes his attention to the *content* of the ancient literatures. It is true, of course, that in reading an author for purposes of vocabulary and style the student cannot fail to gather something besides. But I have in my mind much more than this when I speak of studying "contents." For I affirm that with slight qualification the whole of attainable knowledge lies enclosed within the literary monuments of ancient Greece. This great inheritance I will compare to a limpid spring of whose undefiled waters it behoves all who truly thirst to drink and be restored.

§ 4. THE SUBJECT-MATTER AND THE METHODS WHICH
    ARE MOST SUITABLE TO BEGINNERS.   522 A—E.

Before touching upon the order in which the various
disciplines should be acquired, and the choice of Masters,
I will say something on the instruction of beginners.   In
reading the authors above mentioned for the purposes of
vocabulary, ornament and style, you can have no better guide
than Lorenzo Valla.   His *Elegantiae* will shew you what to
look for and note down in your Latin reading.   But do not
merely echo his rules ;   make headings for yourself as well.
Refer also to Donatus and Diomedes for syntax.   Rules of
prosody, and the rudiments of rhetoric, such as the method of
direct statement, of proof, of ornament, of expansion, of transition, are important both for the intelligent study of authors
and for composition.   Such grounding in grammar and in style
will enable you to note with precision such matters as these :
an unusual word, archaisms, and innovations, ingenuity in
handling material, distinction of style, historical or moral
instances, proverbial expressions :   the note-book being ready
to hand to record them.   Notes of this kind should not be
jotted down at hap-hazard, but carefully devised so as to recall
to the mind the pith of what is read.

If it is claimed that Logic should find a place in the course
proposed I do not seriously demur ;   but I refuse to go beyond
Aristotle and I prohibit the verbiage of the schools.   Do not
let us forget that Dialectic is an elusive maiden, a Siren, indeed,
in quest of whom a man may easily suffer intellectual ship-
wreck.   Not here is the secret of style to be discovered.   That
lies in the use of the pen ;   whatever the form, whether prose
or verse, or whatever the theme, write, write, and again write.
Supplement writing by learning by heart   Upon this latter
question, memory depends at bottom upon three conditions :
thorough understanding of the subject, logical ordering of the

contents, repetition to ourselves. Without these we can neither
retain securely nor reproduce promptly. Read, then, atten-
tively, read over and over again, test your memory vigorously
and minutely. Verbal memory may with advantage be aided
by ocular impressions; thus, for instance, we can have charts
of geographical facts, genealogical trees, large-typed tables of
rules of syntax and prosody, which we can hang on the walls.
Or again, the scholar may make a practice of copying striking
quotations at the top of his exercise books. I have known
a proverb inscribed upon a ring, or a cup, sentences worth
remembering painted on a door or a window. These are
all devices for adding to our intellectual stores, which, trivial
as they may seem individually, have a distinct cumulative
value.

Lastly, I urge, as undeniably the surest method of acquisition, the practice of teaching what we know : in no other way
can we so certainly learn the difference between what we *know*,
and what we *think we know*; whilst that which we actually
know we come to know better.

§ 5.   Instruction Generally : Choice of Subjects of
     Instruction.   The Range of Study Necessary to
     a Well-read Master.   522 E—523 F.

This brings me to treat of the art of instruction generally,
though it seems a mere impertinence in me to handle afresh a
subject which has been made so conspicuously his own by the
great Quintilian.

As regards the choice of *material*, it is essential that from
the outset the child be made acquainted only with the best
that is available. This implies that the Master is competent
to recognise the best in the mass of erudition open to him,
which in turn signifies that he has read far more widely than
the range of authors to be taught by him. This applies even
to the tutor of beginners. The Master should, therefore,

acquaint himself with authors of every type, with a view to contents rather than to style; and the better to classify what he reads he must adopt the system of classifying his matter by means of note-books, upon the plan suggested by me in *De Copia*. As examples of the authors I refer to I put Pliny first, then Macrobius, Aulus Gellius, and, in Greek, Athenaeus. Indeed to lay in a store of ancient wisdom the studious master must go straight to the Greeks: to Plato, Aristotle, Theophrastus and Plotinus; to Origen, Chrysostom, Basil. Of the Latin Fathers, Ambrosius will be found most fertile in classical allusions. Jerome has the greatest command of Holy Scripture. I cannot, however, enumerate the entire extent of reading which a competent knowledge of antiquity demands. I can only indicate a few directions which study ought to take.

For the right understanding of the poets, the *Legends* of Gods and Heroes must be mastered: Homer, Hesiod, Ovid, and the Italian Boccaccio should be read for this. A knowledge of *Geography* is of prime importance, for the study both of ancient poets and of historians. Pomponius Mela makes a useful compendium; Pliny and Ptolemy are learned and elaborate writers; Strabo is something more than a geographer. This subject includes two parts, a knowledge, first, of the names, ancient and modern, of mountains, rivers, cities; secondly, of names of trees, plants, animals, of dress, appliances, precious stones, in which the average writer of to-day shews a strange ignorance. Here we gain help from the works which have come down to us upon agriculture, architecture, the art of war, cookery, precious stones, and natural history. We can make good use, in the same subject, of etymology (the name " unicorn " is an example). Or again we can trace word-change in names through modern Greek, or Italian and Spanish (Tiber, now " Tevere," is an example). I may say that modern French has wandered too far from its classical mother-speech to be of much help to us in recognising and identifying ancient names.

Material for the study of Archaeology is to be found not only in literary sources, but in ancient coins, inscriptions, and monuments. Astrology—futile as it is in itself—must be understood for the sake of many poetical allusions. Of special importance is the study of History, for its own sake as well as for the reason that it is the key to many references in other writings. Finally, to understand such a poet as Prudentius, the one Christian poet of real literary taste, a knowledge of Sacred History is indispensable.

And indeed we may say that a genuine student ought to grasp the meaning and force of every fact or idea that he meets with in his reading, otherwise their literary treatment through epithet, metaphor, or simile will be to him obscure and confused. There is thus no discipline, no field of study, —whether music, architecture, agriculture or war—which may not prove of use to the teacher in expounding the Poets and Orators of antiquity. "But," you rejoin, "you expect all this of your scholar?" Yes, if he propose to become a teacher; for he thus secures that his own erudition will lighten the toil of acquisition for those under his charge.

§ 6. THE ART OF TEACHING THE RUDIMENTS OF LANGUAGE
    UP TO THE STAGE WHEN COMPOSITION IS BEGUN.
    523 F—524 C.

As regards the methods of the rudiments—that is, of learning to talk and knowing the alphabet—I can add nothing to what Quintilian has laid down. For my own part I advise that when this stage is reached the child begin to hear and imitate the sounds of *Latin* speech. Why should it be more difficult to acquire Roman words or even Greek, rather than the vernacular? No doubt my prescription demands the environment of a cultivated home-circle. But the master may secure even under the conditions of school-life that boys be brought to speak Latin with precision, if patience be shown in encouraging and correcting uncertain efforts, and in insisting upon careful observation of the Teacher's own usage. By degrees devices for increasing fluency may be introduced; as, for instance, a game of forfeits and prizes for faults and corrections, the Master choosing the judges from amongst the top boys. The more common phrases suitable for play, for social life, for meal-times, must be early learned and be apt, and ready to hand.

The time will now have come when the able teacher must select certain of the more necessary rules of accidence and syntax, and state them simply, arrange them in proper order and dictate them for entry in note-books. An author may now be attempted, but of the easiest sort; choose one likely to be helpful in composition and conversation. Through this text the rules just referred to will be driven home, and the examples of syntactical usages therein contained carefully worked out; all this of course with an eye to the later stages when regular exercises in prose and verse are required.

§ 7. The importance of the Art of Composition; its method set out. 524 c—525 c.

When this time has arrived care must be taken to propound themes not only worthy in subject but suitable, as being within the range of the boy's interests. For in this way he may acquire not only training in style, but also a certain store of facts and ideas for future use. For example, such a subject as the following would prove attractive: "The rash self-confidence of Marcellus imperilled the fortunes of Rome; they were retrieved by the caution of Fabius." Here we see the underlying sentiment, that reckless counsels hasten towards disaster. Here is another: "Which of the two shewed less wisdom, Crates who cast his gold into the sea, or Midas who cherished it as his supreme good?"   Or, "Eloquence too little restrained brought Demosthenes and Cicero to their ruin."   One more: "No encomium can exceed the deserts of Codrus, who held that the safety of his subjects claimed even the life of the King himself."   But Valerius Maximus will provide you with ample choice of such themes.   At first these may be set in the vernacular.

Mythology and fable will also serve your purpose.   "Hercules gained immortal fame as the destroyer of monsters." "The Muses delight in the fountain and the grove; they shrink from the crowded haunts of men."   "One should not burden a friend with a difficulty which it is a duty to solve ourselves." "All men are conscious of the wallet which hangs in front, but ignore that which they carry behind them."   Proverb and moral will suggest such themes as these: "It is not every one's good fortune to visit Corinth."   "How far above the type of to-day was he who counted a man worthy not for his wealth but for his manhood!"   "Socrates despises those who live in order to eat; he applauds those who eat in order to live." My book *Adagia* will supply you with instances enough. Other themes may be suggested from the properties of natural objects, such as the attraction of the magnet or the mimicry of the polypus.   Similes, also, allegories, sententious sayings, smart turns of expression, will lend themselves to exercises in composition.   The Master in the course of his reading will be careful to note instances which present themselves as models suitable for imitation.

The pupil will now have attained a certain facility in speaking and in writing Latin.   He will be ready, therefore, to proceed to a more advanced stage in Grammar, which must be learnt by means of rules aptly illustrated by quotations: the rules being expressed as tersely as may be consistent with clearness.   I would add that in all that concerns Greek constructions we should do well to follow the guidance of Gaza's grammar.

§ 8. THE METHODS TO BE PURSUED IN WRITING ADVANCED
EXERCISES IN COMPOSITION.   525 C—F.

But I must repeat that when once the simpler rules of
composition, in prose and verse, and the commoner figures of
speech have been mastered, the whole stress of teaching must
be laid upon a close yet wide study of the greater writers.
Fortified with this the student can produce *original* work in
prose, under the criticism (this is most important) of a thoroughly
skilled instructor.

Practice in the epistolary style, both in Greek and Latin,
may be gained by writing to an argument propounded in the
vernacular. This will come first. Then the whole range of
rhetorical prose is open to the student who must gain acquaintance with the different varieties of style ; for instance, that
demanded in the production of the Fable, or the moral
Commonplace, or the short Story, or the Dilemma ; the art
of expressing an Encomium, or a Denunciation ; a Parallel,
a Simile, a Description. Another exercise will take the form
of paraphrasing poetry into prose and the reverse process.
There is also much advantage in attempting the same subject,
say an epistle, in two diverse styles. Or one motive may be
expressed in four or five different metres. Further, an identical
topic may be propounded both for verse and for prose, alike in
Latin and in Greek. An affirmation may be set to be proved
by three or four differing lines of argument. Perhaps the most
useful exercise of all consists in construing from Greek into
Latin, practice in which demands diligent attention. For in
this exercise we are committed to three distinct operations :
first, we have to analyse the construction of the passage in the
older tongue : next, we are forced to appreciate carefully the
peculiar genius of each language and to note the principles
which are common to both : thirdly, in producing an accurate
rendering from the Greek we are exercised in moving freely

amidst the resources of Roman vocabulary and sentence-structure. So exacting a task claims whatever stimulus, encouragement and skilled aid the master has to offer to the pupil; who will further find inspiration in the reading of model passages of a similar theme to that which he has in hand.

§ 9.   ORIGINAL COMPOSITION; ITS VARIETY; THE METHOD OF AIDING THE STUDENT; CORRECTION OF EXERCISES. 525 F—526 F.

It is now time to call for original composition: in which we leave the task of developing a stated theme to the taste and industry of the pupil himself. The right choice of subjects for such exercises is a test of the Master's talent. Suppose an *Epistle* to be required, say of congratulation, or of condolence, or expostulation, or of some other recognised type, the Master should limit himself to indicating certain characteristics of structure or phrasing, common to each variety, and then those which may be specially appropriate to the kind of letter actually proposed. The same method will apply to exercises in *formal Oratory*,—a declamation in praise of Socrates, or in denunciation of Caesar; against reliance on riches, or in favour of Greek Letters; for the married life or against it; against pilgrimages, or in praise of them.

This will lead to the study of the *art* of Oratory as laid down by Cicero and Quintilian. For the subjects proposed as above must be treated in accordance with accepted methods. The master should suggest the number of propositions to be set out on a given theme, of the arguments to be employed, and of the proofs to be adduced in support of each; and the sources from which these may be drawn. This constitutes a kind of skeleton-form of the oration, to be filled in to suit the actual subject selected. Further, the pupil should be led to consider the various methods by which he may adorn his treatment of the argument, such as simile and contrast, parallel cases, moral reflection, adages, anecdotes, parables, and so on; and he should have some guidance in choice of figure and metaphor as aids to ornament in style. In regard to the logical ordering of argument as a whole, the student should be taught to attend to the niceties of exposition,—the exordium, the transition, the peroration; for each of these has its own peculiar excellence, and each, moreover, admits of the merit not only of precision but also of elegance.

Seven or eight exercises of this kind done under careful supervision should be sufficient to enable the pupil to lay out matter for original prose composition without help. Amongst suitable subjects for the purpose are those drawn from legend and ancient history, such as these: "Menelaus before a Trojan assembly claims the restoration of Helen"; "Phalaris presses the priests of Delphi to accept his Brazen Bull as an offering to the god"; "Cicero is warned to reject the offers of Mark Antony." As regards the *correction* of compositions, the Master will note his approval of passages which shew ingenuity in *selection* of material, and in its *treatment*, and in *imitation.* He will censure omission or bad arrangement of matter, exaggerations, carelessness, awkwardness of expression. He will at the same time point out how corrections may be suitably made, and ask for a re-writing of the exercise. Yet, after all, his chief aim will be to stimulate his pupils by calling attention to the progress made by this one or by the other, thus arousing the spirit of emulation in the class.

§ 10. The Best Methods of Procedure in Reading an Author in Class: 526 f—528 c.

In reading a classic let the Master avoid the practice, common to inferior teachers, of taking it as the text for universal and irrelevant commentary. Respect the writer, and let it be your rule to rest content with explaining and illustrating his meaning. This would be the method I advise, say, in taking a class through a play of Terence. You begin by offering an appreciation of the author, and state what is necessary concerning his life and surroundings, his talent, and the characteristics of his style. You next consider comedy as an example of a particular form of literature, and its interest for the student : the origin and meaning of the term itself, the varieties of Comedy, and the Terentian prosody. Now you proceed to treat briefly and clearly the argument of the play, taking each situation in due course. Side by side with this you will handle the diction of the writer ; noting any conspicuous elegance, or such peculiarities as archaism, novel usage, Graecisms ; bringing out anything that is involved or obscure in phrases or sentence-forms ; marking, where necessary, derivations and orthography, metaphors and other rhetorical artifices. Parallel passages should next be brought under notice, similarities and contrasts in treatment observed, and direct borrowings traced—no difficult task when we are comparing a Latin poet with his Greek predecessors. The last factor in the lesson consists in the moral applications which it suggests ; the story of Orestes and Pylades, or of Tantalus, are obvious examples.

It may be wise in some cases to open the reading of a fresh book by arousing interest in its broader significance. For instance, the Second Eclogue of Vergil must be treated as something more than a purely grammatical or literary exercise. " The essence of friendship," the Master would begin, " lies in similarity. Violently contradictory natures are incapable of mutual affection. The stronger and the more numerous the ties of taste and interest the more durable is the bond." This, amplified by apt adages and wise reflections, of which literature is full, will serve to draw the pupil's thought to the more general aspects of his reading. But it is only a Master of ability, insight and wide culture, to whom such a method is possible. A store of pertinent quotations is the product of careful reading. For instance, in illustration of this particular theme, he will adduce such quotations as this : " cascus cascam ducit : balbus balbum rectius intelligit : semper graculus arridet graculo," and others of the same import. Again, the master will have learnt from his knowledge of men that extreme differences of fortunes or of intellectual tastes do not consist with abiding friendship, that a fool laughs at a man of education, a boor has nothing in common with a courtier. He knows that there is a complete lack of sympathy between the Stoic and the Epicurean, the philosopher and the attorney, the poet and the divine, the orator and the recluse. See, too, what advantage learning gives to the master in enforcing the same theme from tradition and from history. He can refer to Castor and Pollux, to Romulus and Remus, to Cain and Abel. The beautiful myth of Narcissus will, in able hands, prove a parable of striking force. What has more likeness to ourselves than our own reflection ? Thus, when one man of learning feels drawn to another, is he not in truth attracted by the reflection of himself ? And so of a man of wise temperance, or a man of integrity, conscious of similar excellence in another. Upon such recognition of identical qualities is friendship based,—I mean the frank, open and abiding friendship which alone deserves the name. The Platonic myth of the two types of Aphrodite, the celestial and the profane, may be adduced to prove that true affection can subsist between the good alone. For where excellence is only upon one side, friendship is but a fleeting and insecure thing. Now it is as a parable of unstable friendship that the Master should treat this Eclogue. Alexis is of the town, Corydon a countryman ; Corydon a shepherd, Alexis a man of society. Alexis cultivated, young, graceful ; Corydon rude, crippled, his youth far behind him. Hence the impossibility of a true friendship. The lesson finally left on the mind of the pupil is that it is the prudent part to choose friends among those whose tastes and characters agree with our own. Such methods of treating a classical story, by forcing attention to the moral to be deduced from it, will serve to counteract any harm which a more literal interpretation might possibly convey. After all, it is what a reader brings to a passage rather than what he finds there which is the real source of mischief.

§ 11. An Introduction to Literary Criticism is afforded by such a Method of Classical Instruction. 528 C—529 B.

Speaking generally, it is advisable to introduce every new book read by indicating its chief characteristics, and then setting out its argument. The characteristics of *Epigram* are aptness and point; of *Tragedy* emotion, the various types of which and their exciting causes must be distinguished. In a great play the argument of each speech, the logical fence of the dialogue, the scene where the action is laid, the period, and the surroundings, call for attention in due order. *Comedy* suggests a different method of introductory treatment: a more familiar setting, lighter, less strenuous emotions, are common to every comedy, though each play will require its own prefatory discussion. In beginning the " Andria," the master will note the contrast of Chremes and Simo, as types of old age, of Pamphilus and Charinus as examples of young men. And so through other plays. The Eclogues of Vergil will be shewn to have their setting in a Golden Age; their ideas, similes, comparisons, are drawn from pastoral life; the emotions depicted are far from complex; the shepherd's delight is in simple melody and the wisdom of maxim and proverb, his reverence is for traditional lore and augury. A historical book, epic or satire, dialogue or fable, will be introduced each in its appropriate way, before the text is touched upon, and the excellence or the defect of the piece emphasised.

Most important is it that the student be brought to learn

for himself the true method of such criticism, that he may distinguish good literature from mediocrity.   Hence the value of
acquaintance with the judgments to be found in the oratorical
writings of Cicero and Quintilian ; in Seneca and in the old
grammarians such as Donatus.   Once acquired, this power of
insight into the mind of the great writers will lead to a habit
of general criticism of character and situation.   The student
will put such questions to himself as these : Why did Cicero
feign to be afraid in his defence of Milo ?   Why did Vergil
depict Turnus as a second hero ?   But enough to indicate what
I mean by literary criticism.

§ 12.   Progress in Classical Knowledge depends upon
    the Learning and the Skill of the Master.
    529 B—530 A.

What has been laid down above as the function of the
schoolmaster implies, I allow, that he be a person of no slight
learning and experience.   But, given these qualities, I have no
doubt that the class will speedily absorb the kind of knowledge
which I have indicated.   The first steps may be slow and
laborious, but exercise and right instruction make progress
certain.   I only stipulate that the material selected be of
sound classical excellence (nothing mediaeval), and the method
skilfully adapted to the growing comprehension ; the teacher
forcing nothing, but working forward gradually from the
broader aspects of his subject to the more minute.   Success
then is assured.   One further counsel, however.   The master
must not omit to set as an exercise the reproduction of what
he has given to the class.   It involves time and trouble to the
teacher, I know well, but it is essential.   A literal reproduction
of the matter taught is, of course, not required, but the
substance of it presented in the pupil's own way.   Personally
I disapprove of the practice of taking down a lecture just as it

is delivered.   For this prevents reliance upon memory which should, as time goes on, need less and less of that external aid which note-taking supplies.

§ 13.   CONCLUSION.   530 A—B.

Such weight do I ascribe to right method in instruction—and I include herein choice of material as well as of modes of imparting it—that I undertake by its means to carry forward youths of merely average intelligence to a creditable standard of scholarship, and of conversation also, in Latin and Greek, at an age when, under the common schoolmaster of to-day, the same youths would be just stammering through their Primer. With the foundations thus rightly laid a boy may confidently look forward to success in the higher range of learning.   He will, when he looks back, admit that the essential condition of his attainment was the care which was devoted to the beginnings of his education.

THE TREATISE

De Pueris statim ac liberaliter instituendis,

WILLIAM, DUKE OF CLEVES, 1529.

ERAS. *Op.* i. 489.

CHAPTER VII.

*DE PUERIS STATIM AC LIBERALITER INSTITUEN-
DIS* LIBELLUS; *or,* THE ARGUMENT OF ERASMUS
OF ROTTERDAM, *THAT CHILDREN SHOULD
STRAIGHTWAY FROM THEIR EARLIEST YEARS
BE TRAINED IN VIRTUE AND SOUND LEARN-
ING.* 1529. Addressed to WILLIAM, DUKE OF CLEVES.

§ 1. THE ARGUMENT AT LARGE: i. 489 A—D.

I DESIRE to urge upon you, Illustrious Duke, to take into
your early and serious consideration the future nurture and
training of the son lately born to you. For, with Chrysippus,
I contend that the young child must be led to sound learning
whilst his wit is yet unwarped, his age tender, his mind flexible
and tenacious. In manhood we remember nothing so well as
the truths which we imbibed in our youth. Wherefore I beg
you to put aside all idle chatter which would persuade you that
this early childhood is unmeet for the discipline and the effort
of studies.

The arguments which I shall enlarge upon are the following.
First, the beginnings of learning are the work of memory, which
in young children is most tenacious. Next, as nature has
implanted in us the instinct to seek for knowledge, can we be
too early in obeying her behest? Thirdly, there are not a few
things which it imports greatly that we should know well, and
which we can learn far more readily in our tender years.
I speak of the elements of Letters, Grammar, and the fables

and stories found in the ancient Poets. Fourthly, since children, as all agree, are fit to acquire manners, why may they not acquire the rudiments of learning? And seeing that they must needs be busy about something, what else can; be better approved? For how much wiser to amuse their hours with Letters, than to see them frittered away in aimless trifling!

It is, however, objected, first, that such knowledge as can be thus early got is of slight value. But even so, why despise it, if so be it serve as the foundation for much greater things? For if in early childhood a boy acquire such useful elements he will be free to apply his youth to higher knowledge, to the saving of his time. Moreover, whilst he is thus occupied in sound learning he will perforce be kept from some of the temptations which befall youth, seeing that nothing engages the whole mind more than studies. And this I count a high gain in such times as ours.

Next, it is urged that by such application health may be somewhat endangered. Supposing this to be true, still the compensation is great, for by discipline the mind gains far more in alertness and in vigour than the body is ever likely to lose. Watchfulness, however, will prevent any such risk as is imagined. Also, for this tender age you will employ a teacher who will win and not drive, just as you will choose such subjects as are pleasant and attractive, in which the young mind will find recreation rather than toil.

Furthermore, I bid you remember that a man ignorant of Letters is no man at all, that human life is a fleeting thing, that youth is easily enticed into sin, that early manhood is absorbed by clashing interests, that old age is unproductive, and that few reach it. How then can you allow your child, in whom you yourself live again, to lose even one of those precious years in which he may begin to acquire those means whereby he may elevate his whole life and keep at arm's length temptation and evil?

§ 2. The First Law : Education must begin from the very earliest years. 486 D—490 A.

I rejoice at your determination that your son shall be early initiated into the arts of true learning and the wisdom of sound philosophy. Herein consists the full duty of fatherhood, the care and guidance of the spirit of him for whose creation you are responsible. And now for my first precept. Do not follow the fashion, which is too common amongst us, of allowing the early years of childhood to pass without fruit of instruction, and of deferring its first steps until the allurements of indulgence have made application more difficult.

§ 3. The Importance of skilled Control from the outset. 490 A—491 D.

I urge you, therefore, to look even now for a scholar of high character and attainment to whom you may commit the charge of your boy's mind and disposition, leaving to wisely chosen nurses the care of his bodily welfare. By thus dividing control the child will be saved from the mischievous kindnesses and indulgence of foolish serving-women, and of weak relatives, who decry learning as so much poison, and babble about the unfitness of the growing boy for Letters. To such chatter you will turn a deaf ear. For, remembering that the welfare of your son demands not less circumspection from you than a man will gladly bestow upon his horse, his castle, his estate, you will take heed only to the wisest counsel which you can secure, and ponder that with yourself. Consider, in this regard, the care which a boy's mother will lavish upon his bodily frame, how she will take thought should she but faintly suspect in him a tendency to become wry-necked, cross-eyed, crook-backed or splay-footed, or by any mischance prove ill-formed in proportions of his figure. Think, too, how she is apt to busy herself about his milk, his meat, his bath, his exercise, following herein the wise foresight of Galen; will she defer this carefulness until the seventh year? No, from the very day of his birth charge is taken lest mischief hap, and wisely, knowing that a weakly manhood may be thus avoided. Nay, even before the child be born, how diligent is the wise mother to see that no harm come to herself for her child's sake.

No one blames this as undue or untimely care for the young life. Why then do men neglect that part of our nature, the nobler part, whereby we are rightly called *men*; we bestow, justly, our effort upon the mortal body; yet have we but slight regard for the immortal spirit.

Are other instances needed? Then think of the training of a colt, how early it is begun; or of the work of the husbandman who fashions and trains the sapling to suit his taste or to further the fruitfulness of the tree. This is a task of human skill and purpose; and the sooner these are applied the more sure the result.

§ 4. The Supreme Importance of Education to human Well-being, 491 D—492 A.

To dumb creatures Mother Nature has given an innate power or instinct, whereby they may in great part attain to their right capacities. But Providence in granting to man alone the privilege of reason has thrown the burden of development of the human being upon training. Well, therefore, has it been said that the first means, the second, and the third means to happiness is right training or education. Sound education is the condition of real wisdom. And if an education which is soundly planned and carefully carried out is the very fount of all human excellence, so, on the other hand, careless and unworthy training is the true source of folly and vice. This *capacity for training* is, indeed, the chief aptitude which has been bestowed upon humanity. Unto the animals nature has given swiftness of foot or of wing, keenness of sight, strength or size of frame, and various weapons of defence. To Man, instead of physical powers, is given a mind apt for training; in this single gift all others are comprised, for him, at least, who turns it to due profit. We see that where native instinct is strong—as in squirrels or bees—capacity for being taught is wanting. Man, lacking instinct, can do little or nothing of innate power; scarce can he eat, or walk, or speak, unless he be guided thereto. How then can we expect that he should become competent to the duties of life unless straightway and with much diligence he be brought under the discipline of a worthy education? Let me enforce this by the well-known story of Lycurgus, who, to convince the Spartans, brought out two hounds, one of good mettle, but untrained and therefore useless in the field, and the other poorly bred and well-drilled at his work; "Nature," he said, "may be strong, yet Education is more powerful still."

§ 5. PARENTS WILL NOT SEE THAT IN THEIR CHILDREN'S INTERESTS EDUCATION MATTERS MOST. 492 A—C.

Yet we see a father, who bestows no little heed to ensure that his horses and dogs are of the right breed, careless whether his son be properly trained that he may prove an honour to his parents, and helpful to them in their later years, a worthy husband, a brave and useful citizen. Yet for whom does such a father plant and build? for whose behoof does he contrive wealth by land and by sea? For his children, forsooth. But what profit or honour lies in inheriting such things if their possessor has no skill to use them aright? Who will fashion ingeniously a harp for one who has not learnt to play upon it? Or furnish a library for one who knows or cares nothing for books? Why, therefore, heap up riches for one who knows not how to employ them? For note this well: that he who

provides for a son who is worthily educated, provides means to
virtue : but whoso saves for a child endowed with rude
temper and uncultivated wit is but ministering to opportunities of indulgence and mischief. It is the height of folly
that one should train the body to be comely, and wholly
neglect that excellence of mind which alone can guide it
aright. For I hesitate not to affirm that those things which
men covet for their sons—health, riches, and repute—are more
surely secured by virtue and learning—the gifts of education—
than by any other means. True, the highest gifts of all no
man can give to another, even to his child ; but we can store his
mind with that sound wisdom and learning whereby he may
attain to the best.

§ 6.   Other Parents neglect the duty of Education
until too late.   492 c—493 b.

Further, there are those—sometimes men of repute for
practical wisdom—who err in deferring education till the stage
when the boy finds the rudiments of learning irksome to
acquire. Yet these same fathers will be over-anxious for their
children's future fortune even before they be born. We hear
of astrologers called in : " the child," it is affirmed, " will be a
born soldier." " Then let us plan to enter him into the king's
service." " He will be the very type of a churchman." " Then
let us work for a bishopric or an abbey for him." And this is
not thought to be taking care prematurely for a career yet far-
distant. Why then refuse to provide not less early that the
boy may be worthily prepared to fill it : so that he grow up not
only to be a captain of a troop, but a fit and reputable officer
of the commonwealth ; not merely to be called a bishop, but
to be made worthy of his charge ? Men seem to me to have
regard to nothing less than to that end to which all these
other ends are subordinate. Lands, castles, furnishings, dress,
servants, all are well cared for, and are of the best : the son of

the house alone is left untrained, untaught, ignorant, boorish. A man buys a slave; he may be useless at first, as knowing nothing. Straightway he is tried, and it is quickly found what he can best do, and to that craft he is diligently trained. But the same man will wholly neglect his son's up-bringing. "He will have enough to live upon," he will say. "But *not* enough to live a worthy life," I rejoin. "What need of learning? He will have wealth." "Then the more need of all the guidance that Letters and Philosophy can bestow." How active, for instance, do princes show themselves to get for their sons as large a dominion as they can, whilst no men seem to care less that their heirs should be duly educated to fulfil the responsibility that must fall to them. The saying of Alexander is often quoted: "Were I not Alexander I would be Diogenes." But Plutarch is right in his reflection, that the very fact that he was lord of so great an empire was, had he known it, reason enough for him to desire to be a philosopher as well. How much more does that father give his son who gives him that by which he may *live worthily* than he who merely gives that whereby he may *live*!

§ 7. REASON THE TRUE MARK OF MAN. 493 B—494 A.

Now it is the possession of Reason which constitutes a Man. If trees or wild beasts grow, men, believe me, are fashioned. Men in olden time who led their life in forests, driven by the mere needs and desires of their natures, guided by no laws, with no ordering in communities, are to be judged rather as savage beasts than as men. For Reason, the mark of humanity, has no place where all is determined by appetite. It is beyond dispute that a man not instructed through reason in philosophy and sound learning is a creature lower than a brute, seeing that there is no beast more wild or more harmful than a man who is driven hither and thither by ambition, or desire, anger or envy, or lawless temper. Therefore do I conclude that he that provides not that his own son may presently be instructed in the best learning is neither a man nor the son of a man.   Would it not be a horror to look upon a human soul clad in the form of a beast, as Circe is fabled to have done by her spells?   But is it not worse that a father should see his own image slowly but surely becoming the dwelling-place of a brute's nature?   It is said a bear's cub is at birth but an ill-formed lump which by a long process of licking is brought into shape.   Nature, in giving you a son, presents you, let me say, a rude, unformed creature, which it is your part to fashion so that it may become indeed a man. If this fashioning be neglected you have but an animal still : if it be contrived earnestly and wisely, you have, I had almost said, what may prove a being not far from a God.

§ 8.   EDUCATION OF THEIR CHILDREN IS A DUTY OWED BY
       PARENTS TO THE COMMONWEALTH AND TO GOD.
       494 A—495 A.

Straightway from the child's birth it is meet that he should begin to learn the things which properly belong to his well-being.   Therefore, bestow especial pains upon his tenderest years, as Vergil teaches.   Handle the wax whilst it is soft, mould the clay whilst it is moist, dye the fleece before it gather stains.   It is no light task to educate our children aright. Yet think—to lighten the burden—how much comfort and honour parents derive from children well brought up : and reflect how much sorrow is engendered of them that grow up evilly.   And further, no man is born to himself, no man is born to idleness.   Your children are begotten not to yourself alone, but to your country : not to your country alone, but to God.   Paul teaches that women are saved by reason that they bring up their children in the pursuit of virtue.   God will straitly charge the parents with their children's faults ; there-fore, except they bring up their little ones from the very first to live aright, they themselves will share the penalty. For a child rightly educated is a comfort and a joy to his parents, but a foolish child brings upon them shame, it may be poverty, and old age before their time. Nay, I know not a few men of note and place who have lost their sons by lamentable deaths, the results of evil life; some fathers, indeed, which out of many children had scarce one surviving. And this from no other cause than that they have made portions for their sons, but have taken no heed to train them. They are called murderers who kill their new-born children: but such kill the mere body. How great, then, is their crime who destroy the soul? For what other thing is the death of the soul than to live in folly and sin? Such fathers do no less wrong to their country, to which, as far as in them lies, they give pestilent citizens. They do, equally, a wrong against God, at whose hands they receive their offspring to bring it up to ' His service.

§ 9. Vicious Habits in which parents encourage their children. 495 B—496 A.

But there is an education which is worse than none at all. For how shall we describe those who go about to imbue the tender mind with wickedness, before it be able to know what wickedness is? For example, how can a child grow up to modesty and humility who in his very infancy totters in the purple? He cannot yet sound his letters, but he knows what cramoisie is, and brocade: he craves for dainty dishes and disdainfully pushes away simple food. The tailor contrives some new marvel in cap or tunic; straightway we must dress up the child therein; we tickle his vanity, and then we wonder that he develops irritation and self-conceit! The serving-women teach him evil words, and for their amusement tempt him to repeat them. He is brought up to sit through long feastings; he hears the noise of jesters, minstrels, and dancers. The guests, nay, his own father, sprawl drunkenly in his presence. And yet you pray that he may grow up honest, temperate, and pure. I would also denounce those who bring up their sons to a love of war. Straight from their mother's arms they are bidden to finger swords and shields, to thrust and strike. With such tastes, already deeply rooted with years, they are handed over to a master, who is blamed for their indifference to worthy interests. If it be urged that parents find some pleasure in this evil precocity of their children, let me ask if any true father will rather that his son pick up gross speech, and copy some shameful act, than hear him, with stammering tongue, utter something worthy and true? Nature has made the first years of our life prone to imitation—though perhaps it is easier to that age to copy evil than good—and with imitativeness she has given also tenacity in retention. Hence the mischief that accrues when mothers are allowed to keep their children in their lap until they are seven years of age: if they want playthings do they not see that monkeys or toy-dogs would serve them just as well? For no one can exaggerate the importance of these years for character, nor the difficulty which such enervating, debasing up-bringing at this stage creates for the teachers who then take over the task. Menander and Paul were perfectly right: such "evil communications corrupt good manners."

§ 10. SAVAGE NATURE TEACHES THE SAME LESSON OF CARE FOR EARLY TRAINING OF THE YOUNG.   496 A—E.

But if neither love nor reason suffice to teach us our duty, let us turn to the example of the brute creation. For mankind has admittedly learned therefrom much useful knowledge. For instance, the hippopotamus has shown us the method of cutting a vein; the ibis the use of the clyster, so much approved by physicians. The stag has taught men that dittany is helpful in drawing out arrows, and that the eating of crabs is an antidote to the poison of spiders.   Goats have proved that ivy is a remedy in certain affections.   Lizards use dittany against the bite of snakes, their standing foes.   From the weasel we learnt the use of rue, from the serpent the use of fennel in affections of the eye.   The dragon is our warrant for employing lettuce in sickness.   Much more of such knowledge have we derived from dumb animals.   Practical arts also have been acquired from them to our great profit.   Nay, I might almost say that there is nothing which advantages the life of man of which nature has not shown us some example in wild creatures, to the end that they who have not learnt philosophy and the rational arts may be admonished by them what men may do.   Attend, therefore, to that which we may learn from them as to the training of children.   We see that every savage creature is not content only to produce its young, but teaches it, and shapes it to fulfil its proper function.   A bird is, indeed, created with instinct for flight, but we see how the fledgling is led on and guided in its first attempts by the parent birds.   The cat teaches her kittens to watch, to spring, to kill. The stag leads her young in chase, brings them to the leap, shows the methods of escape from pursuit.   Authors have recounted to us that the elephant and the dolphin exhibit a veritable art in educating their young ones.   So of nightingales—the old bird goes in front, calls back to, and corrects, the young one, which in turn follows and obeys.   And I affirm that, as the instinct of the dog is to hunt, of the bird to fly, of the horse to gallop, so the natural bent of man is to philosophy and right conduct.   As every creature most readily learns that for which it is created, therefore will Man, with but slight effort, be brought to follow that to which Nature has given him so strong an instinct, viz. excellence, *but on one condition* : that Nature be reinforced by the wise energy of the Educator.

§ 11. THE THREE FACTORS IN INDIVIDUAL PROGRESS:
NATURE, METHOD, PRACTICE. 496 E—497 A.

Can anything be more deplorable than to have to admit
that, whilst an unreasoning animal performs by instinct its
duty towards its offspring, Man, the creature of Reason, is
blind to what he owes to Nature, to parental responsibility,
and to God? But I will now consider definitely the three
conditions which determine individual progress. They are
Nature, Training and Practice. By *Nature*, I mean, partly,
innate capacity for being trained, partly, native bent towards
excellence. By *Training*, I mean the skilled application of
instruction and guidance. By *Practice*, the free exercise on
our own part of that activity which has been implanted by
Nature and is furthered by Training. Nature without skilled
Training must be imperfect, and Practice without the method
which Training supplies leads to hopeless confusion.

§ 12. THE ERROR OF THOSE WHO THINK THAT EXPERIENCE
GIVES ALL THE EDUCATION THAT MEN NEED. 497 A—F.

They err, therefore, who affirm that wisdom is won by
handling affairs and by contact with life, without aid from the
teaching of philosophy. Tell me, can a man run his best in
the dark? Or, can a gladiator conquer if he be blindfold?
The precepts of philosophy—which is knowledge applied to
life—are, as it were, the eyes of the mind, and lighten us to the
consciousness of what we may do and may not do. A long and
manifold experience is, beyond doubt, of great profit, but only
to such as by the wisdom of learning have acquired an intelligent and informed judgment. Besides, philosophy teaches us
more in one year than our own individual experience can teach
us in thirty, and its teaching carries none of the risks which the

method of learning by experience of necessity brings with it. For example, you educate your son to the mystery of medicine. Do you allow him to rely on the method of "experience" in order that he may learn to distinguish between poisons and healing drugs? Or, do you send him to the treatises? It is an unhappy education which teaches the master mariner the rudiments of navigation by shipwrecks: or the Prince the true way of kingship by revolutions, invasions or slaughter. Is it not the wise part to learn beforehand how to avoid mischiefs rather than with the pains of experience to remedy them? Thus Philip of Macedon put his son Alexander to school with Aristotle that he might learn philosophy of him, to the end that when a king he should be saved from doing things which must be repented of. Thus education shews us in brief what we should follow, what avoid; she does not wait till we have suffered the evil results of our mistakes, but warns us in advance against courses which will lead to failure and misery. Let us, therefore, firmly knit up this threefold cord: let Nature be by Training guided to wise ends, let Nature and Training, thus united, be made perfect by right Practice.

When we observe animal life, we notice that each creature learns, first of all, to perform those things which preserve life and to avoid those things which make for pain and destruction. This is true not less of plants, as we can see when we contrast the close-knit tree of the exposed sea-coast and its fellow spreading luxuriantly in warmth and shelter. All living things strive to develop according to their proper nature. What is the proper nature of Man? Surely it is to live the life of Reason, for reason is the peculiar prerogative of man. And what is it that in man makes for pain and destruction? Surely it is Folly, which is life without reason. It is, then, certain that desire for excellence and aversion to folly come readily to man if only his nature, as yet empty of content, be from the outset of life filled with right activities. Yet we hear extravagant complaints "how prone is child-nature to wrong, how hard to win to excellence." But herein men accuse nature unjustly. Parents themselves are to blame in taking little heed for that which the child imbibes in his early years.

§ 13. The Importance of choosing aright the Child's first Master: Obstacles arising from Ignorance, Indifference, Parsimony.   497 f—498 e.

I affirm that at the present day three grave mistakes are rife in respect of the first stage of education. Either, there is no education at all: or it is begun too late: or it is entrusted to wrong hands.

With the first of these I have already dealt, and have proved that fathers guilty of this neglect are no fathers at all. And I have shewn that the second error is only less perilous. It remains now to discuss the third. Parents fall into the mistake of making a wrong choice of teacher through ignorance, or rather, perhaps, indifference. A man would not plead that he does not know what kind of man has charge of his stud, or his farm; but he seems content to know nothing about the man who has charge of a far more precious possession, his own son. He will shew much sense in ordering the several duties of his servants. The bailiff, the house-steward, the cook, are chosen with much discretion. The son of the house, on the other hand, is turned over to some dullard or idler, who is regarded as useless for a more serious task. And then people talk about "Nature's fault"!

Or take the case of a father who grudges the pay of a decent tutor, whom he puts off with a lower wage than he gives his groom. Yet the same niggard will spend a fortune upon banquets and wine, upon play, jesters and his mistress. "The cheapest thing going to-day," says the Satirist, "is education." "I pay my cook," said Crates ironically, "four pounds a year; but a philosopher can be hired for about sixpence, and a tutor for three half-pence." So to-day a man stands aghast at the

w.   13 thought of paying for his boy's education a sum which would buy a foal or hire a farm servant. At a single feast and the dicing that follows he will lose two hundred pounds, but he complains of extravagance if his son's education cost him twenty. Frugality? Yes, by all means : but in this matter of all others frugality is no economy ; it is another name for madness.

Again, there are those who are ready to consider well the choice of a master, but are ready to select a man merely to oblige a friend. The suitable man is rejected ; the incompetent person fixed upon ; easy compliance, lacking any sense of responsibility, decides it all. This is the indifference I spoke of ; but it is more, it is outrageous folly. For, after all, it is not only a question of the boy himself, but of his parents, his house, nay, of the commonwealth itself to which he will belong.

§ 14. THE NURSLING.   498 E—499 A.

The child's *nature*, as we have said before, is the primitive endowment with which he is born, which human purpose can do nothing to determine in advance. Still there may be some qualification to this. For instance, it imports much in regard to the child that the father have chosen a wife of sound health and of good stock, with wholesome and virtuous habits. The links that bind together mind and body are so close that it cannot be but that the physical nature affects the spiritual. Again, as the child reflects the disposition of its parents, let them observe moderation in appetites and keep strict guard over themselves that they should be temperate, not given to anger ; the father sober, the mother, especially during the months preceding the child's birth, of good conscience and free from anxieties. Further, it will be good for the child that it be nursed by the mother ; should necessity arise for a foster-mother, she must be strong and of right disposition. Neglect in this respect may have enduring results for harm, physical and moral. For it is at this period that education truly begins; not, as some would have it, at the seventh year— or the seventeenth!

§ 15. THE TUTOR AND HIS RELATION TO THE PARENTS. 499 A—C.

But the most important of the forces that mould the development of the child is the influence of the tutor. In choosing him we cannot show too great diligence, enquire too carefully, or apply too rigorous tests. The right person once secured, we are not to conclude that all is done. Two cautions, indeed, seem necessary. First, that masters, like doctors, must not be changed except for serious cause. The repeated be- ginnings-afresh are as the weaving and unweaving of Penelope's web. I have known children who have, by the folly of their parents, had as many as a dozen masters before they were as many years of age. Secondly, the responsibility of parents for the education of their children in no way ceases with the appointment of the master. Let the father often visit the schoolroom and note the progress made. Amongst the virtues praised in Aemilius Paulus this is recorded, that as often as his duties to the State allowed he would be present at the lessons of his sons. This was also the custom of Pliny. I speak, however, now of young children: as they grow up it is wiser to remove them somewhat more from their parents' eye.

§ 16. INDIVIDUALITY OF THE CHILD; ITS RECOGNITION BY THE TEACHER; ITS IMPORTANCE IN DETERMINING THE CHOICE OF SUBJECTS TO BE TAUGHT. 499 C—500 A.

By the *nature* of a man we mean, as a rule, that which is common to Man as such: the characteristic, namely, of being guided by Reason. But we may mean something less broad than this : the characteristic peculiar to each personality, which we may call *individuality*. Thus one child may shew a native bent to Mathematics, another to Divinity, another to Rhetoric, or Poetry, another to War. So strongly disposed are certain types of mind to certain studies that they cannot be won to others ; the very attempt in that direction sets up a positive repulsion. I was once very intimate with a student, who, having attained a high level in Greek and Latin scholarship, and in some other of the liberal arts, was sent by his patron the Archbishop to the University to study Law. But this discipline he found wholly repugnant to his nature. " I am," he told me, " so averse to the Law that when I force myself to its study I feel as if a sword were being driven through my heart." Minds of that strong determination ought not to be forced against their instinct ; it is almost as though we should train a cow to box or a donkey to play the violin.

The Master will be wise to observe such natural inclination, such individuality, in the early stages of child life, since we learn most easily the things which conform to it. It is not, I believe, a vain thing to try and infer from the face and bearing of a boy what disposition he will show. Nature has not omitted to give us marks for our guidance in this respect. Aristotle wrote a work on physiognomy ; and Vergil bids us recognise the differences which distinguish one type of cattle from another in regard to the uses to which we may put them. However, I am personally of opinion that where the method is sound, where teaching and practice go hand in hand, any discipline may ordinarily be acquired by the flexible intellect of man. What, indeed, should be beyond his powers when, as we are told, an elephant has been trained to walk a tight-rope ?

§ 17.   THE EFFECTS OF TRAINING UPON NATURE IN HUMAN
BEINGS ARE CERTAIN AND ARE FAR-REACHING.   500 A—
501 A.

Making all allowance, however, for the factor of nature in
education, which is, as we said, self-determined, it is not
questioned that the other two, Training and Practice, are
under human control.   Training, or Reason brought to bear
upon Nature, implies capacity for learning; practice, readiness
to self-exertion.   "But," it is asked, "can you begin Education
at an age when capacity for learning has not yet developed,
and when continuous exertion cannot be expected?"   My
reply to this is that children are universally taught manners
and conduct at the same age; and this implies capacity for
effort and for learning.   A rudimentary capacity, I admit:
but we are only considering rudiments of Letters and of
philosophy, or of morals and duty.   Animals are trained by
degrees according to their powers, and so should children be
inured slowly to study.   Nature has implanted in the young
an ability of their own.   It is not for them, I allow, to learn
the *Ethics* of Aristotle or the *Epistles* of St Paul.   But if, for
instance, you correct their manners at table, they obey and
amend; when they go to church they learn to bend the knee
and to bear themselves reverently.   Such rudiments of modesty
and piety the child acquires before he can speak properly, and,
thus early learnt, they abide in mind and habit until, as the
boy grows older, they form a living part of his higher nature.
Notice Nature's teaching.   We see how at first the newly-born
child knows no difference between his parents and strangers.
By degrees he distinguishes his mother, then his father.
Respect, obedience, affection follow.   From his parents he
learns to repress anger and vindictiveness, to make up a
quarrel with a kiss; he learns to listen without chattering;
to rise in the presence of his elders; to lift his cap as he

passes a Calvary. Thus it is established that what is poured into our nature, so to say, in our earliest years becomes an integral part of us. Hence the error, the grave error, of the opinion which maintains that the halting steps of the child avail nothing to the progress of the boy. "It is always best to use the best," even from the very first. For that habit will endure longest which you impart whilst the nature is yet tender, void, and eager to imitate the actions of others. Clay, perhaps, may be sometimes made too moist to retain the mould impressed upon it; but I doubt if there be any period of a child's progress when he is too young to learn. "No age," said Seneca, "is too late for learning." Perhaps. But it is my conviction that no age is too *early*, in respect, that is, of that knowledge which Nature has fittingly prescribed for it. By which I mean, that nature has planted in the youngest child an ape-like instinct of imitation and a delight in activity. From this quality springs his first capacity for learning. Hence as soon as he is born the child may be trained in conduct; and as soon as he can talk he may by virtue of the same imitative instinct be trained in speech and letters. Now note this analogy. As in the nursling action anticipates speech, so throughout life conduct takes the prior place, and learning and the liberal arts must prove themselves her hand-maidens, lest erudition haply work ill rather than good to him who pursues it.

§ 18. The Age at which Instruction should begin
to be considered. 501 A—C.

The opinion is widely held that children should not be set to learn till they are seven years of age. Hesiod is said to have been the author of this view, but even if that be true, I should not follow him against my own judgment. It is probable, however, that this contention implies no more than this, that the laborious side of studies, such as learning by heart, repetition, long written exercises, should be avoided as far as possible in early education. If figures are to be mentioned at all, we may remember that Chrysippus judges the first *three* years to be the province of the nurse, during which period the child should imbibe right habits and lay the foundations for that edifice of character and learning which will be raised later. And I freely allow that this stage of home education is of profound importance.

§ 19.   RIGHT EXPRESSION AS THE MAIN END OF EARLY INSTRUCTION, AND ITS IMPORTANCE FOR SUBSEQUENT PROGRESS.   501 C—502 B.

The aim of instruction at the first stage should be to teach children to speak clearly and accurately, a matter in which both parent and nurse share the responsibility. Language, indeed, is not simply an end in itself, as we see when we reflect that through its neglect whole disciplines have been lost, or, at least, corrupted. Think what Theology, Medicine and Law have lost from this cause. Upon the question of early training in expression, Cicero tells us that those famous orators, the Gracchi, owed their distinction largely to Cornelia : "their first school was their mother's knee." Laelia is a similar instance, for she, like Mutia and Licinia, was brought up as a girl in an atmosphere of dignified and refined conversation. We must not forget that besides parents, tutors, serving-women, and playfellows, all have marked influence upon a child's manner of speaking. For it is in speech that the imitative instinct is specially active. We know that a German boy will pick up French unconsciously almost, but most successfully, if only he have opportunity when very young. Now if this be possible in a language which is barbarous and unformed, in which spelling never follows pronunciation, whose sounds are mere noises for which the throat of man was never framed, how much more readily should he learn the tongues of Greece and Rome? Mithridates could administer justice in two-and-twenty dialects and languages: Themistocles, when well advanced in years, learnt Persian in a twelvemonth. To what, then, may not the plastic mind and tongue of a boy attain? For the learning of a language is partly, as we have suggested, a matter of *imitation*; and it is partly a matter of *memory*. It is as instinctive with children to imitate as it is easy for them to remember; while to a man of my age it is difficult to recall exactly a fact read two days ago. How few people do we meet who have been able to learn a new language, especially in respect of accent, in middle life! Cato the elder may be quoted as one of these; but his namesake of Utica is a far more trustworthy pattern for us, as he was the more learned and eloquent of the two, and he was taught Greek from the cradle.

§ 20. The Importance of this Early Training ought to lead Parents to ask themselves how far they can follow the example of the Ancients in becoming themselves the Instructors of their Children. 502 B—503 B.

But we may not forget that children are prone to follow the allurement of the senses rather than the rule of reason; to store up in mind what is trivial or bad rather than what is of enduring worth. This fact of human nature sorely puzzled the ancient philosophers, but has its key in the Christian doctrine of Original Sin. True as this explanation is, we are not to forget the part played by faulty training, particularly in the first and most impressionable stage. Wherefore, I bid you recall how Alexander allowed that he had been unable to forget some things which he had learnt, to his hurt, from his tutor in early boyhood; and how the Romans in the days of their prime refused to yield the charge of their sons to any hired person. In those days the parents and other kinsmen taught the growing boy; for instance, it was held the truest honour to the family that as many children as possible of the name should have repute for learning.   Nowadays the mark of a noble house seems to consist in exhibiting coats of arms, in giving feasts, in play and sport; and the only service which elders perform for their sons is to provide them with rich marriages.   Meantime it is thought natural that as a child he should be left in charge of a man ignorant of learning and of illiberal condition.   In old days careful parents trained up a slave specially fit in learning that he might act as a tutor, or they bought one already skilled.   But it were wiser that the parents should qualify themselves to this task.   If it be objected that time is lacking, I point to the flagrant waste of leisure in play and entertainments, and in the stupid social "duties of our station."   He has but lukewarm love for his son who grudges the time for teaching him.   I admit that the Romans had the great advantage of a single tongue under-stood universally; but, in spite of drawbacks in our own day, certain parents of distinction have undertaken the duty of training their own children.   Amongst these I name Thomas More.   He, although deeply occupied in affairs of the State, devoted his leisure to the instruction of his wife, his son, and his daughters, both in the uprightness of life and in the liberal studies of Greek and Latin.   The common tongue of the people may be left to be picked up in the ordinary intercourse of life.

Should, however, neither parent be a suitable instructor to the child, then, I admit, we must secure the services of an able and experienced teacher.   But the father should hesitate to take an untried man.   In many things, perhaps, negligence may find its pardon; but here the eyes of Argus himself are wanted.   There is a proverb that teaches us that in war a general may not make *two* mistakes.   In planning his son's education a father dare hardly make *one*.

§ 21. THE OBJECTION THAT HEALTH IS ENDANGERED BY
CLOSE APPLICATION ON THE PART OF THE YOUNG
CHILD.   503 B—E.

We have to meet an argument against early training drawn
from the superior importance of health.   Personally I venture
to regard the mental advantages gained as outweighing some
slight risks in the matter of physical vigour.   We are not
concerned with developing athletes, but scholars and men
competent to affairs, for whom we desire adequate constitu-
tions indeed, but not the physique of a Milo.   I should,
certainly, always advise moderation in the amount of mental
exertion demanded, but I have little patience with critics who
only become anxious about the youthful constitution when
education is mooted; but who are indifferent to the far more
certain risks of over-feeding, late hours, and unsuitable dressing, which are the common indulgences allowed to children in
the classes about whom I am here concerned.   In the same
way some parents profess alarm lest premature study affect the
complexion or figure of their child.   This is justifiable to
some degree, but we ought not to think too much of such
attractions in a boy.   Here again evil habits, brawling, and
intemperance are far more serious causes of this kind of
mischief.

But if the teaching be of a wise sort the danger of harm
will be wholly negligeable.   For the effort required will be but
slight, subjects will be few, attractively taught, and adapted to
the age and tastes of the scholar.   Such study may hardly be
distinguished from play, and is a source of enjoyment to the
child.

§ 22.   THE DISPOSITION OF THE TEACHER.   503 E—504 A.

Seeing, then, that children in the earliest stage must be beguiled and not driven to learning, the first requisite in the Master is a gentle sympathetic manner, the second a knowledge of wise and attractive methods. Possessing these two important qualifications he will be able to win the pupil to find pleasure in his task.   It is a hindrance to a boy's progress, which nothing will ever nullify, when the master succeeds in making his pupil hate learning before he is old enough to like it for its own sake.   For a boy is often drawn to a subject first for his master's sake, and afterwards for its own.   Learning, like many other things, wins our liking for the reason that it is offered to us by one we love.   But, on the other hand, there is a type of man of manners so uncouth, of expression so forbidding, of speech so surly, that he repels even when he by no means intends it.   Now men of that stamp are wholly unfit to be teachers of children ; a man who loves his horse would hardly put such a man to have charge of his stable. Yet there are parents who think such a temper as I have described well adapted to breaking in the young child, thinking, perhaps, that seriousness of that sort betokens a proper gravity.   Therein may lie a great error, inasmuch as that demeanour may cloak a depraved nature, which, delighting in tyranny, cows and breaks the spirit of the pupil.   *Fear is of no real avail in education* : not even parents can train their children by this motive.   Love must be the first influence ; followed and completed by a trustful and affectionate respect, which compels obedience far more surely than dread can ever do.

§ 23. The Evil Condition of the Schools, especially the Private Schools, in the Present Day. 504 A—D.

What shall we say then of the type of school too common at the present time ? A boy scarce four years old is sent to school to a master about whose qualifications for the work no one knows anything. Often he is a man of uncouth manners, not always sober ; maybe he is an invalid, or crippled, or even mentally deficient. Anyone is good enough to put over the grammar school in popular opinion. Such a man, finding himself clothed with an unlooked for and unaccustomed authority, treats his charges as we should expect. The school is, in effect, a torture chamber ; blows and shouts, sobs and howls, fill the air. Then it is wondered that the growing boy hates learning ; and that in riper years he hates it still. There are parents who will send their children to learn reading and writing at a dame's school, kept by some incompetent, ill-tempered, perhaps drunken creature. Now as a general principle I should affirm that it is contrary to Nature that men should be placed under the exclusive control of women ; for women are not only lacking in the necessary self-control, but when aroused are prone to extreme vindictiveness and cruelty. Nor can I personally, though few agree with me, advise parents to send their sons to school in Monasteries or in the Houses of the Brethren. For, whilst allowing the teaching Brothers to be often good, kindly men, they are usually too narrow and ignorant to be fit to educate children. The monks make a good income out of their schools, which are conducted no one knows how, and are jealously hidden away in the inner recesses of the convent. So I strongly urge : Choose for your boy a *public* school, or keep him at home.

§ 24. EXCESSIVE PUNISHMENT THE CHARACTERISTIC OF
WORTHLESS SCHOOLS AND OF WEAK TEACHERS. 504 D
—507 E.

A poor master, we are prepared to find, relies almost
wholly upon fear of punishment as the motive to work. To
frighten an entire class is easier than to teach one boy properly:
for the latter is, and always must be, a task as serious as it is
honourable. It is equally true of States: the rule which
carries the respect and consent of the citizens demands higher
qualities in the Prince than does the tyranny of force.

Scotsmen say that they find the French schoolmaster the
most thorough-going flogger in Europe: to which the Gaul
replies that, if it is true, it is because the Frenchman knows his
Scot. Perhaps there is a difference in the method by which
the youth of different countries needs to be handled, though
for my part I consider it far more a matter of individual than
of national temperament. For instance, there are natures
which you will rather break than bend by flogging: whilst by
kindness and wise stimulus you may do anything with them.
I confess that I personally am constituted in this way. Once,
my master, with whom I was really on very good terms, a man,
too, who had formed a flattering idea of my capacities, conceived a wish to try how far I could stand the test of a very severe
discipline. So, watching his opportunity, he charged me with
some offence that I had not even dreamt of committing, and
thrashed me. Now, that piece of tyranny then and there
annihilated in me all further interest in learning, and so
dejected, so broken was I, that I gradually fell into a low
feverish state. So when my master—no fool and not a bad
man at heart, as I have said—realised what he had done, he
came forward and admitted his mistake. " I nearly succeeded
in ruining his disposition before I had learnt to understand it,"

he said. But his repentance came too late to alter the consequences, so far as my attitude to him was concerned.

Do schoolmasters consider how many earnest, studious natures have been by treatment of this type—the hangman type—crushed into indifference? Masters who are conscious of their own incompetence are generally the worst floggers. What else, indeed, can they do? They cannot teach, so they beat. By degrees it becomes a positive pleasure to them to torture, especially when they are self-indulgent men, or slothful or cruel by nature.

I know particularly well a certain Churchman of great distinction who selected the masters of his school from amongst the more accomplished wielders of the birch. Flogging, in his educational doctrine, was the prime instrument for "softening and purifying" boys' natures. It was his practice when the mid-day meal was over to order one or other of the boys to be brought out and cruelly thrashed: the innocence or guilt of the boy was not in question. I was present on one occasion when he had before him a lad of about ten years of age, only just admitted to the school. My churchman proceeded to tell us that the boy had been carefully brought up, and had been specially commended to his charge by his mother. A wholly groundless complaint was laid against him. The birch was thereupon handed to the wretched ministrant charged with this duty, who so lost all self-control in his task that the churchman himself had to call halt. The boy swooned away. Then said the divine : " The lad, of course, has done nothing to deserve all this, but it is necessary to curb his spirit by wholesome discipline." But who would dream of training a horse or a slave after this fashion? By patience and kindliness, and not by violence, men tame the lion's whelp and the young elephant. No beast is so wild but that it may be subdued by gentle handling, and none so tame but that cruelty will rouse it to anger.

It is, indeed, the mark of the servile nature to be drilled by

fear; why then do we suffer children (whose very name imports free men, "liberi"—those born fit for a "liberal"
training—), to be treated as slaves might be? Yet even slaves,
who are men like the rest of us, are by wise masters freed
from something of their servile state by humane control. Let
a father stand towards his son in a more kindly relation than
that of a master to his serfs. If we put away tyrants from
their thrones, why do we erect a new tyranny for our own sons?
Is it not meet that Christian peoples cast forth from their
midst the whole doctrine of slavery in all its forms? Paul
shews us that a slave is a "dear brother"; and that all
Christian believers, whether bond or free, are fellow-servants
to one Lord. In speaking of parents as regards their children
the Apostle warns them that they "provoke not their children
to wrath, but bring them up in the chastening and admonition
of the Lord." And what the "chastening" of the Lord Jesus
should imply, he may readily perceive who considers with what
gentleness, forgiveness, affection, He trained, cherished, and
bore with, his own disciples. Contrast with this the story of
Auxon, a Roman knight, who for cruelty towards his own son
was dragged by the crowd into the Forum, fiercely handled,
and with difficulty rescued with his life. I fear that there
be many Auxons living still. I could tell you certain stories of
wicked cruelty by schoolmasters which it is hard to believe, but
for which I vouch my own personal knowledge. In one case
in especial, where foul torture was employed, the child, whom I
knew,—he was twelve years of age—very nearly died from the
ill-usage. He was the innocent victim of some prank played
by a school-fellow, who was a favourite with the master, an
incompetent and worthless creature, and, therefore, given to
violent floggings to enforce his authority. I can only say that
hanging the luckless child up by the arms and flogging him
as he hung till the brutal master was too tired to go on, was
the least disgusting part of the punishment. The Scythians
or Phrygians of old were less inhuman. Once more, I cannot

forget the rough horse-play which awaited every newly-arrived student at my old College. The brutality of it and the intolerable torments devised by the youthful wits I do not care to particularise. Risks of permanent bodily injury were constantly experienced : and the ceremony ended in a noisy carouse. It was an "initiation," forsooth, into a course of training in the liberal arts : it was naturally well-adapted to turn out the flogging masters whom I have just described. The worst of it was that the authorities winked at the scandal; it was "the tradition," and it was, therefore, "unwise to interfere," and so on. As though the fact that an evil tradition is deep-rooted in the past does not make the stronger call upon sensible men for its abolition. Should not they who pursue the studies we term "liberal" cultivate a type of humour also to match ?

§ 25. THE PERMISSIBLE INSTRUMENTS OF DISCIPLINE.
507 E—508 D.

Teaching by beating, therefore, is not a liberal education. Nor should the schoolmaster indulge in too strong and too frequent *language* of blame. Medicine constantly repeated loses its force. You may quote against me the old proverb : "He that spareth the rod hateth his own son." Well, perhaps, that may have been true of Jews. But I do not accept it as true for Christians to-day. If we are to "bow the necks" and "chastise," as we are bidden to do, let us see to it that the rod we use is the word of guidance or of rebuke, such as a free man may obey, that our discipline be of kindness and not of vindictiveness. Lycon, the philosopher, sets forward these two spurs to industry : shame, and desire for praise. Shame is the fear of just reproach ; by praise a boy is quickened to excel in all he does. Let these, then, be the schoolmaster's weapons to-day. And I can add another : "unwearied pains conquer all things," says the poet. Let us watch, let us encourage, let us press and yet again press, that by learning, by repeating, by diligent listening, the boy may feel himself carried onward towards his goal.   Let him learn to respect and to love integrity and knowledge, to hate ignorance and dishonour.   Bid him regard those who are lauded for their virtues, be warned by those who are denounced for their ill-doing.   Set before him the example of men to whom learning has brought high praise, dignity, repute and position. Warn him of the fate of those who by the neglect of high wisdom have sunk into contempt, poverty, disgrace and evil life.   These are your instruments of discipline, my Christian teacher, worthy of your calling and of your flock.   But should none of these avail, then, if it must be so, let the rod be used with due regard to self-respect in the manner of it.   But I am, at heart, with Quintilian in deprecating flogging under any conditions.   If then you ask, " What is to be done with boys who respond to no other spur ? "   My answer is : " What would you do if an ox or an ass strayed into your schoolroom ? "   Turn him out to the plough or the pack-saddle, no doubt.   Well, so there are boys good only for the farm and manual toil : send your dunces there for their own good. "Yes," says the master, "but I want my fees."   There I cannot help you : your duty is to the boy.   But I fear that this matter of profit lies at the root of the whole matter.

§ 26. THE PROVISION OF FIT TEACHERS OF YOUTH IS A NATIONAL DUTY IN WHICH BOTH CHURCH AND STATE SHOULD SHARE THE JOINT RESPONSIBILITY. 508 D—E.

The ancients drew the ideal of the wise man and of the Orator—types never realised in fact.   So it is easier to outline the ideal schoolmaster than to find him in reality.   Which brings me to claim it as a duty incumbent on Statesmen and Churchmen alike to provide that there be a due supply of men qualified to educate the youth of the nation.   It is a public obligation in no way inferior, say, to the ordering of the army. Vespasian is an example, in that out of his Treasury he maintained Greek and Latin teachers; and the younger Pliny of his private fortune did the same. And if the community be backward in this respect, yet should every head of a household do all that he can to provide for the education of his own.

Now you may rejoin, that men of poor station, whose efforts are absorbed in nurturing their families, can do nothing for them besides. I have nothing to say except this: " We must do as we may, when we cannot do as we would." But the liberality of the rich can be most wisely exercised here, in enabling innate powers to attain their due development by removing the hindrance imposed by poverty.

§ 27. THE QUALITIES DESIRABLE IN A GOOD MASTER.
508 E—509 B.

Although I have urged the need of gentleness, let it not decline into unwise familiarity towards the pupil; a degree of formal authority must be maintained, such as marked the relation of Sarpedon towards the young Cato, who rendered his master great affection and equal reverence. What would the master do who can only teach by flogging, if he were set up as tutor in a royal household, where no such discipline is for a moment allowed? "Oh," he rejoins, "such pupils are not of the common order." "How then? Are not the children of a citizen *men*? Do not citizens love their sons no less than kings?" If they be poor men, the more need have they of learning in order to minister to their deficiency; if they be rich, in order to learn to govern their wealth aright. Not a few born in low estate are called to high station, as to Bishoprics. All men do not rise to so great distinction, yet ought all to gain by right education the opportunity of so

rising.   Now I have said enough of that evil class of schoolmaster which only knows how to beat: but I cannot too
seriously deplore that the scandal is in our day so widely
spread.

§ 28.   THE NEED OF SYMPATHY IN ONE WHO SHALL
TEACH YOUNG CHILDREN.   509 B—F.

It is the mark of a good teacher to stand towards his
charge somewhat in the relation of a parent: both learning
and teaching are made easier thereby.   He will also in a
sense become a boy again that he may draw his pupil to
himself.   Though this by no means justifies the choice of the
old and infirm as teachers of youth: these indeed have no
need to simulate a childish temper, they are only too truly
once more in their second infancy.   Rather should the master
be in the full vigour of early manhood, able to sympathise
naturally with youth, ready to adapt himself to its demands.
He will follow in his first instruction the methods of the
mother in the earliest training of her nursling.   As she
prattles baby language, stirs and softens baby food, stoops and
guides the tottering steps—so will the master act in things of
the mind.   Slowly is the transition made to walking alone, or
to eating solid food; the tender frame is thus carefully
hardened.   In exactly the same manner instruction is at first
simple, taught by way of play, taught by degrees.   The sense
of effort is lost in the pleasure of such natural exercise: insensibly the mind becomes equal to harder tasks.   Wholly
wrong are those masters who expect their little pupils to act as
though they were but diminutive adults, who forget the
meaning of *youth*, who have no standard of what can be done
or be understood except that of their own minds.   Such a
master will upbraid, exact, punish, as though he were dealing
with students as old as himself, and forgets that he was ever
himself a child.   Pliny warned such a one when he spoke thus

14—2

to a master: "Remember that your pupil is but a youth still, and that you were once one yourself." But how often does the schoolmaster of to-day prove by his harsh discipline that he wholly forgets this simple truth!

§ 29. What subjects may be most suitably chosen for the First Steps in Education. 509 F—510 D.

To treat next of the matter which may be wisely taught the little child. First of all, I give the leading place to practice in spoken language, which it is so great a task for adults to accomplish. As I have already said, this is an exercise of the child's powers of imitation, which it shares with certain birds. As an aid to this study can anything be better adapted to the youthful capacity than the reading of ancient Fables? For they appeal by their romance, they are good for moral lessons, they help vocabulary. There is nothing a boy more readily listens to than an apologue of Aesop, who under cover of pleasant story teaches the youth the very essence of philosophy. You relate, again, how Circe transforms the comrades of Ulysses into swine and other animals. It is a story to rouse interest and, perhaps, amusement; but the lesson is therein driven home that men who will not yield to the guidance of reason, but follow the enticements of the senses, are no more than brute beasts. Could a stoic philosopher preach a graver truth? The poetry styled Bucolic is easy to understand; Comedy is intelligible to boys, and teaches them many deep truths of life in its lighter vein. Then it is time to teach the names of objects—a subject in which even learned men are apt to be uncertain. Lastly, short sentences containing quaint conceits, proverbs, pithy sayings, such as in ancient times were the current coin of philosophy.

But do not forget that children are not seldom seen to show a peculiar bent to particular disciplines, such as Music, Arithmetic or Geography. I have myself known young pupils

who, though backward in all that concerned Grammar or Rhetoric, had much facility in these less rigid yet more recondite
subjects.   Nature, therefore, claims the help of the schoolmaster in carrying forward the special gifts with which she has
endowed the child.   By following the path which she points
out the toil of learning is reduced : whilst on the other hand
nothing can be well accomplished *invita Minerva.*

§ 30.   PLEASURABLE METHODS MUST BE DEVISED IN THE
FIRST STAGES OF TEACHING.   510 D—511 C.

Progress in learning a language is much furthered if the
child be brought up amongst people who are gifted talkers.
Descriptions and stories are impressed the better if to good
narrative power the teacher or parent can add the help of
pictorial illustration.   The same method can be more particularly applied to the teaching of natural objects.   Names
and characteristics of trees, flowers, and animals can be thus
learnt : specially is this plan needful where the creature described is wholly unfamiliar to the child, as for instance the
rhinoceros, the tragelaphus, the onocrotalus, the Indian ass,
and the elephant.   A picture is shown, containing an elephant,
in combat with a dragon.   At once the class shows curiosity.
How shall the master proceed ?   He states the Greek and Latin
names for elephant, giving the Latin genitive case as well.   He
then points to the trunk, giving the Greek and Latin for it, and
the purpose of the organ : he will explain that the elephant
breathes as well as feeds by its means.   The tusks are next
dealt with, the uses and rarity of ivory ; if possible he will
produce something made of it.   The dragon is shown to be of
the large Indian species.   He states the Greek and Latin
equivalents for 'dragon,' their similarity in form, and their
feminines.   He will instil the fact that between the dragon and
the elephant there is, instinctively and constantly, a ruthless
war.   If any boy is keen for further knowledge in the subject,

the Master will add many other facts concerning the nature and habits of these two great beasts. Boys, too, will generally be attracted by pictures of hunting scenes, through which a wealth of information about trees, plants, birds, and animals may be imparted in a most delightful and yet instructive manner. In choosing subject-matter of this kind it is desirable to take some pains to discuss what is naturally attractive to the youthful mind, and discard what is of too advanced a kind. Remember always that youth is the springtime of life, when harvests are sown and flowers bloom. But autumn is the season for ripe fruits and laden wains. Hence, as only folly will look for purple grapes in May, so no Master who understands his task will demand the tastes and powers of maturity from the growing child. Brightness, attractiveness, these make the only appeals to a boy in the field of learning. Is not this why the ancients fabled the Muses to be comely maidens, given to the song and the dance, and companions to the Graces? It was their doctrine also that excellence in true learning was only to be attained by those who find pleasure in its pursuit; and for this cause the liberal arts were by them called 'Humanitas.'

Yet there is no reason why in this early stage of education utility should not go hand in hand with delight. On the method which I have here sketched nothing hinders that a boy learn a pretty story from the ancient poets, or a memorable tale from history, just as readily as the stupid and vulgar ballad, or the old wives' fairy rubbish such as most children are steeped in nowadays by nurses and serving women. Who can think without shame of the precious time and energy squandered in listening to ridiculous riddles, stories of dreams, of ghosts, witches, fairies, demons; of foolish tales drawn from popular annals; worthless, nay, mischievous stuff of the kind which is poured into children in their nursery days?

§ 31. THE WORK OF EDUCATING THE YOUNG IS A PART
OF THE SERVICE WE OWE TO GOD. 511 C—D.

" Granting your contention "—so it may be said—" that we
should sweep away this rubbish and place education of the
very young on a higher plane, who will consent to stoop to this
trying task?" " Well," I reply, " Aristotle, Cheiron, Eli, are
examples to my hand. I only ask for the same kind of effort
that people are willing to bestow upon training a parrot to
talk." What of the pious folk who will make long and dangerous pilgrimages and perform exacting penances to please
the Deity? And yet can any duty be more agreeable to God
than the right up-bringing of the young? No gloom, no self-
mortification, no exhausting effort is demanded in this service :
diligence, patience, a cheerful demeanour, will accomplish all.
Nay, the very shadow of harsh, exacting toil and compulsion
should be banished from the field.

§ 32. METHODS OF EARLY INSTRUCTION AGAIN TOUCHED
UPON. 511 D—512 E.

Ability to speak is easily learned by use. Next come the
arts of reading and writing, where the skill of the teacher can
do much to lighten the monotony of learning. Much time is
commonly wasted in teaching the child to know his letters and
to pronounce words, which could be spent on more important
matters to far greater profit. Reading, indeed, should be
attacked on methods practised in Roman schools. Letters
were made in biscuit form and when learnt were allowed to be
eaten. Ivory letters were used, by means of which words were
composed by the scholar. And other devices could be employed. In England I heard of a father who taught his boy to
aim with bow and arrow at Greek or Roman letters painted on
a target; a hit meant a cherry for the archer. This could be

carried out as a competition in a class of boys : for as it was, the boy learnt all his letters, their names and sounds, in a few days instead of as many months.

I would not, however, encourage learning by games of chess or dice ; nor any devices whose complexity is such that the "aid" costs more to learn than the subject itself.   There are machines so intricate that they hinder work rather than shorten it.   Amongst the devices I have in mind is the whole class of mnemonic puzzles, put forth merely for their ingenuity, or as a means of making money.   Believe me, there is only one sound mnemonic art, and it has three rules : understand, arrange, repeat.

A clever Teacher will utilise the motive of emulation amongst children ; for this will often be found effective with boys who will not respond to warnings, to encouragement, or to the offer of rewards.   Now the award of the prize must by no means preclude the losers from the chances of proving themselves winners later on : and there may be circumstances under which the master will be wise in granting the first place to one who is not ahead in actual attainment.   The due alternation of praise and blame will often provoke keenness.   Should you reply that a master may be unwilling to take these pains to adapt his teaching to the youthful mind, I rejoin that, in such case, he is in my judgment unfit for his work.

I allow that the first steps in Latin Grammar are not in themselves attractive to boys.   But for this I blame, not a little, the lack of judgment in the master.   He should confine his teaching to the things that matter.   But as a rule the young beginner is worried, let us say, about the names of the letters, before he knows one of them by sight, or about the case of "Musae," or the tense of "legeris," before he has learnt his accidence.   And what beatings are apt to follow failure ! Again, a shallow mind will, in order to parade its thin layer of knowledge before the class, import wholly unnecessary difficulty into a lesson ; this happens especially in teaching Logic.

They are ways by which the rudiments are made harder than
they need be.   No doubt I shall be told, "*I* had to learn
Latin in this manner when I was a boy; what was good enough
for me must do for him."

§ 33.   DIFFICULTIES SHOULD BE ATTACKED PATIENTLY.
512 E—513 A.

My principles of method then are briefly these.   First, do
not hurry, for learning comes easily when the proper stage is
reached.   Second, avoid a difficulty which can be safely
ignored or at least postponed.   Third, when the difficulty
must be handled, make the boy's approach to it as gradual
and as interesting as you can.   Lucretius tells us that doctors
used to sweeten the rim of the medicine glass with honey.   We
know that imagination often magnifies a difficulty in life.   So
in teaching, lead the beginner to face his unfamiliar matter
with self-confidence, to attack it slowly but with persistence.
We must not under-rate the capacity of youth to respond to
suitable demands upon the intelligence.   Youth indeed lacks
that sheer force which marks the bull, but on the other hand
Nature has given it something of the tenacity and industry of
the ant.   The child, like every other creature, excels in the
precise activity which belongs to it.   How else could he race
about for hours and not be tired?   But such exercise is instinctive, it is play to him, there is no sense of toil about it, no
compulsion.   Follow Nature, therefore, in this, and so far as is
possible take from the work of the school all that implies toil-
someness, and strive to give to learning the quality of freedom
and of enjoyment.   Systematic games must be encouraged as
a needful relaxation when boys reach the higher stages of their
subject, and can no longer postpone close application and hard
work.   Such subjects are Greek composition, Latin composition
from the Greek, and cosmography.   But I would say that no

aid to progress is more effectual than are the boy's reverent affection for his master, his love of learning, and his ambition to rank with the best.

§ 34. THE ARGUMENT THAT THE EDUCATIONAL RESULT ATTAINABLE DURING THESE EARLY YEARS DOES NOT JUSTIFY THE TROUBLE OR EXPENSE INVOLVED. 513 A—514 A.

The contention that the time and the outlay involved in this early education are wasted is unworthy of anyone who realises what true fatherhood implies. Grant, with Quintilian, that the boy may acquire in one year after he has passed his fifth birthday as much as he can during the whole of the previous years, is that a reason for sacrificing what you admit to be equivalent to the harvest of a twelvemonth? Nor is the alternative merely that the boy may learn nothing; for he will undoubtedly be learning that which he must later unlearn. The training which I propose will serve to interest and occupy the growing child from the time when he can understand and be understood. The youthful mind is ever acquiring something—good or evil. The progress made, slight as it may be, is a saving of labour at a later stage, when the entire time and energy of the pupil are set free, as Quintilian says, for work of greater difficulty. Need I repeat what has been said concerning the aptitude of early childhood to some studies? I cannot, indeed, allow that it is a trivial gain that a child should win acquaintance with two languages, and learn to read and write. A merchant is far from despising the day of small things; he knows that "little" is the necessary beginning of "much."

Can we, in fact, afford to throw away four years of our children's lives, when we know that the two hardest things to overtake in this world are time lost and learning neglected? We can never be said to begin too soon a task which we can never live to finish: for a man may cease to learn only when he ceases to live. In all other departments of life we may succeed in recovering what we have lost by neglect. Time, however, when once it has flown by—and it flies very quickly— obeys no summons to return. There is no such miracle as a fountain of perpetual youth : no physic which can make old men young again. Of time, then, let us always be sparing ; of youthful years most of all, for this is the best part of man's life, the most profitable, if it be rightly guarded. No farmer will see his land lying fallow, not even a little field, but he will sow it with young grasses, or lay it down to pasture, or use it as a garden. And shall we suffer the best part of our life to pass without any fruit of wisdom ? Land, as we know, when newly ploughed up must be sown with some crop, lest it bear a harvest of weed. So the tender mind, unless it be forthwith sown with true instruction, will harbour evil seeds. The child grows up either to goodness or to unworthiness : if the latter, there is the hard task of up-rooting. The child has gained no small thing who has escaped evil. See, then, how in various ways it profits that he be early brought up in learning.

§ 35. EXAMPLES OF THE PROFICIENCY OF YOUTH AND ITS IMPORTANCE FOR LATER LIFE. 514 A—E.

But is there need to labour this ? How steeped in learning from their very infancy were men of old time ! How helpless are their successors to-day ! Ovid and Lucan composed not a little of their poetry in their youth : who can now boast the same ? Lucan when but six months old was brought to Rome and was soon after placed under the two best teachers of Grammar in the city. For companions he had Bassus and Persius : the former a historian, the latter the famous satirist. No doubt we have here the secret of that notable learning and eloquence, whereby Lucan is distinguished as the typical ora- torical poet of ancient Rome. In modern days how rare are examples of similar distinction! Poliziano has celebrated the erudition of Cassandra: and in a letter of elegant Latinity has recorded the genius of the boy Orsini, who at the age of eleven could dictate two Latin letters at once, letters which in composition and scholarly diction struck scholars with admiration. This experiment he on one occasion repeated five times, a feat which some observers ascribed to witchcraft. Well, I will allow this explanation, if by it you mean the "enchantment" that is worked by setting the boy from earliest childhood to work under the example and stimulus of a learned, sincere, and conscientious Master.

By such "enchantments" Alexander of Macedon shewed himself master alike of eloquence and of philosophy; in which indeed he might have attained great distinction had he not been lured away by ambition and by passionate ardour for war. By the same arts Julius Caesar became proficient in oratory and in the mathematical disciplines. Cicero, Vergil, and Horace, not a few of the earlier Emperors, became men of approved learning and of classic style, by reason of the diligent use they were led to make of their early years. For they were taught by their parents from the very nursery the art of refined speech, and were afterwards passed on to masters by whom they were grounded in the liberal arts, in Poetry, Rhetoric, History, Antiquity; in Arithmetic; in Geography, and in Philosophy, both moral and political.

§ 36. THE SAD CONDITION OF TEACHING AND OF SCHOOLS
IN MODERN DAYS. 514 E—516 A.

What a contrast when we look around to-day! We see boys kept at home in idleness and self-indulgence until they are fourteen or fifteen years of age. They are then sent to some school or other. There, if they are lucky, they gain some touch of Grammar, the simpler inflections, the agreement of noun and adjective. They are then supposed to "know"

Latin, and are put on to some terrible text in Logic, which will spoil what little good Latin accidence or syntax they have acquired. My own childhood was tortured by logical subtleties which had no reference to anything that was true in fact or sound in expression. Not a few Masters postponed Grammar to Logic and Metaphysic, but found that they had to revert to the rudiments of Latin when their pupils were fast growing up. Great heavens, what a time was that when with vast pretension the verses of John Garland, eked out with amazing commentary, were dictated to the class, learnt by heart, and said as repetition! When Florista and the Floretus were set as lessons! Alexander de Villa Dei, compared with such a crowd, is worthy of positive commendation. Again, how much time was spent in sophistries and vain mazes of logic! Further, as to the manner of teaching, what confused methods, what needless toil, characterised instruction! How common it was for a master, for mere display, to cram his lesson with irrelevant matter, wise or foolish, but all equally out of place! All this made for needless difficulty; for there is no virtue in *difficulty*, as such, in instruction. And even to-day schoolmasters are not seldom men of no learning at all, or, what is worse, of no character. They have taken to teaching as a means to a life of ease and money-making. If this has been, and is, the true state of education in our schools, no wonder that learning perishes amongst us. The critical years of a boy's life are allowed to run to waste; he acquires the habit, which cannot be cured, of giving but a fraction of his time and thought to serious pursuits, the rest he squanders on vulgar pleasures. The parent looks on and does nothing. And yet we hear talk of the "tender youth," "undeveloped capacity," "meagre results,"—all so many excuses for wicked neglect of the child in his early years!

§ 37.   CONCLUSION.   516 A.

Now I have done.   I make my appeal to that practical wisdom which you have always exhibited in affairs.   Consider how dear a possession is your son; how many-sided is learning; how exacting its pursuit, and how honourable!   Think how instinctive is the child's wish to learn, how plastic his mind, how responsive to judicious training, if only he be entrusted to instructors at once sympathetic and skilled to ease the first steps in knowledge.   Let me recall to you the durability of early impressions, made upon the unformed mind, as compared with those acquired in later life.   You know also how hard it is to overtake time lost; how wise, in all things, to begin our tasks in season; how great is the power of *persistence* in accumulating what we prize; how fleeting a thing is the life of man, how busy is youth, how inapt for learning is age.   In face, then, of all these serious facts you will not suffer, I do not say seven years, but three days even, of your son's life to pass, before you take into earnest consideration his nurture and future education.

CHAPTER VIII.

I. FROM THE *DE CONSCRIBENDIS EPISTOLIS.*

THE following passage forms one of the model letters comprised in the treatise on *Epistolary Composition.* It is inserted here in the original as a good specimen of Erasmian Latin of the later period (1522).

The advice given has primary reference to private study, but it is obviously equally applicable to class work. It should be read in conjunction with the section above on *The Method of reading an Author*, and with the *De Ratione Studii.*

QUI SIT MODUS REPETENDAE LECTIONIS, that is, HOW TO MASTER A PASSAGE FROM A CLASSICAL AUTHOR. *Op.* i. 447.

§ I. IT IS A MISTAKE TO BEGIN BY LEARNING THE PASSAGE BY HEART.

Quibusdam prima ac unica fere cura est statim ad verbum ediscere; quod equidem non probo, est enim tum magni laboris, tum fructus prope nullius. Quorsum enim attinet, psittaci more, verba non intellecta reddere? Commodiorem igitur viam accipe.

§ 2. A FIRST READING SHOULD AIM MERELY AT SECURING THE GENERAL SENSE OF THE PASSAGE.

Lectionem quidem auditam continuo relege, ita ut universam sententiam paulo altius animo infigas.

§ 3. A SECOND READING IS CONCERNED WITH GRAMMATICAL STRUCTURE AND WORD-FORMS.

Deinde a calce rursus ad caput redibis, et singula verba excutere incipies, ea duntaxat inquirens quae ad grammaticam curam attinent: videlicet, si quod verbum obscurum, aut ancipitis derivationis, si heteroclitae conjugationis; quod supinum, quod praeteritum faciat: quos habeat maiores, quos nepotes, quam constructionem; quid significet; et huiusmodi nonnulla.

§ 4. A THIRD READING IS DEVOTED TO ANALYSIS OF THE RHETORICAL ARTIFICE DISPLAYED.

Hoc ubi egeris, rursum de integro percurrito, ea iam potissimum inquirens quae ad artificium rhetoricum spectant. Si quid venustius, si quid elegantius, si quid concinnius dictum videbitur, annotabis indice aut asterisco apposito. Verborum compositionem inspicies, orationis decora scrutabere. Auctoris consilium indagabis, qua quidque ratione dixerit. Ubi quid te delectaverit vehementius cave praeter casam, quod aiunt, fugias. Fige pedem, ac abs te ipso rationem exige quare tantopere sis ea oratione delectatus, cur non ex ceteris quoque parem ceperis voluptatem. Invenies te acumine aut exornatione aliqua oratoria, aut compositionis harmonia, aut (ne omnia persequar) simili quapiam causa, commotum fuisse. Quod si aliquod adagium, si qua sententia, si quod proverbium vetus, si qua historia, si qua fabula, si qua similitudo non inepta, si quid breviter, acute, aut alioqui ingeniose dictum esse videbitur, id tanquam thesaurum quendam animo diligenter reponendum ducito ad usum et ad imitationem.

§ 5. A FOURTH READING NOTES THE USES WHICH THE
PASSAGE ADMITS OF FOR PRACTICAL, AND ESPECIALLY
MORAL, APPLICATION.

His diligenter curatis ne pigeat quarto iterare.   Nam hoc
habent eruditorum virorum, summo ingenio, summis vigiliis
elucubrata scripta, ut millies relecta magis magisque placeant,
semperque admiratori suo novum miraculum ostendant—id
quod tibi in tabula tua, saepenumero nec sine causa laudata,
evenire solet—quod antea non animadvertisses.   Idem tibi
multo amplius in bonis auctoribus eveniet.   Releges igitur
quarto, ac quae ad philosophiam, maxime vero ethicen, referri
posse videantur, circumspicies, si quod exemplum, quod
moribus accommodari possit.   Quid autem est, ex quo non
vel exemplum vivendi, vel imago quaedam vel occasio sumi
queat?   Nam in aliorum pulchre ac turpiter factis, quid deceat
quid non iuxta videmus.

§ 6. THE PASSAGE THUS THOROUGHLY UNDERSTOOD WILL
NEED LITTLE EFFORT TO COMMIT IT TO MEMORY, SHOULD
THAT BE DESIRED.

Haec si facies iam vel edidiceris, quanquam aliud egisti.
Tum demum, si libet, ad ediscendi laborem accedito, qui tum
aut nullus erit aut certe perquam exiguus.

§ 7. DISCUSSION IS USEFUL AS AID TO ESTABLISHING OR
REVISING YOUR INTERPRETATION AND YOUR CRITICISMS.

Quid deinde?   Restat ut, cum studiosis congrediaris, tuas
annotationes in medium proferas, vicissimque illorum audias,
alia laudabis, alia reprehendes; tua partim defendes, partim
castigari permittes.   Postremo, quod in aliis laudasti tuis in
scriptis imitari conaberis.   Secreta studia a doctis laudantur,
at ita ut postea e latebris in arenam prodeamus viriumque

nostrarum periculum faciamus.   Id quod sapientissime a
Socrate est dictum.   Experiamur utrum partus ingeniorum
vitales sint, nimirum obstetricum industriam imitati.   Quare
alternatim utrisque utetur, qui non vulgariter volet evadere
doctus.   Vale.

II. FROM THE *CONVIVIUM RELIGIOSUM.*

The following passage from the Colloquy entitled *Convivium Religiosum* is a typical illustration of the Erasmian
method of handling Natural History and pictorial illustrations
of Nature, History and Religion for purposes of teaching.
The *Colloquies*, the recognised school Reading-book of the
16th century, provided an introduction to *eruditio* or general
knowledge as well as practice in Latin.   But not less obvious
than either was its function of inculcating moral lessons.

CONVIVIUM RELIGIOSUM, that is, A SERIOUS ENTERTAINMENT.
Op. i. 662.

The host Eusebius is entertaining friends from the Town
at his villa, and before breakfast is served shows them the
gardens.

Eusebius: This part of the grounds was planned as a
pleasure garden, but for honest pleasure; for the worthy
gratification of the senses, yet not less for the recreation of
the mind.   None but sweet-smelling flowers and herbs are
planted here, and of these only the finest kinds.   Each variety
has a bed to itself.

A guest: It is plain that your plants are not dumb creatures.

Eusebius: That is true.   My villa I built for converse,
and here everything has its fit utterance, as you will perceive.
The various plants, for instance, are marshalled in troops,
each with its ensign, and its motto.   The marjoram, I see,
gives warning by inscription : *Abstine, sus, non tibi spiro* :
Keep off, sow, my perfume is not for you.   For however

fragrant, marjoram repels a sow.   And in the same way each
variety has its appropriate title, indicating its peculiar virtue.

A guest: How charming is this fountain, and the marble-
lined channel which dividing its course marks out the different
sections of the garden, reflecting the flowers as in a mirror!
I see that your artificial fences are green, like the plants.

Eusebius: Yes, green is my own choice, and in his garden
a man should follow his fancy.   For here I study, or walk,
or converse, or sometimes even take my meals, as I feel
disposed.

A guest: Having so pleasant, so well-furnished a garden,
wherein reality and nature have done so much for your delight,
what need have you for that other pleasaunce which I see
yonder painted on the wall?

Eusebius: First, because no one garden can contain the
plants of all climates; next, I like to see the art of the painter
pitted against the direct product of the Creator, though both
art and nature are the gifts of the same divine goodness, and
intended for man's use.   Lastly, a garden is not always green:
flowers fade with the seasons: this garden remains fresh when
the other is bare....In the path beneath our feet, which I have
had paved with wood, you can see the beauty of painted flowers
standing forth from the green background.   Turn to the wall
which shelters us.   Here we have unfamiliar trees, each tree
there drawn to the life is a distinct species; the same is the
case with the birds shown in the branches, most of them we
could not see in our own northern gardens: and some of them
are of extraordinary types.   Below the trees are animals that
haunt the ground.

A guest: Wonderful is the variety; and each one is in
movement, doing, or at least saying, something.   Here is an
Owl, what says she?

Eusebius: She speaks Greek: Σωφρόνει, οὐ πᾶσιν ἵπτημι.
That is, "Learn wisdom from me: I do not fly to everyone."
It is a lesson against recklessness.   There is an eagle devouring

a hare, and a beetle stands by interceding, but in vain. By the beetle stands a wren, the eagle's inveterate foe. The swallow has a leaf of celandine in her beak, which she is taking to her nest to give sight to her blind unfledged young. Near is the chameleon always gaping, because always hungry. The wild fig close by is his aversion.

A guest: How does he change his colour?

Eusebius: Only when he moves from one place to another. See the camel dancing as the monkey pipes to him. But we should need three days to go through each object depicted here. In that compartment are all kinds of remarkable plants, amongst them the poisonous trees, which we may here approach and examine without danger to ourselves.

A guest: See, here is a scorpion, an animal we rarely see in this country, but common enough in Italy, and apt to be malignant. The colour in the picture, however, seems hardly true to nature. Those in Italy are much darker.

Eusebius: But do you not recognise the plant upon which it has hapt? It is the wolfsbane: so deadly a poison that at the first touch of it the scorpion is stupefied and suddenly grows pale. But it is his habit when oppressed by one poison to seek an antidote in another. Hard by the scorpion are hellebore plants, if the scorpion can but struggle clear of the wolfsbane and reach the white hellebore, he will recover, for the one will counteract the other.

A guest: And do your scorpions speak?

Eusebius: Yes, and they speak Greek: Εὗρε θεὸς τὸν ἀλι-τρόν: God hath found out the guilty. Here also you may see serpents of all kinds, such as the basilisk, which is not only formidable for his poisonous bite, for the mere glance of his eye is mortal. His motto is, *Oderint dum metuant*: Let them hate, if only they fear me.

A guest: He speaks like a king.

Eusebius: Like a Tyrant rather: but not a true King. Here is a lizard fighting an adder, and another variety of snake

just on the spring. Notice the polity of the ants, whom we
are bidden to imitate by Solomon and Horace. The Indian
ants are busy carrying off gold to hoard it up. But turn to
look beyond, where is a third wall facing us. There are lakes,
rivers, and seas, with the appropriate fishes shown swimming
in the water. The Nile for instance, in which is a dolphin,
that natural friend of man, fighting with the deadly enemy of
man, the crocodile. Upon the banks are such creatures as
crabs, beavers and seals. Here is a polypus, nipped by an
oyster. Αἰρῶν αἰροῦμαι, he cries, "the biter bit." Close by
there is a second polypus floating on the surface; and a
torpedo-fish lying on the sands and hardly discernible. They
are dangerous enough, but not to us. I will now show you
the kitchen-garden, and an inner garden planted with healing
herbs. Upon the right hand there is an orchard, where you
shall see a great variety of foreign trees which have been
acclimatised by care. At the end of the upper walk is the
aviary. Now amongst its denizens you will see birds of many
forms, of various note, and of divers humours. Some are
bound to each other by mutual affection, and are again parted
from others by deep aversion. Then they are so tame and
friendly that when I am at supper they will fly in at the
window and take food from my hands. At times they will
sit listening as I talk to a friend, or perch upon my shoulders
without any fear, knowing that no one will harm them. At
the end of the orchard I have my bees, a sight worth seeing.
......Observe this summer apartment, which looks out upon
the gardens in three directions, and in each of them a foreground of delicate green meets the eye. When I dine here
I seem to be dining in the garden itself: nay, the very walls
are painted in green, with flowers intermixed. There are
subject pictures also: our Saviour celebrating his Last Supper:
Herod keeping his birthday: Dives in the midst of his luxury:
Lazarus driven from his doors.

A guest: Here are other stories.

Eusebius: This is Cleopatra, vying with Antony in a race of extravagance; she has swallowed the draught containing the pearl.   Here is the battle of the Centaurs; there Alexander the Great kills Clytus with the lance.   These examples teach us sobriety at table, and warn against gluttony and excess.   We will now pass into my Library, my chiefest treasure.   This hanging Globe is a presentation of the whole world.   Here upon the wall are the several regions of it described more at large.   Upon those other walls you have pictures of the most eminent authors.   First among them is Christ sitting upon the Mount, stretching forth his hand.   The Father speaks, *Hear ye Him*: the Holy Spirit overshadows Him with outstretched wing....The Library has a little gallery looking upon the garden, and an oratory adjoining it.   Let us pass now to the covered gallery that you have not yet seen.   Here upon the left hand is depicted the whole life of Jesus down to the descent of the Spirit upon the Apostles.   And there are notes upon the places, so that the spectator may see by what lake or upon what mountain such or such an event occurred.   There are also titles to every story.   Over against this you have figured the types and prophecies of the Old Testament.   Upon the upper border are portraits of the Popes and of the Caesars, there placed as aids to the due remembering of history.   At each corner is a belvedere, where I can sit down, and view my gardens and my birds; or in summer can take my breakfast.......

BIBLIOGRAPHICAL LISTS.

(i) TITLES OF WORKS QUOTED AND REFERRED TO.

The following List has been compiled to facilitate the identification of, and reference to, the works actually quoted in the text and notes of the present volume. It in no way represents the whole body of available authorities, or of those which have been consulted for the purpose of this work.

ABDY (Mrs H.). *Isabella d'Este.* 2 voll. 8°. London 1903.

ALEXANDER DE VILLA DEI (Grammaticus). *Doctrinale,* Kritisch-exegetische Ausgabe, bearbeitet von Dietrich Reichling. 8°. Berlin 1893.

ANON. *Vocabularius Breviloquus.* f°. Argent. 1491.

ARNAUD (Car.). *Quid de Pueris Instituendis senserit Ludovicus Vives.* 8°. Paris 1887.

BAILEY (N.). *The Colloquies of Erasmus,* translated by N. Bailey (1725). 2 voll. 8°. London 1878.

BECHER (Richard). *Die Ansichten des Desiderius Erasmus über die Erziehung und den ersten Unterricht der Kinder.* 8°. Leipzig 1890.

BEMBO (Pietro). *Opere tutte.* 4 voll. f°. Ven. 1729.

BEMBO (Pietro). *Della Volgar Lingua Libri III.* f°. Venezia 1525.

BENOIST (A.). *Quid de puerorum institutione senserit Erasmus.* 8°. Parisiis 1876.

BRUNI (L.). *Ad P. Paulum Istrum Dialogus.* 8°. Greifswald 1888.

BURCKHARDT (Jacob). *The Civilisation of the period of the Renaissance in Italy,* translated by S. G. C. Middlemore. 8°. London 1892.

BURNET (J.). *Aristotle on Education, being extracts from the Ethics and Politics.* 8vo. Cambridge 1902.

CLERVAL (L'Abbé A.). *Les Écoles de Chartres au Moyen Age du Ve au XVIe Siècle. (Mémoires de la Société Archéologique d'Eure-et-Loire,* tome XI.) 8°. Chartres 1895.

CORDERIUS (Maturinus). *School Colloquies, English and Latine, divided into several classes.... That children by the help of their Mother-Tongue may the better learn to speak Latine in ordinary discourse,* by Charles Hoole, M.A. 12°. London 1657.

DOLET (Étienne).   *De Imitatione Ciceroniana adversus Erasmum Rot. pro C. Longolio.*   8⁰. Lugd. 1535.

DOMINICI (Giovanni).   *Regola del Governo di Cura Familiare.*   Testo... illustrato con note dal Prof. Donato Salvi.   8⁰. Firenze 1860.

DRUMMOND (Robert B.).   *Erasmus, his Life and Character as shown in his Correspondence and Works.*   2 voll. 8⁰. London 1873.

ELYOT (Sir Thomas).   *The Boke named the Governour.*   Ed. Crofts.   2 voll. 8⁰. London 1880.

ELYOT (Sir Thomas).   *The Defence of Good Women.*   T. Berthelet.   8⁰. London [1540].

EMERTON (Ephraim).   *Desiderius Erasmus of Rotterdam.*   New York 1899.

ERASMUS (Desiderius).   *Opera omnia, emendatiora et auctiora: cura J. Clerici.*   10 voll.   f⁰. Lugd. Bat. 1703—6.

FAIRBAIRN (A. M.).   *Tendencies of European Thought in the age of the Reformation* (ch. xix. in the *Cambridge Modern History*, vol. ii.).   8⁰. Cambridge, 1904.

FEUGÈRE (Gaston).   *Érasme.   Étude sur sa vie et ses ouvrages.*   8⁰. Paris 1874.

FLORIDUS SABINUS (Franciscus).   *In Latinae linguae scriptorum calumniatores Apologia.*   f⁰. Bas. 1540.

FORTUNIO (Giovanni Francisco).   *Regole Grammaticali della volgar lingua.*   8⁰. Ancona 1516.

FROUDE (James Anthony).   *Life and Letters of Erasmus*: Lectures at Oxford 1893—4.   8⁰. London 1894.

GASPARY (Ad.).   *Storia della Letteratura Italiana* (from the German).   3 voll.   8⁰. Torino 1887—1901.

GEIGER (Ludwig).   *Rinascimento e Umanismo in Italia e in Germania: traduzione Italiana del Valbusa.*   8⁰. Milano 1891.

GHENT, University of.   *Bibliotheca Erasmiana.*   4⁰. 2 pts., and 8⁰. 3 voll. Gand 1893 etc.

GLOECKNER (Dr G.).   *Das Ideal der Bildung und Erziehung bei Erasmus von Rotterdam.*   8⁰. Dresden 1889.

HORAWITZ (Adalbert).   *Erasmiana* (in *Sitzungsberichte der K. Akademie der Wissenschaften*).   8⁰. Wien 1878—1885.

ISRAEL (A.).   *Sammlung selten gewordener pädagogischer Schriften des 16 und 17 Jahrhunderts.*   8⁰. Zschopau 1893 etc.

JEBB (R. C.).   *The Classical Renaissance* (being ch. xvi. in the *Cambridge Modern History*, vol. i.).   8⁰. Cambridge 1902.

JEBB (R. C.)   *Erasmus* (Rede Lecture 1890), 2nd edition.   8⁰. Cambridge 1897.

KUECKELHAHN (L.).   *Johannes Sturm, Strassburg's erster Schulrector.*   8⁰. Leipzig 1872.

LOWNDES (M. E.). *Michel de Montaigne, a biographical study.* 8°. Cambridge 1898.

LUPTON (J. H.). *A Life of John Colet, D.D.* 8°. London 1887.

MELANCHTHON (P.). *De Corrigendis Studiis* (1518) in *Corpus Reformatorum*, xi. p. 15. 8°. Halle 1834—1860.

MIRANDULA (Giovanni Pico della). *De Imitatione.* 8°. Venet. 1530.

MUELLER (Johannes). *Vor- und frühreformatorische Schulordnungen und Schulverträge in Deutscher und Niederländischer Sprache.* 8°. Zschopau 1885.

NAUSEA (Fridericus), Bishop of Vienna. *De Puero literis instituendo.* Col. 1536.

NICHOLS (Francis Morgan). *The Epistles of Erasmus, from his earliest letters to his fifty-first year.* Vol. i. 8°. London 1901.

NOLHAC (Pierre de). *Érasme en Italie.* 8°. Paris 1888.

PATER (W.). *Marius the Epicurean.* Second ed. 2 voll. 8vo. London 1885.

PAULSEN (Friedrich). *Geschichte des Gelehrten Unterrichts auf den Deutschen Schulen und Universitäten vom Ausgang des Mittelalters bis zur Gegenwart.* 8°. Leipzig 1885.

PICCOLOMINI (Aeneas Sylvius). *Opera.* f°. Basil. 1551.

POLITIANUS (Angelus). *Omnia Opera.* f°. Venet. 1498.

QUINTILIANUS (M. Fabius). *Institutionis oratoriae Liber Decimus.* Ed. W. Peterson, M.A. 8°. Oxford 1891.

RALEIGH (Walter). *The Book of the Courtier,* translated by Thomas Hoby, with Introduction by the Editor. 8°. London 1900.

RAUMER. *Geschichte der Pädagogik.* 2 voll. 8°. Berlin 1880.

RICHTER (Dr Arthur). *Erasmus-Studien.* 8°. Dresden 1891.

ROESLER (A.). *Kardinal Johannes Dominicis Erziehungslehre.* 8°. Freiburg 1894.

ROSSIGNOL (J.-P.). *De l'Éducation et de l'Instruction des Hommes et des Femmes chez les Anciens.* 8°. Paris 1888.

SABBADINI (R.). *Franciscus Floridus Sabinus.* Article in the *Giornale Storico della Letteratura Italiana,* vol. viii. p. 333. 8°. Torino.

SABBADINI (R.). *La Scuola e gli Studi di Guarino Guarini Veronese.* 8°. Catania 1896.

SABBADINI (R.). *Prolusione al corso di Letteratura Italiana nella R. Università di Catania.* Catania 1894.

SABBADINI (R.). *Storia del Ciceronianismo e di altre questioni letterarie nell' età della Rinascenza.* 8°. Torino 1885.

SADOLETO (J.). *De Liberis recte instituendis* in *J. Sadoleti...opera,* tom. iii. p. 66. 4to. Veronae 1738.

SANDYS (John Edwin). *A History of Classical Scholarship from the Sixth Century* B.C. *to the end of the Middle Ages.* 8°. Cambridge 1903.

SCALIGER (Julius Caesar). *Pro M. T. Cicerone contra Desiderium Erasmum Roter. Oratio I.* 8°. Tolosae 1620.
The same. *Oratio II.* Tolosae 1620.

SCHMID (K.). *Encyklopädie des gesamten Erziehungs- und Unterrichtswesens.* 11 vols. 8°. Gotha 1858 etc.

SEEBOHM (Frederic). *The Oxford Reformers of 1498: Colet, Erasmus, More.* 3rd ed. 8°. London 1867.

SPITZNER (Johannes). *Beitrag zur Kritik der Unterrichts- und Erziehungslehre des Desiderius Erasmus auf Grund seiner " Declamatio de Pueris liberaliter instituendis."* 8°. Leipzig 1893.

STURM (Johannes). *De Literarum Ludis recte aperiendis Liber.* 12°. Argent. 1543.

SYLVIUS (Aeneas). *See* Piccolomini.

THUROT (Charles). *Notices et Extraits des Manuscrits de la Bibliothèque Impériale etc.* Tome xxii. 4°. Paris 1868.

TÖGEL (Dr Hermann). *Die pädagogischen Anschauungen des Erasmus in ihrer psychologischen Begründung.* 8°. Dresden 1896.

TOPSELL (Edward). *The Historie of Foure-Footed Beastes.* f°. London 1607.

VALLA (Laurentius). *Elegantiae Linguae Latinae.* 4°. Venet. (Jenson) 1471.

VEIL (H.). *Zum Gedächtnis Joh. Sturms* in *Festschrift zur Feier des 350-jährigen Bestehens des Protestantischen Gymnasiums zu Strassburg* (Erster Theil). 8°. Strassburg 1888.

VILLARI (P.). *The Life and Times of Niccolò Machiavelli.* Translated by Linda Villari. 2 voll. 8°. London 1892.

VIVES (J. L.). *De disciplinis libri XX.* J. Gymnicus. Coloniae 1532.

VIVES (J. L.). *De officio mariti.* 8°. Brugis 1529.

VIVES (J. L.). *De institutione foeminae Christianae.* 4°. Antverpiae 1524.

VOIGT (G.). *Die Wiederbelebung des Classischen Alterthums.* 2 voll. 8°. Berlin 1893.

WARD (A. W.). *The Netherlands* (being ch. xiii. in the *Cambridge Modern History*, vol. i.). 8°. Cambridge 1902.

WATSON (Foster). *The Curriculum and Text-books of English Schools in the first half of the Seventeenth Century.* 4°. London 1903.

WOODWARD (William Harrison). *Vittorino da Feltre and other Humanist Educators.* 8°. Cambridge 1897.

NOTE.—A useful bibliography of German humanism will be found in Paulsen's *Geschichte des Gelehrten Unterrichts*, and others in the *Cambridge Modern History*, voll. i. and ii.

(ii) FIRST EDITIONS OF ERASMUS IN ENGLISH, XVI. CENTURY.

The following List of first editions of English Versions of works by Erasmus is certainly incomplete, but it is less so than any hitherto available. Biblical works are excepted. I shall be grateful for all information which may aid in enlarging or correcting the particulars here given. W. H. W.

ADAGIA.

Proverbes or adagies with newe addicions gathered out of the Chiliades of Erasmus, by R. Taverner. Hereunto be also added Mimi Publiani. 8°. [R. Bankes:] London 1539.

APOLOGIA PRO DECLAMATIONE DE LAUDE MATRIMONII.

A modest meane to marriage, translated into englishe by N[icholas] L[eigh]. 16°. London 1568.

APOPHTHEGMATA.

Apophthegmes, that is to saie, prompte, quicke, wittie and sentencious saiynges of certain Emperours, Kynges...into englyshe by N. Udall. 8°. R. Grafton: London 1542.

A translation of Books III. and IV. only.

Dicta Sapientium. The sayenges of the wyse men of Grece, in Latin with the Englysshe followyng...interprete...by...Erasmus Rote.... 12°. T. Berthelet: London [c. 1550].

Berthelet printed 1530—1555.

Flores aliquot sententiarum ex variis collecti scriptoribus. The flowers of sentencies gathered out of sundry wryters by Erasmus in Latine, and englished by Richard Taverner. 8°. R. Bankes: London 1540.

The colophon reads "Printed in Fletestrete very diligently under the correction of the selfe R. Taverner by R: Bankes...." "The work is not really by Erasmus, though partly founded on his *Apophthegmata*. The author was Taverner." E. G. D.

Sage and Prudent saiynges of the seaven Wyse Men; Wyse saiynges and Prety Tauntes of Publius. R. Grafton: London 1545.

Certain flours of most notable sentences of wise men, gathered together by Erasmus of Roterdam, and translated into English. [A supplement to An Introducion to wysedome made by Ludovicus Vives.] 8°. John Daye: London (? 1546).

BELLUM. (Ex *Adagiis*.)

Bellum, trans. into englyshe. 8°. Tho. Berthelet: London 1533-4.

CATO PRO PUERIS.

Preceptes of Cato, with annotations of D. Erasmus of Roterodame, very profytable for all men. Newly imprynted and corrected ; Translated out of Latyn into Englysshe by Robert Burrant. R. Grafton: London 1545.

COLLOQUIA.

A dialogue or communication of two persons...pylgremage of pure devotion.... 8°. [John Byddell: London c. 1538].

Byddell printed 1533–44.

A mery dialogue, declaringe the propertyes of shrowde shrewes and honest wyves. 8°. Antony Kytson: London 1557.

A mery dialogue declaryng the properties of shrowde shrewes and honest wyves. 4°. Abr. Vele: London [c. 1557].

Apparently the same impression as the above. Cf. Hazlitt, III. 76.

Vele or Veale printed 1551–86.

A seraphical dirige, disclosing the 7 secret priviledges graunted to S. Francis and all his progenie for ever. 8°. John Byddell: London [c. 1538].

Epicureus, translated by Philyppe Gerard. 16°. Rich. Grafton: London 1545.

[Erasmus Rotordamus contaynynge a moste pleasaunt Dialoge towchynge the entertaynment and vsage of gaystes in comen Innes etc.] [? W. Griffith: London c. 1566.]

"No copy of this work is known to me ; but the book was licensed to W. Griffith in 1566. Cf. Arber's *Stationers' Register* I. 334." E.G.D.

Funus, lately traducte...at the request of a certayne gentylman. 16°. John Skot: London 1534.

One dialogue or colloquy (intituled "Diversoria") translated...by E. H. 4°. W. Griffyth: London 1566.

Two dyalogues...one called Polyphemus...the other dysposyng of thynges and names, trans. by E. Becke. 8°. J. Mychell: Canterbury [c. 1550].

Mychell printed 1549–56.

CONCIO DE PUERO JESU.

A sermon of the chyld Jesus. 8°. Rob. Redman: London [c. 1531].

Redman printed 1523–40.

DE CIVILITATE MORUM PUERILIUM LIBELLUS.

A lytell Booke of good Maners for chyldren...with Interpretacion... into the vulgare Englysshe Tonge by Robert Whytynton, Laureate Poete. 16°. W. de Worde: London 1532.

DE CONTEMPTU MUNDI.

    De contemptu mundi epistola, translated in to englysshe [by T. Paynell]. 16⁰. Tho. Berthelet: London 1533.

DE IMMENSA DEI MISERICORDIA CONCIO.

    De immensa dei misericordia (trans. at the request of the lady Margaret Countese of Salisburye by Gentian Hervet). 8⁰. Tho. Berthelet: London 1533.

    De immensa Dei misericordia. Trans. from the Latin of Erasmus by Gentian Hervet. 4⁰. T. Berthelet: London [c. 1543].

                    Berthelet printed 1530–1555.

DE MORTE DECLAMATIO.

    A treatise perswadyng a man paciently to suffer the death of his freend [preceded by the Tables of Cebes, the philosopher, trans. by Sir F. Poyngz; and How one may take profit of his enemies, trans. out of Plutarch]. 16⁰. Tho. Berthelet: London [c. 1550].

DE PRAEPARATIONE AD MORTEM.

    Preparation to deathe, a boke as devout as eloquent. 8⁰. Tho. Berthelet: London 1543.

ENCHIRIDION MILITIS CHRISTIANI.

    A booke called in Latyn Enchiridion militis Christiani and in englysshe the manuel of the christen knyght, plenysshed with most holsome preceptes....To the which is added a newe and mervaylous profytable preface [trans. attributed to W. Tyndale]. 8⁰. Wynkin de Worde, for Johan Byddell, otherwyse Salisbury: London, Nov. 15, 1533.

    An edition is given in *Bibliotheca Erasmiana*. 8⁰. Basel (? London, W. de Worde) 1518.

    "There is no authority for the edition of 1518." E. G. D.

ENCOMIUM MATRIMONII.

    A ryght frutefull epystle...in laude and prayse of matrymony, trans. by R. Tavernour. 8⁰. Robert Redman: London [c. 1530].

                    Redman printed 1523–40.

EPISTOLA AD BALTHASAREM EPISC.

    An epistle of...Erasmus...concernynge the veryte of the sacrament of Christus body and bloude...dedycated...unto...Balthasar bysshop of Hyldesheimensem. 8⁰. R. Wyer: [London 1535].

EPISTOLA APOLOGETICA AD CHRISTOPHORUM EP. BASIL.

    An epystell...unto...Christofer bysshop of Basyl, cŏcernyng the forbedynge of eatynge of flesshe, and lyke constitutyons of men. 8⁰. Thom. Godfray: London [c. 1532].

                Godfray printed in 1532.

EXOMOLOGESIS SIVE MODUS CONFITENDI.

A lytle treatise of the maner and forme of confession. 8°. J. Byddell: London [c. 1538].

EXPLANATIO SYMBOLI APOSTOLORUM.

A playne and godly expossytion or declaration of the commune crede...and of the ten commaundements of Goddes law; at the request of Thomas, erle of Wyltshyre. 12°. R. Redman: [London] 1533.

INSTITUTUM HOMINIS CHRISTIANI.

The godly and pious institution of a christen man. 8°. Thom. Berthelet: London 1537.

An English translation of Erasmus' metrical version of Colet's *Cathecyzon.*

LIBELLUS DE PUERIS LIBERALITER INSTITUENDIS.

That chyldren oughte to be taught and broughte up gētly in vertue and learnynge [preceded by A treatise of schemes and tropes, gathered out of the best grammarians and oratours by Rychard Sherry, Londoner]. 8°. John Day: London [c. 1555].

John Day printed 1546–84.

MORIAE ENCOMIUM.

The praise of folie...englished by Sir Thom. Chaloner. 4°. Th. Berthelet: London 1549.

(In the colophon the date is printed MDLXIX.)

PARACLESIS.

An exhortation to the diligent studye of scripture...translated in to englissh (by W. Roy?). 8°. Hans Luft: Malborow 1529.

"Very probably printed at Cologne." E. G. D.

An exhortacyon to the dylygent study of scripture, made by Erasmus of Roterdam, and lately translated into Englyshe, which he fixed before the new testament. 12°. Robert Wyer: London [c. 1535].

Erasmus on the sacrament, and an exhortation to the study and readynge of the gospell....Done at Basle 1522. 12°. Robert Wyer: London [c. 1535].

Wyer printed 1527–42.

PRECATIO DOMINICA.

A devout treatise upon the Pater noster. 4°. W. de Worde: London 1524.

"This edition is doubtful." E. G. D.

A devout treatise upon the Pater noster. [With a preface by R. Hyrde dated Oct. 1, 1524.] Th. Berthelet: London [c. 1530].

QUERELA PACIS.

The complaint of peace, trans. by T. Paynell   8°. John Cawoode: London 1559.

RESPONSIO AD DISPUTATIONEM CUJUSDAM PHIMO-STOMI DE DIVORTIIS.

The censure and judgement of Erasmus: Whyther dyvorsemente betweene man and wyfe stondeth with the law of God...trans. by N. Lesse.   8°. Printed by the widowe of John Herforde: London [c. 1550].

The widow of J. Herforde printed 1549–50.

SILENI ALCIBIADIS (Ex *Adagiis* chiliad. III, cent. III).

A scornful image or monstrous shape of a marvelous strange figure called Sileni Alcibiadis presenting ye state and condicion of this present world.... 16°. John Goughe: London [c. 1535].

"Gough apparently never printed, but was in business as a book-seller, 1526–1543." E. G. D.

VIRGINIS ET MARTYRIS COMPARATIO.

A comparation of a vyrgin and a marter, trans. by Thomas Paynel. 8°. T. Berthelet: London 1537.

INDEX.

CAMBRIDGE: PRINTED BY J. AND C. F. CLAY, AT THE UNIVERSITY PRESS.

CRAIG R. THOMPSON, Professor of English and History at Haverford College, was born in Carlisle, Pennsylvania, in 1911. He received his B.A. from Dickinson College and his M.A. and Ph.D. from Princeton University. Professor Thompson taught English at Cornell University, Yale University, and Lawrence College before joining the Haverford faculty in 1960. His writings include *The English Church in the Sixteenth Century* (1958), *The Bible in English, 1525–1611* (1958), *Schools in Tudor England* (1958), and *Universities in Tudor England* (1959), in addition to translations of Erasmus' *Inquisitio de Fide* (1950) and complete *Colloquies* (1964).

Da

3-17-66
4-1-66
4-21-66
NO 18
DE 4-78
NOV 2 6
DEC 14 1982

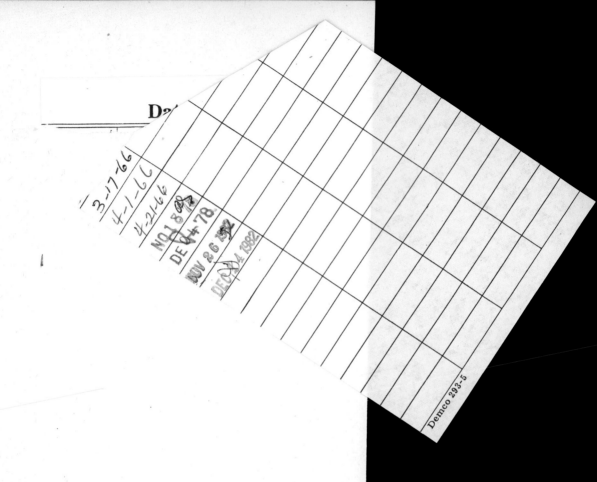

Demco 293-5